The Course of Islam in Africa

Mervyn Hiskett

EDINBURGH UNIVERSITY PRESS

Edinburgh University Press Ltd
22 George Square, Edinburgh

Typeset in Linotron Trump Mediaeval
by Koinonia Ltd, Bury, and
printed and bound in Great Britain
by Hartnolls Ltd, Bodmin

A CIP record for this book is available
from the British Library

ISBN 0 7486 0461 8 (paper)
ISBN 0 7486 0464 2 (cased)

Contents

List of Maps

Preface

This book sets out to trace the course of Islam in Africa from its beginnings there until the present day. While dynastic history must have a place in such a study, since Islam is inseparable from politics and government, it is always subordinate to the main theme of Islamic belief and culture. Likewise, details of colonial administrations are dealt with only insofar as they affect Islam.

Annotation is normally limited to direct quotation or to citation of a specific kind. Beyond that, the Bibliographic Essay is intended as an acknowledgement to the works of those scholars to whom I am indebted in the writing of this book.

The transcription of Arabic words and names always presents a problem. In general I have followed the system used in the *Bulletin of the School of Oriental and African Studies* (BSOAS). Arabic personal names are transcribed according to this system when they occur before AD 1900. After that date they are spelt according to the most familiar modern rendering: thus, 'al-Turabi', not 'al-Turābī'; 'Khomeini' not 'al-Khumaynī'; 'Ibraheem', not Ibrāhīm' and so on.

Dates are normally given as the year of the *Hijra* (AH) followed by the date AD – thus, 906/1500. But where the incident in question took place primarily in a non-Islamic context – for instance, when discussing the Ethiopian Christian Church – I give only the date AD.

I am most grateful to the following friends and scholars who have encouraged me to write this book and have helped me in many ways: Professor Edmund Bosworth of Manchester University; Professor Jan Knappert, formerly of the School of Oriental and African Studies, University of London; Dr Humphrey Fisher and his colleagues, who have so warmly welcomed me back to the SOAS African History Seminary after several years' absence; Mrs Jean Boyd, whose knowledge of Nigerian history has been constantly at my disposal; and Mr Christopher Moore, who so expertly drew the maps – a task totally beyond me!

I am also most grateful to Mrs Mary Twynham for drawing my attention to Braybrooke's *The Concise Pepys* (from which I have quoted), for photocopying my typescript and for her interest in this work. I am beholden to the publishers, Edinburgh University Press, for the facilities they have put at my disposal; and to Dr Carole Hillenbrand for her kind encouragement in certain moments of gloom. Finally, I am deeply grateful to my wife for her patience and understanding.

Despite the generous help that I have enjoyed from friends and colleagues, all errors and deficiencies in this book are mine and I assume responsibility for them.

Mervyn Hiskett

1

North Africa

NORTH AFRICA TO *C.* 673–4/1275

The North African coast from Morocco to Libya was known to Europeans from the sixteenth century AD onwards as the 'Barbary Coast', after the Turkish corsair, Barbarossa. The hinterland, comprising what are now Morocco, Algeria, Tunisia and Libya, was known as the 'Barbary states'. But from a much earlier date the Arabs had used the term *maghrib* (Maghrib or Maghreb), a noun of place from the Arabic root 'Gh R B', 'west', to refer specifically to Morocco. They then subdivided this into *al-maghrib al-awsaṭ*, 'the central *maghrib*', approximately present-day Algeria, and *al-maghrib al-aqṣā'*, 'the hinder *maghrib*', approximately present-day Morocco. The eastern end of the littoral, including present-day Tunisia and Libya, was known to them as 'Ifrīqiya'.

The Arab conquest of North Africa

This area, then in every way part of the Mediterranean world, had been held at various times by the Carthaginians, the Romans, and briefly by the Vandals, before being reconquered by the Byzantines under the redoubtable Belisarius in 533–4. Yet though it was dominated by all of these overlords, it was never won over culturally by any of them as in vast areas of the countryside the ancestral Berbers, people with ancient roots in North Africa who spoke an Hamito-Semitic language, retained much of their political independence and cultural identity.

In AH 26/AD 647, the Arabs, fired by their new and militant faith of Islam, burst out of Egypt into North Africa. At the battle of Sbeitla in present Tunisia, they easily defeated the Byzantines, whose hold on North Africa was in any case already fragile. But the Arabs were for the moment intent on no more than a raid, and content with the spoils of Sbeitla, they withdrew with their booty, not disturbing North Africa again for some seventeen years. Then, in 43/663–4 a certain ʿUqba b. Nāfiʿ al-Fihrī, an Arab chief, arrived at the head of an army bent on conquest He set up a military base at Qayrawān (Kairouan), at the eastern end of the littoral in present-day Tunisia, which later became one of the main religious and cultural centres of Islamic North Africa. At first he encountered fierce opposition from the Byzantines and certain Berber tribes. Under their leader Kusayla, these Berbers succeeded in driving the Arabs out of the eastern littoral, but this time, however, the Muslim Arabs did not withdraw. They fought back under a new leader, Ḥassān b. al-Nuʿmān, who reconquered the territory lost to Kusayla. He was then faced by another Berber revolt led by al-Kāhina, a Berber woman whose name means 'soothsayer'. This elderly lady, so reminiscent of the British Boudicca of an earlier age, harassed al-Nuʿmān for many years. But it appears the ancestral cult she represented had run its course, for by 79/698 Ḥassān b. al-Nuʿmān had finally succeeded in crushing this last serious resistance on the part of the Berbers, as well as that of the residual Byzantines.

The conversion of the Berbers

The Arabs' victory seemed complete and the conquerors turned to consolidating their position, especially in Qayrawān, which now became both a fortress city and a centre of learning. Events then took a remarkable turn. The Berbers, far from rejecting the religion of the conquerors, as one might have expected, began to come over to Islam in great numbers, rapidly becoming its most zealous adherents.

History is not without other examples of such apparently inconsistent behaviour, when conquered people have avidly embraced the culture of the conquerors while rejecting their political domination, and continuing to assert their own ethnic identity and independence. It was a frequent enough phenomenon of the Roman empire, as the cases of the British and other subject peoples of that empire show. Similarly, the Persians adopted the Islam of their conquerors and used it to revive their own imperial tradition.

It seems probable that such behaviour springs from an apperception that the ancient ancestral gods have let their people down, and that the demonstrably successful alien culture can be internalised and turned to the use of the vanquished, to redress the military and political balance in their own favour. In the Berber case, this strategy of purloining the conquerors' culture and religion and turning it against them may well have been provoked by the failure of Kusayla and al-Kāhina, both of whom seem to have been identified with the ancient animism of the Berbers, to achieve a lasting victory against the alien invaders. Hence the religion and the culture of Islam now made rapid strides across Ifrīqiya and the Maghrib throughout the first half of the first–second/eighth century. Moreover, while Arabic did not – and has never subsequently – extinguished the Berber dialects, it quickly replaced Latin as the administrative language and the language of the towns.

The Khārijī Revolt

In 122/740 the Berbers rose again, this time under a leader named Maysara. The Arabs were once again virtually driven out of North Africa. Only in their eastern stronghold of Qayrawān, on the very edge of the littoral, did they manage to hold out. Arab military domination was at an end; the spiritual hold of Islam was not.

Maysara and his followers were inspired by one of the earliest and most potent of Islam's dissident ideologies – Kharijism (from the Arabic root 'Kh R J', 'go out', thus 'dissent'). The *Khārijīs*, who had first arisen in Iraq in the turmoil of the first century of the Hijra were strict and puritanical, interpreting Islam in a fiercely egalitarian manner. In particular, they disputed the claim of the *Sunnīs* – those who follow strictly the 'Path' (*sunna*) of the Prophet Muḥammad – that the caliph (Arabic *khalīfa*), the supreme ruler of Islam, must be elected from the line of Quraysh, the Prophet's clan, and insisted that this office be open to all deemed deserving of it. Their ideology captured the imaginations of certain Berber activists, resentful of the haughty Arabism of the conquerors.

This Islamic egalitarianism, however, sank roots among only a minority of Berber zealots who proved capable of firing their fellow tribesmen for long enough to drive the majority of the Arabs back behind the walls of Qayrawān. Beyond that point it was not sustainable. Islam among the Berbers declined, becoming little more than a faint adherence that only tinged their traditional way of life at that time.

Early Islamic dynasties

Meanwhile, against this unsettled background, adventurers from the Islamic heartlands, contrived to set up a number of discrete Islamic principalities in North Africa: the Rustamids of Persian origin, in a Tahert (Tiaret), in what is now Algeria, the Idrisids from Arabia in the west, in what is now Morocco, and the Aghlabids, also of Arabia, centred on Qayrawān in Ifrīqiya (now Tunisia). The Rustamids professed Kharijism while the Idrisids were *Shīʿīs*. The Aghlabids, however, were *Sunnīs* who established centres of learning in which *Sunnī* Islam of the Mālikī *madhhab* (legal rite) was consolidated and from which it was slowly propagated among the half-converted Berbers of the countryside. By the end of the third/ninth century *Sunnī* Islam prevailed throughout most of North Africa although its victory was not yet secure.

The Fāṭimids

Later in that century a representative of another Islamic dissident sect arrived in Ifrīqiya, Abū ʿAbd Allāh al-Shīʿī. As this name implies, he was a member of the *Shīʿa*, a breakaway faction with strong Persian connections. The *Shiʿis*, too, dispute the *Sunnī* doctrine of the succession to the caliphate – namely that it resides with those who can claim the Prophet's Qurayshī blood. But unlike the Khārijīs, who wished to open it to all Muslims, they interpreted it in an even more restrictive fashion than the *Sunnīs*, insisting it belonged exclusively to the Prophet's son-in-law, ʿAlī b. Abī Ṭālib, and his descendants. This faction also looked for an *Imām*, an Islamic Deliverer who would appear from ʿAlī's line to claim the leadership of Islam. A similar notion was to arise among the *Sunnīs* who looked for a *Mahdī*, the final messiah, who would be precursed once in every century by a *mujaddid*, 'renewer'. The *Shīʿī* and the *Sunnī* versions of this idea differed essentially only in that the *Shīʿīs* believed their *Imām* had to come from the line of ʿAlī, while the *Sunnīs* expected their *Mahdī* to arise from the wider Qurayshite genealogy. Once sown in the soil of North Africa, this belief in a coming messiah became central to the characteristically eschatological politics of the area.

Al-Shīʿī won over certain Berbers to his cause and then launched an uprising that overthrew the Aghlabids opening the way for members of the *Shīʿī* family of the Faṭimids (descendants of Fāṭima, the Prophet's daughter and the wife of ʿAlī b. Abī Ṭālib) to migrate from the Middle East and establish a *Shīʿī*, Fāṭimid dynasty in Tunis, in 297/910. From here they defeated the last uprising of the Berber Khārijīs, led by a certain Abū Yazīd, known as the 'Man on the Donkey'. This gentle creature, perhaps mimicking the Christian tradition of Palm Sunday, now became a symbol of egalitarian revolt not only in North Africa but also elsewhere in Africa where Islam spread. More ambitiously, the Faṭimids also challenged the ʿAbbāsids in Baghdad, who had now replaced the Umayyads in Syria, for the leadership of the whole Islamic *umma* (the world-wide Islamic community).

In pursuit of these wider ambitions, in 362/973 the Fāṭimids moved from Mahdiyya, which they had by now built as their centre of government in Ifrīqiya, to Egypt. They left the administration of their North African palatinate to the Zīrids, Berbers of the Sanhaja group, who had been their allies throughout. But the Zīrids turned on their erstwhile patrons *c.* 440/1047, renounced the *Shīʿa,* returned to the *Sunnī* fold and declared their allegiance to the ʿAbbāsids, the Fāṭimids' great rivals. This move was no doubt as much one of convenience as of conviction, designed to win the support of the *Sunnī ʿulamāʾ*, Muslim literates, of Qayrawān which was by now not only a formidable fortress city but also an influential seat of learning devoted to the *Sunnī* form of Islam. Its scholarly community was bitterly opposed to what its members regarded as the heretical doctrines of the *Shīʿī* Fāṭimids, as well as their oppressive treatment of their *Sunnī* subjects.

The Hilalian invasion of North Africa

Since the Egyptian Fāṭimids were too weak to retaliate against Zīrid treachery by resort to arms, they turned to a tribe of nomadic Arabs – the Banū Hilāl – who were at that time raiding in Upper Egypt, and induced them to invade Ifrīqiya. By 443/1052 they had overrun the Zīrids and, to quote the eighth/fourteenth-century Muslim historian, Ibn Khaldūn, they spread through North Africa 'like a plague of locusts'.

Despite Fāṭimid inducements it is also clear that nomadic Arab pasturalists had already been on the move westwards from their Arabian homelands for some time before the Zīrids turned their coats. They would almost certainly have reached Ifrīqiya in any case, even if the Fāṭimids had not egged them on to do so since it appears that the Hilalian invasion was simply one wave of a longer-term migratory movement of Arab nomads that extended over some four centuries, beginning with the initial Arab incursions into North Africa. That fertile land proved a constant and inviting goal for migrating nomads, especially at times of political instability.

The conventional view of these bedouin invasions – of which Ibn Khaldūn is the chief begetter – is that they were abrupt disasters disrupting what he regarded as the settled and civilised Islamic way of life of that day. In comparing the nomads to locusts, he simply expressed the cultivated townsman's dislike of these rough pasturalists and their uncouth ways. But it is also possible to present the Hilālian 'invasions' in a more benign light, as a process of slow change to which the society of the day easily adjusted. The truth probably lies somewhere in between. No doubt the nomads did cause some immediate devastation. No doubt, too, their overgrazing created dust bowls where once there had been fertile cultivated lands, a process which brought decline to the towns that had depended on a surrounding agricultural economy since Roman times.

On the other hand – and for better or for worse – what the invasions unwittingly achieved in the longer run was the 'arabisation' of Ifrīqiya and the Maghrib. Except in the more remote mountainous areas, which remained Berber strongholds, their Arab tongue now rapidly overlaid the Berber of the countryside, though it did not entirely extinguish it; their Arab way of life permeated Berber society as they intermarried with Berber Muslims. The present, distinctive Arabo-Berber population of North Africa, and the North African dialect of Arabic widely spoken within it, is to be traced back, not so much to the early Arab conquerors, who planted Islam but little else, but to these Hilalian invasions that began in the fifth/eleventh century.

The Almoravids

The western Sahara had for many centuries been the home of Berber tribes belonging to the Sanhaja group. (Sanhaja is an arabised form of a Berber word *iznāgen* meaning 'those who speak Zenaga', a Berber tongue.) Pastoral nomads, they were distinguished by the wearing of the mouth veil, perhaps as a protection against Saharan dust storms. In consequence, they became known to the Arabs as *al-mulath-thamūn*, 'The Veiled Ones'.

One of their chiefs, fired by Islam, performed the Pilgrimage to Mecca *c.* 437/1045 and realised the parlous state of spiritual shortcoming among his own people. Returning by way of Qayrawān, now the site of a university mosque and the main North African school of *Sunnī*, Mālikī Islam, he sought a Muslim teacher and missionary for them, to work their salvation. Since none of the Qayrawān *'ulamā'* appears to have relished the task, he was put in touch with a certain 'Abd Allāh b. Yāsīn, from southern Morocco. This *'ālim* (Muslim scholar)' returned with the Sanhaja chief to the western Sahara. There he subjected the rude Veiled Ones to a regimen of stern and puritanical Islam, which, after some initial discontent, they took to with zeal. Before long 'Abd Allāh b. Yāsīn was leading them in raids, inevitably glossed as *jihād*, 'Holy War', against the settled oases of Dar'a and Sijilmasa, held by him to be awash with vice. These raids rapidly developed into a major invasion of Morocco by the Berber nomads. While there is no doubt about their new-found religious fervour, it is none the less reasonable to see their martial excursion within the wider context of the nomadic invasions by both Arab and Berber tribesmen, of settled, cultivated areas of the littoral, for which Islam provided the touchpaper.

The fiery 'Abd Allāh b. Yāsīn was killed in battle in 451/1059. By now the Veiled Ones, who were already masters of most of southern and central Morocco, had acquired another name – *al-murābiṭūn*. The word arises from the Arabic *ribāt*, 'frontier fortress', itself most appropriately derived from the verbal root 'R B Ṭ' 'to tether (a horse)', surely reflecting the frontier warfare these nomads engaged in. It became latinised as Almoravids, which will be used to refer to them henceforth.

After the death of 'Abd Allāh b. Yāsīn in 451/1059, command of the Almoravids passed to one of their chiefs, Abū Bakr b. 'Umar al-Lamtūnī, who in due course assumed what amounted to the sultanship of Morocco and founded the city of Marrākūsh (Marrakesh) *c.* 462/1070 as his capital. Internal dissension and rivalries among the Almoravids now led to a division of power among them. In consequence al-Lamtūnī turned back into the desert in 463/1071, where he is thought to have led the remaining Saharan Almoravids in a *jihād* against the non-Muslim Sūdānīs, the negroes of the southern Sahara and the Niger Bend, though precisely who these were is uncertain.

Meanwhile, in Morocco, al-Lamtūnī's cousin, Yūsuf b. Tāshufīn, pursued the North African war of conquest. By 462/1070 he had taken Fās (Fez) and subsequently Tilimsān (Tlemcen), thus making the Almoravids masters of *al-maghrib al-aqsā'*, the 'hinder Maghrib'.

By now the Muslim conquest of Spain, begun from North Africa by the Arabs in 91/710, had brought the southern half of the peninsula under Muslim domination. A turbulent history, from the first/eight century to the fifth/eleventh century, had seen the growth of a luxuriant Andalusion Islamic civilisation and the rise and fall of an Arab–Andalusian Umayyad dynasty. Its fall resulted in the fragmentation of Muslim Spain into a number of petty, squabbling principalities, one of which – the ʿAbbādids of Seville – now turned to the Moroccan Almoravids for help against their enemies, who included the Spanish Christians. Thus the Almoravids were given a foothold that in due course led to their own conquest of Muslim Spain; by about 493/1100 the Almoravids controlled a sweep of territory that included southern Spain, Morocco and an area down the western side of the Sahara, as far as the Sudanic state of Ghana. However, their Spanish conquest led these bare-bones Islamic radicals to become seduced by a lush way of life similar to that against which their early master ʿAbd Allāh b. Yāsīn had so ferociously inveighed.

The result of these conquests was the development of a Spanish-Moorish culture that embraced both Spain and Morocco and became especially evident in the towns of Marrākūsh and Fās (Fez). But beyond Morocco the starker, Arabo-Berber culture and mores of earlier days still ruled. For the later Almoravids the wages of succumbing to an indulgent Andalusian way of life proved to be the loss of their puritanical zeal, and with it the military ardour on which their supremacy had been built. They were now to be overtaken by other Muslims, also of Berber origin, for whom a new turn in Islamic theology provided the drive for conquest.

The Almohads

As in the case of the early chief of the Veiled Ones, so in that of the Berber Muh ammad b. ʿAbd Allāh b. Tūmart, it was the experience of Islam beyond North Africa that was the spur to radical reforming zeal. This Berber Muslim, having obeyed the Prophetic injunction to travel the world in search of *ʿilm*, 'religious knowledge', returned to Morocco *c.* 512/1118 in the heyday of Almoravid turpitude. What he found did not please him: wine shops, dancing girls and all the other raptures and roses of decadence abounding in Marrākūsh and Fās, where once there had been Koran recitations and the learned commentaries of grave Mālikī *ʿulamā*. He perceived the Almoravids of his day as having betrayed their sacred trust and set out to preach reform, the 'preaching *jihād*' that should always precede resort to arms. Finding this ineffective, he and his mainly Berber followers turned to a *jihād* of the Sword. By 555/1160 they had ousted the Almoravids and become the masters of the Maghrib, Ifrīqiya and finally of Muslim Spain.

Behind this military conquest – which once again surely reflected at one level the endemic ebb and flow of nomadic Berber pressures on the fertile littoral – lay a most interesting development in Islamic theology. The Almoravids had begun as stark Islamic radicals who applied the teachings of the Koran in a woodenly literalist fashion, uncomplicated by the more spiritual theology that had begun to make itself apparent elsewhere in the Islamic world. This literalism had become more oppressive and less inspiring as the ardour of the founders had given way to the mere formalism of the epigoni. Indeed, the Spanish Almoravids had publicly burned the works of al-Ghazālī, the great mystic theologian of Baghdad (d. 505/1111) in the square of Cordova, on the ground that his ideas were heretical.

Ibn Tūmart, on the other hand, appears to have been strongly influenced by al-Ghazālī, or at least by the climate of ideas he represented. He proclaimed the immanence of Allah, His immediateness and His immaterialness and at the same time he execrated the Almoravids as anthropomorphists who conceived of Allah in grossly human terms and thus came near to idolatry. His insistence that Allah was immanent in all things and could not be thought of as a separate entity from His creation gave rise to the name *al-muwahhidūn* or his followers from the Arabic *wahhada*, 'to assert the Oneness (of Allah)'. The name became latinised to Almohads: it is thus that this Muslim dynasty is now remembered in history.

But there was more to Ibn Tūmart's theology than this Ghazalian mysticism and its incipient pantheism. He also embraced the notion of the *Mahdī*, the Islamic messiah who was to come at the End of Time; and who was to be preceded by his 'Renewer', in Arabic *Mujaddid*.The Almohads thus replaced the cerebral austerity and literalism of the early Almoravids, to say nothing of the hedonism of their unworthy successors, with a form of Islam that emphasised transcendent mysteries, to be experienced and celebrated in the spirit, as well as theological precepts to be comprehended in the mind.

This change of emphasis had something to do with the rise to prominence in North Africa of individual *Ṣūfīs*, that is Muslim mystics, which was contemporaneous with it. Among them were Abū Madyān (d. 594/1197–8) and Abū al Ḥasan al-Shādhilī (d 656/1258), the eponymous founder of the Shādhiliyya *ṭarīqa*, *Ṣūfī* 'way'. Unlike the Almoravids, the Almohads looked benignly on Sufism and patronised its *awliyā'* (Arabic, singular *walī*), 'holy men'). The immense influence that Sufism exercised in the culture and politics of Muslim North Africa is to be traced back to the transcendental mysticism with which the Almohads tempered the stark outlines of Islamic formula-bound, intellectual theology.

Like the Almoravids, the Almohads made themselves masters of Muslim Spain as well as of North Africa. In both areas they quickly became patrons of architecture and learning. The notable Ibn Rushd (Averroes, d. 595/1198), an early rationalist and the primary intellectual opponent of the mystical al-Ghazālī, at one time enjoyed the hospitality of their court at Marrākūsh until his rationalism displeased the Almohads and he was banished for a time.

Yet not even this Almohad intellectual and spiritual flowering endured indefinitely. In their case, as in that of the Almoravids, the early fervour declined into empty ritual; their military ardour was blunted by defeat at the hands of both Christian and Muslim enemies and their political will was fragmented by internal factionalism. The Almohads were gradually replaced, by the family of the Ḥafṣids in Ifrīqiya, the Banū ʿAbd al-Wād (Ziyānids) in Tilimsān, in present-day Algeria and by the Marīnids who conquered Marrākūsh in 667/1269. By 674/1275 the Almohad empire was at an end. These three successor states had carved its North African province up into three principalities that broadly corresponded to the present-day divisions of, from east to west, Tunisia, Algeria and Morocco.

NORTH AFRICA FROM *C.* 673–4/1275 TO *C.* 960/1553

From the mid-seventh/thirteenth century to the mid-tenth/sixteenth century little political change of a far-reaching kind took place in North Africa. What change there was, occurred at a palace level. The various branches of the Hafsids in Ifrīqiya, the Banū ʿAbd al-Wād or Ziyānids as their reigning family was also known, in Algeria and the Marīnids in Morocco, competed within their own families and clans for power in their respective territories. They also alternately allied with one another against their neighbours, or squabbled across their frontiers. Some of their members were able and sought to re-create the unified North African empire of the Almoravids and the Almohads. They failed, largely because of their own internal divisions and their inability to win solid support from the mercurial bedouins, who simply exploited their family and tribal divisions. They were finally overtaken by the Saʿdids, a new dynasty destined to become outstanding in the history of North Africa, (see pp. 13–15 below).

The consolidation of Sunnī Islam

Yet these three centuries were momentous in other respects. In the course of them the hitherto kaleidoscopic pattern of North African Islamic history began to exhibit tendencies that became permanent. Gone were such aberrations as the Kharijism of the early Berber converts – though it lingered on for several generations among the Ibāḍīs, members of a sub-sect of the Khārijis, along the caravan routes, and in the cities of the Sahara and the Sahel. Gone, too, was the *Shīʿa*, which had never taken root in North Africa, even at the height of the Fāṭimid interlude.

What had taken root, over the changing fortunes of the early centuries, was *Sunnī* Islam as enunciated by the *Imām Mālik.* Not only did it become, and remain, the dominant form of Islam in urban North Africa, it also spread southwards into the Sahara, from there along the caravan routes into the Sahel and then, as will be seen, deep into the savannah country of the western Sudan. Surely this firm *Sunnī* Mālikī basis of north African and west African Islam is largely attributable, in the first instance, to the influence of Qayrawān, the early *ribāṭ*, or frontier fortress founded by ʿUqba b. Nāfiʿ al-Fihrī. It subsequently developed during the Almoravid and Almohad periods into a seat of learning where *Sunnī*, Mālikī *ʿulamāʾ* elaborated the doctrines and laws of Islam. From the seventh/thirteenth century to the tenth/sixteenth century, under the three successor dynasties to the Almohads, that is the Ḥafṣids, the Ziyānids and the Marīnids, this *Sunnī* Islam became yet more firmly entrenched thanks to the patronage of scholars and founding of *madrasas* (schools of higher Islamic studies) to which all three, but especially the Marīnids, were given. Indeed, in some measure, this patronage of *Sunnī* Islam was a consequence of the desire to restrain another Islamic tendency that flourished during this period, Islamic mysticism (Sufism), referred to briefly above, which took two forms: Sufism and maraboutism.

Sufism and maraboutism

It was during the Almohad period that the scholarly Sufism of men such as Abū Madyān and al-Shādhilī had become salient. These learned mystics did not wholly reject the cerebral theology of an earlier period, but in the manner of al-Ghazālī, in whose intellectual and spiritual influence their own thought had developed, they taught that it could be fully comprehended only in the light of mystic and intuitive experience. Thus the Muslim must seek to come nearer to Allah not only through the mastery of texts but also through contemplation and asceticism: by experiencing Him in the spirit as well as understanding Him in the mind. There was certainly already a hint of pantheism in their ideas: they believed that the Divine Essence infused the whole creation yet their teachings remained relatively restrained, and pantheistic tendencies were strictly controlled.

The Almoravids, as a dynasty, had risen and waned but the role of the *murābiṭ*, the Muslim frontier fighter, had not died with the ruling house. Holy men, still known as *murābiṭūn*, continued to wander the towns and the countryside of North Africa, not unlike the itinerant friars of medieval Europe. But they had turned, over the passage of time, from fiercely iconoclastic Islamic warriors into purveyors of popular magic. Their stock-in-trade consisted of Koranic amulets and incantations, divination, soothsaying and astrology based upon the Islamic Zodiac. This cult of magic, cast in Koranic mode, burgeoned in the villages and in the countryside of North Africa from late Almohad times onwards. It competed with the strict *Sunnī* formalism of the Mālikī *'ulamā'*; and with the more scholarly mysticism of the *ṭuruq* (Arabic plural of *ṭarīqa*). Later French scholars have distinguished this kind of activity by the name 'maraboutism', from the Arabic *murābiṭ*, explained above. Thus from the end of the seventh/thirteenth century to the beginning of the tenth/sixteenth century, three strands had gradually become institutionalised in North African Islam: the formalistic and largely legalistic Islam of the *Sunnī* *'ulamā'*, the scholarly mysticism of the *ṭuruq* leaders and the popular maraboutism of the countryside. They have remained so ever since.

The return of the Christians

Another characteristic of this period of almost 300 years was what may be thought of as the return of the Christians. The initial Islamic conquests had virtually extinguished any Christian presence along the littoral (there had never been a substantial presence further inland). In consequence, North Africa, once the home of Saint Augustine of Hippo (350–430), had become severed from the rest of the western Mediterranean world to which it had anciently belonged. During this period it was drawn to the culture of the Middle East rather than to that of Christian Europe.

But during the 300 years that followed the collapse of the Almohads, a tenuous European presence, which was at that era also necessarily a Christian presence, slowly began to reassert itself. In the sixth/twelfth century the Normans of Sicily had made an unsuccessful attempt to establish themselves by conquest in North Africa but by 818/1415 Ceuta, in Morocco, had been taken and held by the Portuguese which led to the establishment of a number of Portuguese factories, that is trading posts, in the area. The Portuguese were shortly followed by the Spaniards, who had set themselves up in Melilla by the end of the fifteenth century AD. Both the Portuguese and the Spaniards then began to play an increasingly active part in the tortuous politics of the North African sultanates. In fact, what was taking place at this time was the Christian reaction to the Muslim conquest of North Africa and Spain. In the Spanish case, the *reconquista* was completed by AD 1492 while in the North African case it was to increase in intensity over the centuries until it led to the colonial occupations of North Africa in the late nineteenth century and the early twentieth century AD. These colonial occupations achieved a slow and painful military, political and commercial victory over Islam but in contrast to the Spanish case, Christianity never re-established itself as the dominant religion and culture in North Africa. It remains essentially Islamic to this day.

The Ottomans

It was not only the Europeans who began to take an interest in the territories of the failing Ḥafṣids, Marīnids and other ruling families of the Maghrib and Ifrīqiya. By the beginning of the tenth/sixteenth century, Ottoman Turkish corsairs, contesting Spanish attempts to establish a presence along the coast and operating with the connivance of the distant Ottoman sultan, began to set up unstable petty states of their own in Algeria, Tunisia and Tripoli, which were then recognised by the sultan. This Turkish presence in North Africa was destined to become increasingly powerful as time went on, until in certain areas it developed into Turkish sovereignty that was to prove almost as unpopular with the native North African Muslims as that of the European colonialists who followed. It also had the effect of drawing the European powers into a confrontation with these Ottomans, in order to protect their own interests and influence in North Africa.

NORTH AFRICA FROM THE RISE OF THE SA'DIDS TO THE EVE OF THE COLONIAL OCCUPATIONS (*C.* AD 1830)

The Marīnids of Morocco were replaced by the Banū Wattās, a branch of the same family, *c.* 823/1420. They survived for nearly a century and a half, against a background of increasing encroachment by the Portuguese who, as was said above, had taken Ceuta in AD 1415 and the Spaniards, who had established themselves in Melilla by the end of the fifteenth century AD.

The Banū Sa'd

The consequences of Christian intrusions in North Africa (for the Muslims of the day thought invariably in terms of 'Christians' rather than of Europeans') was increasing resentment, especially among the *Ṣūfī* and maraboutic class, and frustration at the inability of the Wattāsids to act effectively against them. Meanwhile, in southern Morocco, around Sous, in the same stark landscape that had nurtured the Almoravid Sanhaja, a tribe known as the Banū Sa'd allied themselves with maraboutic interests against the Portuguese and the Spaniards, and finally against the Wattāsids themselves. These Banū Sa'd claimed descent from the Prophet, therefore styling themselves *shurafā'* (singular *sharīf*), 'nobles'. Their claim was widely accepted and they became known as the Sharifian Sa'dids. The claim also gained them the support of several other nomadic Arab groups, as well as of the influential Shādhiliyya *ṭarīqa* and the Jazūlī branch of the Qādiriyya *ṭariqā*. With this backing they set up their capital at Marrākūsh whence they succeeded in expelling the Portuguese temporarily from Morocco. They then turned on the Wattāsids and quickly overcame them; by 960/1553 the Sharifian Sa'dids were masters of all Morocco. By *c.* 1019/1610 they had extended the Sharifian empire beyond Morocco to embrace a wide corridor of territory that reached south down the western Sahara and on into the area of the Niger Bend, where it took in the Sudanic city of Timbuktu. The territory itself was styled the *pashalik* of Timbuktu and was ruled on behalf of the Sharifian sultan by a Moroccan *pasha* from 199/1591 to *c.* 1012/1603, after which date Moroccan authority declined.

The Portuguese king, Sebastian (1557–78), a Christian mystic of great religious fervour, now determined to win Morocco for the Cross. The result was the battle of al-Qaṣr al-Kabīr, in northern Morocco, in 986/1578, in which, ill-organised and less than wholehearted in their task, the Portuguese were heavily defeated. The real victor in this battle, the Sharifian sultan 'Abd al-Malik, did not survive it. He suffered a fatal heart attack in the moment of victory. Consequently, the credit for it went to his brother Ah mad, who thereupon assumed the title *al-Manṣūr*, 'The Victorious'. The military success against the Portuguese encouraged North African Muslims to rally against the Christians; Mawlāy Aḥmad al-Manṣūr's reign was launched on a wave of religious enthusiasm.

Mawlāy Aḥmad al-Manṣūr: 986–1012/1578–1603

Under al-Manṣūr the Sharifian Sa'dids reached a glittering zenith. It was during his time that the *pashalik* of Timbuktu was established, giving Mawlāy Aḥmad access to the gold and other riches of the western Sudan. In consequence the Sharifian state became extremely wealthy: its gold coins were greatly valued on European money markets and he was given the nickname *al-Dhahabī*, 'The Golden'. Mawlāy Aḥmad now claimed the right to be recognised as caliph of all Islam, in which capacity he argued, somewhat self interestedly, that the wealth of the Sudan ought to be solely available to him, to finance a *jihād*, 'Holy War', against the Christians. This stance did not prevent him, however, from seeking an alliance with Elizabeth I of England in an attempt to win certain Spanish territories. What it did do was to bring him increasingly into conflict with the Ottoman Turks, who were now becoming ever more involved in North Africa. They did not take kindly to his caliphal ambitions.

Another of his achievements was to set up the well-known Moroccan institution of the *makhzan*, or *dār al-makhzan* (from the Arabic root 'Kh Z N', 'store up'), a treasury and administrative system answerable to the sultan and staffed by *wazīrs* and other civil dignitaries, together with representatives of the *gish* (dialectal form of the classical Arabic *jaysh*, 'army'). It administered taxation and other civil and military matters. The *makhzan* continued as the central administrative institution of the Moroccan state up to and including the period of the French protectorate.

In carrying out these initiatives Mawlāy Aḥmad al-Manṣūr, notwithstanding his militantly Islamic claim to consanguinity with the Prophet, and his call to *jihād* against the infidels, did not scruple to employ an increasing number of Europeans, many of them Christian renegades to Islam, in an effort to balance out the influence of the Turks. Moreover, his commercial activities set up extensive links with both European Christians and Jews. The predictable consequence was rising popular discontent, especially among the *Ṣūfī* orders and the marabouts. From their point of view, it seemed that Mawlāy Aḥmad al-Manṣūr, who had set out to be the hammer of the infidels, had ended by conspiring with them against fellow Muslims. The end of his reign was therefore marked by growing popular discontent.

The succession was now fiercely disputed among his sons. Mawlāy Zaydān, who finally succeeded al-Manṣūr, failed to consolidate his position in the course of what amounted to a Moroccan civil war of which the Spanish took advantage to advance their own interests. A popular religious movement was set in motion that enabled a certain marabout, Abū Mahallī, to occupy Marrākūsh and drive the Saʿdids from it and other maraboutic leaders to set themselves up elsewhere. By the time Mawlāy Zaydān died in 1036/1627, Morocco had been largely broken up among these religious fraternities. By 1064/1654 the Sa'did empire had collapsed in anarchy.

There now ensued a period of rivalry among the religious factions, in which each attempted to assume the mantle of the fallen Sharifians. As a consequence of this political confusion Europeans were encouraged to attempt to establish themselves more firmly in Morocco. But by *c.* 1071/1660 a new and able Muslim dynasty, that of the 'Alawids, emerged out of this confused tangle of competing factions. Their rule survived into the French occupation.

The Turkish corsairs and their successors

Before passing on to the history of the North African sultanates and other principalities in the tenth/sixteenth and eleventh/seventeenth centuries, it will be useful to explain certain Ottoman titles that became current there during this period.

Bey denotes a 'prince' or 'governor' and is an Ottoman title of rank. It first appeared in European sources about AD 1599. It sometimes occur in the alternative form *beg.* A *beylerbey* is a 'Bey-of-beys', a *primus inter pares. Beys* were appointed by Istanbul and posted as governors to provinces of the Ottoman empire, including the Barbary states. A *beylik* is the jurisdiction of a *bey.*

Dey, which became familiar to the Europeans *c.* AD 1659, is the titular appellation of a commander of Janissaries, the professional slave soldiers, usually of Caucasian origin, of the Ottoman state. The word is Turkish and originally meant 'maternal uncle' or 'elder'. In North Africa it became the habit of *deys* to depose *beys*, *pashas* (q.v.) and others and seize the sole rulership for themselves. They frequently received retrospective recognition from the Porte for such *faits accomplis.*

Pasha, anglicised as 'Basha', Bashaw', 'pacha' etc., is also a Turkish title given to military officers of high rank and to governors of provinces. A *pashalik* is the jurisdiction of a *pasha*. The rank has three grades, distinguished by the number of horse tails displayed as insignia of rank. A *pasha* of three tails is the highest in rank. *Pashas* were also dispatched by Istanbul to govern provinces. The title *Pasha Bey* sometimes occurs and the difference between the two titles appears to be mainly a matter of honorifics.

Finally the title *Agha* also occurs. An *agha* was a military officer who commanded Janissaries. It appears to have been used as an alternative to *dey*, though *dey* may have denoted the higher command, while the *agha* commanded subordinate formations, possibly of cavalry. *Agha* sometimes occurs in combination with *pasha* as in Pepys's scathing reference to the hapless 'Basha Shavon Aga' (see p. 20 below).

In Tunisia the Ḥafṣids had retained control of little but the town of Tunis by *c.* 906/1500. For the rest, nomadic Arab tribes had largely taken over. By 947/1540 the noble city of Qayrawān had become a petty principality in the hands of the Shabbiyya tribe of Arabs, while Spaniards, Turks and local representatives of the Ḥafṣids waged a three-cornered struggle for power behind its walls. By 981/1574, the Turkish corsair Kilij ʿAlī Pasha, acting with the approval of Istanbul, put an end to the last of the Ḥafṣids and at the same time drove out the Spaniards. Thereupon Tunisia became a Turkish *pashalik* subsequently governed by usurping *beys* who enjoyed the retrospective authority of Istanbul. By a treaty of AD 1581 with the Porte, the Spaniards retained only certain trading stations in the area.

By the end of the ninth/fifteenth century in Algeria, the Ziyānids had lost control over all except Tilimsan. Once again, this opened the door to Spanish intrusion, as a result of which the Spaniards became masters of the whole Algerian coastline, while anarchy prevailed inland. Again with the connivance of an alarmed Istanbul, the Turkish corsairs ʿArūj and his brother Khayr al-Dīn, know to the Europeans as Barbarossa, 'Red Beard', entered Algeria in 921/1515. ʿArūj defeated the Spaniards and occupied Tilimsān and other coastal cities. Although he was killed in 924/1518 his work was carried on by his brother, Khayr al-Dīn, Barbarossa. This doughty pirate formally accepted the overlordship of the Ottoman sultan, who in turn recognised him and gave him the title *Pasha.* Algeria thus became the *Pashalik*, 'Regency' as the Europeans rendered this term, of Algiers. Khayr al-Dīn next turned his attention to Tunis, where he participated in the struggle resulting from the decline of the Ḥafṣids. Full Ottoman control of Tunisia was not realised, however, until the intervention of Kilij ʿAlī, in 981/1574.

The rule of metropolitan Ottoman representatives in Algeria and Tunisia was fragile and the position of the *pasha* or the *dey* sent by Istanbul became increasingly nominal. In the Algerian case, the situation quickly broke down into a tussle for power between the Janissaries, Turkish professional slave soldiers, brought in by the *beys* sent by the Ottoman sultan, and the largely independent corsairs who by this time had become a powerful political presence whose privateering activities largely sustained the Algerian economy.

These corsairs, who preyed upon the European sea-borne trade of the Mediterranean were made up partly of Turkish seafarers and partly of renegade Europeans, often Greeks, who had thrown in their lot with the Muslims. Although men such as ʿArūj and Khayr al-Dīn Barbarossa professed allegiance to the Ottoman sultan, the corsairs were largely a law unto themselves. Added to these sources of instability – the Janissaries and the corsairs – were these of the *khoulouglis*, descendants of mixed blood from Turkish fathers and Arab or slave women and of the Berbers and the Arab tribes, all of whom were powerful factions seeking their own interests against this turbulent background.

Throughout the eleventh/seventeenth century the hereditary professional slave class of Janissaries controlled the Algerian *dīvān* (classical Arabic *dīwān*), a Turkish administration nominally under the control of the *pasha* but in fact largely in the hands of the *aghas*, the military commanders of the Janissaries. They were, however, an unreliable lot, prone to constant plotting and revolts among themselves. They lost power, *c*. 1082/1671, to a succession of *deys* who were nominally elected by their own supporters. But this system, too, was short lived: in 1123/1711, the tenth *dey*, ʿAlī Shāwūsh, seized power and inaugurated his own regime.

In Tunisia, by now a Turkish *pashalik* founded by Kilij ʿAlī, as noted above, a similar situation quickly arose. The Janissaries again took over the *dīvān*, reducing the *pasha* of the day to a figurehead. Here, too, as in Algeria, a system of government by *deys* emerged and for some time achieved a measure of success. In due course, however, it developed into a hereditary dynasty of which a certain Ḥammūda b. Murād (1040/1631–1070/1659), who took the Turkish title *Bey*, 'Governor', was the outstanding member. The Murādid *beys*, who retained the offices of *dey*s *and pasha*s but reduced them to largely nominal roles, now ruled Tunisia.

The epigoni were, however, less able than the first Murādid *beys*. After a succession struggle and a civil war, a certain Ibrāhīm al-Sharīf, claiming the charismatic role of *Mahdī*, seized power in 1114/1702. He fell foul of Algerian raiders who sought to dominate Tunisia and who defeated and captured him in 1117/1705. He was succeeded by Ḥusayn b. ʿAlī, who received the approval of Istanbul by way of the sonorous title *Beylerbeyi pasha*, 'Bey-of-beys, Pasha'. The dynasty he founded, that of the Husaynids, was to rule Tunisia for the next two centuries, until Tunisia became a colonial possession of the French.

In eastern Ifrīqiya, the collapse of the Ḥafṣids at the end of the ninth/fifteenth century had been followed by a period of rule by local dynasties. By 916/1510 the Spaniards had seized the town of Tripoli, which they fortified and it was later handed over by them to the knights of Saint John of Jerusalem in AD 1530. In the middle of the tenth/sixteenth century, Tripoli suffered the same fate as Algeria and Tunisia in passing under the control of another Turk, Ṭurghut, known to the Europeans as Dragut. A notable corsair and a wily foe of the Spaniards, he was appointed *beylerbeyi* by the Ottomans in 961/1554, and deputed by them to establish Turkish rule over the coast and hinterland of Tripolitania. He was killed in 973/1565 in an attack against the Christians of Malta. He had encountered much opposition from the marabout class, which opposed Turkish rule. A troubled period followed in which the Arab population of Tripolitania led by a marabout called Niyāl revolted. Niyāl briefly became master of Tripoli in 997/1589 until he was defeated. Thereafter the territory was governed by *beylerbeys* sent out by Istanbul. Then the Janissaries revolted in 1018/1609 and set up government by *beys* appointed by themselves.

Meanwhile, the English, French and Dutch constantly intervened, diplomatically and sometimes by naval bombardment, in an attempt to suppress the privateering, for which Tripoli was a particularly notorious centre. A number of treaties were signed between the European powers and the *beys*, which the latter constantly broke – or so the Europeans claimed. In fact, it seems probable that lack of central control rather than deliberate duplicity lay behind the broken treaties. During this period, the *beys* of Tripoli engaged in their own hostilities with neighbouring Tunisia. By *c.* 1123/1711 the dynasty of the Qaramānlīs gained power and ruled Tripoli as a tributary of the Ottoman empire until the thirteenth/nineteenth century.

The age of privateering

The seventeenth century AD was the heyday of privateering off the coast of North Africa. It reached its peak early in that century when corsairs – renowned or infamous, according to one's point of view – operating from the North Africa ports and natural harbours, preyed upon the European shipping in the Mediterranean. Such characters as Barbarossa and Dragut became the great bogymen for generations of Europeans. This privateering supplied much of the revenue of the North African sultanates, *beyliks* and *pashaliks* and also gave rise to the notorious bagnios, the prisons in which European captives, taken in the course of privateering, were held, either for ransom or to work as galley slaves and in other capacities. Christian organisations were founded which were dedicated to the welfare of these unfortunates, and to the securing of their release, though in fact they tended to become agents and middlemen through whom ransoms were negotiated. Thus, in some measure, and despite their undoubted humanitarian intentions they contributed to institutionalising the whole ugly business. Among the more notable were the Trinitarians, the Lazarists and the order of Notre Dame de la Merci.

This enslavement and ransom-taking did not prevent the

European powers from entering into commercial agreements with the Muslims of North Africa, when this suited their purpose. As a result of such agreements, they set up many *funduqs*, or factories, along the coast. About AD 1700 the French established the Compagnie d'Afrique with the agreement of both the Algerians and the Tunisians.

Sometimes, captured Europeans adopted Islam and served the local rulers, though this did not always win Muslim approval since the prospect of a ransom was thereby lost.

North Africa in the Diary of Samuel Pepys

A vivid impression of what all this meant to the men of those times who were caught up in it, and the tortuous relationships between the European powers severally involved in North Africa, the Barbary dynasties and the Ottomans in Istanbul, is to be gained from the diary of Samuel Pepys. He was for many years Secretary to the English Admiralty; and on 20 February 1665 he was appointed Treasurer to the Tangier (Morocco) Committee, having served on that body since 1662. His diary entries contain frequent references to this committee, as well as to Algiers, or Argiers as he sometimes spells it, Tunis and Tripoli. The period he records runs from 1659 to 1669 when, increasingly afflicted by blindness, he was no longer able to continue his diary.

In Morocco the first part of the period was one of anarchy in which a number of petty polities arose – some ruled by corsairs, others centred on *Ṣūfī zāwiyas*, 'seminary-hostels' – and struggled for supremacy. The ʿAlawids emerged about 1070–71/1660 but their authority did not extend over the whole of Morocco until the reign of Mawlāy al-Rashīd (1075/1664–1083/1672), in the course of which Pepys finally had to abandon his diary. It was against this background of near anarchy that the English began their Tangier adventure.

In Algeria the *deys* of the Janissaries held power. The English had unsuccessfully bombarded the town of Algiers in 1622 and again in 1655, in an effort to check their privateering. A renegade Englishman, Ward, had taken on the task of reorganising the Tunisian navy earlier in the century, while the Lazarist, Père Le Vacher, was active there on behalf of the slaves held in Tunisian bagnios. The French, meanwhile, had built a *funduq* in Tunis in 1659.

As for Tripoli, in 1658 the English admiral John Stoakes had arrived there to establish an English consulate and negotiate a treaty which was signed in the name of Charles II with the *bey* of the day, a certain ʿUthmān.

By 1662 Pepys notes with satisfaction that:

> Dunkirke newly sold, and the money brought over; of which we

> hope to get some to pay the navy; which by Sir J. Lawson's having dispatched the business in the Straights, by making peace with Argiers, Tunis and Tripoli (and so his fleet will also shortly come home), will now every day grow less, and so the King's charge be abated; which God send![1]

But this peace was uncertain, according to Pepys, because the 'Duana' (the *Dīvān* of the Janissaries) failed to observe its terms:

> Captain Berkely is come to town with a letter from the Duana of Algier to the King, wherein they do demand again the searching of our ships and taking out of strangers, and their goods; and that what English ships are taken without the Duke's pass they will detain (though it be flat contrary to the words of the peace), as prizes, till they do hear from our King, which they advise him may be speedy. And this they did the very next day after they had received with great joy the Grand Seignor's [the Ottoman sultan?] confirmation of the peace of Constantinople by Captain Berkely; so that there is no command nor certainty to be had of these people.[2]

The instability of the political situation in Algeria at this time when, as was pointed out above, Janissary commanders succeeded one another as a result of palace *coups*, is reflected in a further comment by Pepys as to the English response to this failure of the Algerians to observe the treaty:

> The King is resolved to send his will by a fleet of ships; and it is thought best to send these very ships back again after cleaning, victualling, and paying them. But it is a pleasant thing to think how their Basha [*pasha*] Shavon Aga [*agha*] did tear his hair to see the soldiers order things thus; for ... when they see the evil of war with England, then for certain they complain to the Grand Seignor of him, and cut his head off: this he is sure of, and knows for certain.[3]

A series of such incidents, in which the Algerians allegedly broke the terms of the peace, culminated in the renewal of hostilities. On 3 May 1664, Pepys records:

> Mr Cutler told me how for certain [Admiral Sir John] Lawson hath proclaimed war again with Argiers, though they had at his first coming given back all the ships which they had taken, and all their men; though they refused afterwards to make him restitution for the goods which they had taken out of them.[4]

What life was like for the unfortunates held in the slave bagnios of Algiers is vividly recorded by Pepys in the following passage, dated 8 February 1661:

> Capt Cuttle, and Curtis, and Mootham, and I, went to the

> Fleece Taverne to drink; and there we spent till four o'clock, telling stories of Algiers, and the manner of life of slaves there. And truly Capt. Mootham and Mr Dawes (who have been both slaves there) did make me fully acquainted with their condition there: as, how they eat nothing but bread and water. At their redemption they pay so much for the water they drink at the public fountaynes, during their being slaves. How they are beat upon the soles of their feet and bellies at the liberty of their padron. How they are all, at night, called into their master's Baynard [bagnio]; and there do they lie. How the poorest men do love their slaves best. How some rogues do live well, if they do invent to bring their masters in so much a week by their industry or theft; and then they are put to do other work at all. And theft there is counted no great crime at all.[5]

In 1662 the Portuguese, who at this time controlled part of the coast of Morocco, had given the English the right to station a garrison at Tangier. Measures were taken to maintain the fortress and a great mole was constructed, to improve the harbour. Large sums of money were spent on this project, on behalf of the English Parliament, by the Tangier Committee, of which Pepys was a member, and eventually Treasurer. But the project was a troubled one from the start. On 20 February 1662 Pepys records:

> Letters from Tangier ... telling me how, upon a great defete given to the Portuguese there by the Moors, he had put in 300 men into the towne, and so he is in possession, of which we are very glad, because now the Spaniards' designs of hindering our getting the place are frustrated.[6]

However, the Portuguese were not the only ones to suffer severe losses. For in July 1663 Pepys received news that

> the Moors have made some attaques up the outworks of Tangier; but my Lord Teviott, with the loss of about 200 men, did beat them off, and killed many of them.[7]

But less than a year later, on 1 June 1664, he received

> the very sad news of my Lord Teviott's and nineteen more commission officers being killed at Tangier by the Moores, by an ambush of the enemy upon them, while they were surveying their lines: which is very sad, and he says, afflicts the King very much.[8]

A day later, 2 June, he received a more detailed account:

> It seems my Lord Teviott's design was to go a mile and a half out of town, to cut down a wood in which the enemy did use to lie in ambush. He had sent several spyes: but all brought word that the way was clear, and so it might be for any body's discovery of an enemy before you are upon them. There they were all

> snapt, he and his officers and about 200 men, as they say; there being left now in the garrison but four captains.[9]

He goes on to tell how, three years earlier, 'many brave Englishmen were knocked on the head by the Moores, when Fines made his sally out'. It is clear from such incidents that the Europeans did not always possess the superiority in weaponry and general military efficiency in the course of the seventeenth century that they came to enjoy some two hundred years later.

Overture to colonial conquest

During the seventeenth century AD the balance of power between the North African states and the Europeans was broadly maintained, as Pepys so colourfully illustrates. The Europeans were by no means invincible, although they probably had the edge over the Muslims in naval power even at that time. During the course of the eighteenth century AD, and as the Industrial Revolution gathered pace during its last quarter, that balance began to tip decisively in the Europeans' favour. It continued to do so until *c.* AD 1900, by which time the sultanates, *beylik*s and *pashalik*s of North Africa had become little more than puppets in the hands of their European masters.

In Morocco the ʿAlawids had some early success in restoring order, which had collapsed with the Sharifian Saʿdids' decline. They even managed to regain certain coastal territories from the Europeans between 1681 and 1691. However, a series of palace *coups* set up by slave soldiers between 1139/1727 and 1170/1757, resulted in the proclamation of twelve sultans over that period. Moreover, the *Ṣūfī* orders and the marabouts became increasingly restless at the encroaching European presence in Morocco, which was soon resumed. In the end the ʿAlawids were faced with the choice of excluding the Europeans altogether, as the religious classes wanted, but which was beyond their power, or whole heartedly embracing modernism, at the cost of intensified opposition from these classes. In the event they simply drifted. Yet willy-nilly, they found themselves making increasing political and financial concessions to the Europeans, especially the French. Moreover, Morocco had by now incurred substantial indebtedness to European finance houses by way of large loans that led to increasing European involvement in the Moroccan economy. By AD 1863 the Béclard Convention gave the French the right to intervene extensively in Moroccan affairs. Meanwhile conditions within Morocco deteriorated sharply. The oppressive taxation policies adopted by the sultans provoked constant civil unrest. In March 1912, France negotiated a treaty of protection with the hapless sultan of the day. The French colonial occupation of Morocco had begun.

In Algeria, unlike Morocco, no indigenous dynasty emerged. The Turkish *deys* and *pashas*, despite their Islam, were regarded by the native Algerians as foreign tyrants; there was constant opposition to their rule from the powerful *Ṣūfī ṭuruq*, from the marabouts and from Berber tribesmen, especially the Kabyles. This discontent was aggravated by the increasing financial interference of the Europeans seeking the production of produce purely for export, and the introduction of paper money, which distorted the traditional economy and caused hardship to the peasants. By 1245/1830 unrest in Algeria had reached such a pitch that French commercial interests, which were by now considerable, felt threatened. They pressed for outright occupation. In AD 1830 the French landed, took the town of Algiers and then formally occupied what is now Algeria.

In Tunisia a period of stability was enjoyed under the capable rule of Ḥusayn b. ʿAlī, a Turkish military commander who founded the Ḥusaynid line of *bey*s early in the twelfth/eighteenth century. It lasted uninterruptedly until the French occupation in AD 1881 but the prosperity that attended the early Ḥusaynids quickly declined, due in part to the cutting off of privateering, enforced by the European navies in the wake of the Congress of Aix-la-Chapelle convened by the European powers in AD 1819, and in part to the disruption of the Tunisian economy brought about by European involvement in it. The Ḥusaynid *bey*s attempted to retrieve the situation by turning to modernisation, by accepting ever larger loans from European financiers and by oppressive taxation of the peasants to offset this. This simply made matters worse. In 1280–81/1864 the tribes of the central region of Tunisia revolted. They were severely put down. By now almost bankrupt, the reigning Ḥusaynid *bey* accepted the oversight of Tunisian affairs by an International Financial Commission, composed of the major European sea powers in July 1869. This was followed, in May 1881, by the Convention of the Bardo, between the French and the Ḥusaynids which amounted to a *de facto* French protectorate over Tunisia.

A return to the world of the Mediterranean?

Some scholars, perhaps influenced by the ideas of the great French historian, Fernand Braudel, have thought to see in the colonial occupations the re-establishment of North Africa in a Mediterranean world from which it was temporarily torn away by the Islamic conquest of the first/seventh century – the culmination of the 'return of the Christians' referred to above. All three Barbary states were now under direct French control. One might indeed be forgiven for assuming that the wheel had turned full cycle, that the ravishing of Christian basilicas to set up the plagiarised columns of the Grand Mosque of Qayrawān had been avenged. The actual situation was not as straightforward.

Seen simply as a economic and commercial phenomenon, the history of the Barbary states does seem to have involved a severance of ties between North Africa and the rest of the Mediterranean world, which were then gradually renewed over the following centuries. By the ninth/fifteenth century, at the latest, Mediterranean Europeans had begun to trickle back in search of their share of the fruits of this prosperous land; by the sixteenth century AD, this had become a flood. Far from resisting it, many of the rulers of the area had embraced the opportunity for enrichment that participation in the trade of the Mediterranean offered, both by legitimate commerce and by privateering. Mawlāy Aḥmad al-Manṣūr, 'The Golden', was an outstanding example. He preached *jihād* against the Christians with one of his tongues while with the other he blandished the Virgin Queen of England for her help against the Spaniards. During his reign the gold of the Sudan flowed as abundantly into the European money markets as it did into those of the Middle East. Only the *Ṣūfī* and marabout classes – those committed to an exclusive Islamic spirituality that fortunately coincided with their material interests – had resisted what they believed to be the infidel encroachments this had entailed.

The privateering of the Muslims certainly proved damaging to the Europeans but it was ineffective in the long run in checking their determination to dominate the economy of the Barbary states. Such Europeans were little interested, however, in matters of religion and culture. These were of concern to certain single-minded idealists such as King Sebastian of Portugal and Philip II of Spain but mariners like Sir John Lawson and my Lord Teviott, not to say Samuel Pepys and his cronies quaffing their ale in the Fleece Taverne, were interested in cargoes and profits, not the cure of souls.

It is therefore reasonable to argue that, at a material level, one arm of the mainstream Mediterranean culture that began by being the aggressive mercantilism of Philip II's Spain, and gathered pace with the increasingly secular forces released by the industrial revolution, had imposed itself upon North Africa by *c.* 1900 and that it has continued to impinge upon it ever since. But at a spiritual and intellectual level, the triumph of the Mediterranean world over the world of the Middle East that spread across North Africa in the course of the Islamic conquest in the seventh century AD, is less evident. The ghost of Saint Augustine still waits in vain for Christianity to return to its ancient North African cloisters. Islam is surely unassailable in North Africa today; moreover, Sufism and maraboutism continue to give North

African politics that peculiarly eschatological quality characteristic of it.

To think of 'the Mediterranean world' as unified by climate, by the nature of the habitat and by the trade it generates, is valid. To imagine that it has ever returned to a cultural unity that was shattered, once and for all in the seventh century AD, is not.

NORTH AFRICA FROM *C.* AD 1830 TO INDEPENDENCE (AD 1956–1962)

Algerian resistance to the French

Despite the apparent ease of their initial occupation, the subsequent progress of the French was far from unopposed. For the Algerian people, the French were 'infidels' (they had yet to learn to think in such terms as 'colonialists' and other more modern expressions of obloquy). The proper response to them was *jihād*, 'Holy War'. What they looked for was a leader strong and able enough first to unite them around himself and then to lead them against the formidable French army under its ruthless commander, General Bugeaud. Understandably, they turned to the *Ṣūfī shaykhs*, the leading functionaries of the *Ṣūfī* orders, their traditional champions against the infidels, to fulfil this role. Their choice fell on a certain Shaykh Muhyī al-Dīn, a scion of a notable twelfth/eighteenth-century family of *Ṣūfīs* who had founded a Qādirī *zāwiya* at al-Qayṭān, in Algeria. This elderly scholar and mystic bravely declared holy war against the invading French. In rallying his forces he tried to enlist the help of the neighbouring Moroccans, who proved unreliable while the Tijānī *Ṣufīs* of ʿAyn Māḍī also withheld their support owing to an ancestral quarrel with the Qādirīs. None the less, Shaykh Muhyī al-Dīn and his son, the Amīr ʿAbd al-Qādir, fought the French in two battles near Oran, in 1248/1832, in which the French were defeated and in which ʿAbd al-Qādir distinguished himself. He now took over direction of the *jihād* from his ageing father.

The Amīr ʿAbd al-Qādir was not a mystic but a learned theologian. None the less, it is probable that the eschatological symbolism of the year 1200/1785–6 (the turn of the century of the *hijra*) 'prefigures the activities of the Amīr ʿAbd al-Qādir'.[10] ʿAbd al-Qādir sought to legitimise his position not by claiming to be a *mahdī* but by the more cerebral use of learned *Sunnī* metaphors. First, he attempted to recreate the early Islamic caliphate, as a means of unifying the Algerians in the fight against the infidels. This pleased the *'ulamā'*, long dissatisfied with the modernising policies of compromising *beys*. Secondly, he adopted the Prophet's example when faced with infidel opposition that could not be immediately overcome, namely *hijra*, 'emigration', out of infidel reach. He made his capital at Mascara in western

Algeria, but when this was burned down by the French General Clauzel in AD 1835, the Amīr and his entourage withdrew in *hijra* to the mountainous areas of Algeria and the Sahel. From here they waged guerrilla war against the French.

The Amīr ʿAbd al-Qādir commanded a substantial army, for which he obtained ample weapons and supplies from a number of sources, some European and, reputedly, even French. Although he held the French at bay for nearly fifteen years, his efforts were largely vitiated by the chronic inability of the Algerian Muslims to unite. He was obliged to fight a 'second front' against a certain Muḥammad b. ʿAbd Allāh al-Baghdādī who, in contrast to the Amīr's more sober pretensions, did claim to be the *Mahdī* and led a revolt against the Amīr in protest at his attempts to raise taxation – an unavoidable requirement of his war effort against the French.

Yet another charismatic emerged to muddy the waters. He too was called, or adopted the name, Muḥammad b. ʿAbd Allāh, but became known as 'Bū Ma'aza', 'The Man with the Goat', for this little creature, like the donkey, had often served as a millennial symbol for the Muslims. Bū Ma'aza and his followers, those who resented the French occupation, suffered heavily at the hands of the French and he later abandoned his initial claim to be the *Mahdī* and co-operated with the Amīr ʿAbd al-Qādir. He was subsequently captured by the French and imprisoned.

In AD 1847, the Amīr ʿAbd al-Qādir, frustrated by the fissile nature of his support, was forced to surrender to General Bugeaud. None the less, spasmodic armed resistance continued until *c.* AD 1880 including major uprisings in Kabylia between AD 1852 and 1864 and in the Sahara from AD 1864 to 1870. In 1871 a certain al-Ḥājj Muḥammad al-Muqrānī revolted again, at the head of a loose confederation of tribes from southern Algeria. The revolt was severely put down. By 1880 the French had virtually completed their pacification of Algeria.

Reflections on the French in Algeria

The period of the French administration in Algeria that followed the suppression of these risings and preceded the final granting of independence in 1962, has earned a somewhat unfavourable presentation from some historians. There is, of course, no doubt that French financial interests were prominent in egging on often half hearted French governments to undertake the outright conquest of Algeria, as well as the rest of North Africa during a period of considerable domestic political turmoil. Yet in finally succumbing to such pressures the French government was no different from several other European powers of the day, who behaved similarly elsewhere in the

Mediterranean and Africa. Most of the major European powers – and some minor ones – also cherished their own ideals of what the French thought of as their *mission civilisatrice* and the British as 'order and good government'. They were sincere ideals in their day, colonial adventuring not having attracted the odium that later became associated with it. It is surely anachronistic to indict the ethics of an era in the light of those that evolved long after its passing.

The long history of privateering played a large part in provoking the Europeans' eventual armed intervention. While it is true that both Christians and Muslims constantly engaged in piracy throughout the Middle Ages and the Renaissance period, the problem was more deep rooted than just a cycle of retaliation. Muslim preying on Christian shipping in the Mediterranean had begun almost as soon as the Muslims had become established in North Africa. It was inseparable from the whole theocratic, Koranic perception of the Muslims, which left them with the unshakable belief that to attack the infidel as and where he was to be found was consistent with the Will of Allah. As in the case of enslavement, so also in that of piracy, there was no moral restraint on Muslim behaviour, only the constraints of expediency. Agreements to restrain privateering were not honoured since the fissiparous structure of the Islamic polities in North Africa rendered the enforcement of such agreements by any central authority nugatory as Pepys's account so clearly shows. Under such circumstances the eventual occupation of the area by one or other of the European powers seems, in hindsight, to have been both inevitable and understandable. The alternative was to cease trading in the Mediterranean.

The French conquest of Algeria was followed by a policy of colonisation that undoubtedly deprived the indigenous Muslim cultivators of much land, by sequestration or outright purchase. This was not due to any policy of bare-faced dispossession, as might be imagined from the moral indignation that transfuses some accounts. It was more a case of cultural clash than deliberate tyranny being a consequence of the application by the French, of western legal norms governing private ownership – a status that, as far as land was concerned, was largely unknown in Islam, land being held under complex customary laws of clientship and immemorial tenant rights. Vast numbers of North Africans did continue, in the mountains and in the Sahel, to live their lives in the traditional fashion undisturbed by these developments; and under a more equitable, less arbitrary administration than had been their lot under the Turkish *beys*.

Nevertheless, French government, however even-handed, had the undoubted disadvantage that it was administered by unbelievers, not by believing Turks, however oppressive. It may well be that it is perceived to be better to be misgoverned by those who share one's own culture, than to be governed well by cultural aliens.

As for the *colons*, the European settlers in North Africa, they were pawns in the same game as the Muslims. Many settled in the coastal towns, where they made no direct demands on agricultural land, most being shopkeepers and artisans. These towns expanded rapidly and quickly took on the characteristics of European towns on the Christian side of the Mediterranean divide. Some speculation in land inevitably followed, which caused economic dislocation. The European population, Italian and Spanish as well as French, grew from 272,000 in AD 1870 to 681,000 by 1911 while the native Algerian population also grew considerably over the same period until, by 1911, it numbered 4,686,000. These figures hardly support the notion of an oppressed and disinherited people exploited by a European colonial elite.

Such comments as:

> On the French side, there was a distinct willingness to show a strong hand against a people who were considered 'inferior'. A clear racist tone emerged here, coupled with a wish to test new French weapons of the time,[11]

and:

> The new type of colonist [apparently later town-dwellers as opposed to earlier village-dwellers] became hardened in a racialism which sometimes took violent forms against the native Algerians,[12]

seem to ignore the fact that the vast majority of the *colons* were simple peasants whose way of life differed little, at a material level, from that of the indigenous Algerians. While tension surely existed from time to time between the Algerian Muslims and the *colons*, it is very doubtful whether this ought to be described as 'racism', which is essentially a modern concept that has developed since the Second World War. These *colons* were, however, almost to a man, Roman Catholics of many generations' standing. For centuries the Muslims of North Africa, and indeed throughout the whole Islamic *umma*, had been used to referring to such people as 'infidels', except when it suited them to regard them as 'People of the Book'. The Catholic peasants, on the other hand, had been accustomed to think of the Muslims as 'followers of Anti-Christ' at least since Dante Alighieri had so unkindly consigned the Prophet Muḥammad to the Seventh Hell, together with the rest of those he considered to be Christian heretics! It is to such essentially religious and cultural prejudices, on both sides, and not to some anachronistic, secular concept such as racism – an attitude that was barely conceived of *c.* AD 1830 – that one should look for an understanding of the antagonisms that existed between these two groups of people of totally different religions and cultures: antagonisms towards which an empirical, not a censorious approach is appropriate.

Further aspects of the French administration

The French governed Algeria by a system of *bureaux arabes*, which they set up in AD 1844. These institutions included both French officials and Arabs: *'ulamā'*, tribal *shaykhs* and other dignitaries, most of whom appear to have served willingly. The system worked well, fostering mutual understanding between Arabs and French. It enabled many Arabs to come into contact with French culture, which often fascinated them. There thus developed in Algeria a class of Arab who, while retaining Islam, none the less adopted aspects of the French life-style, especially the language and literature. This is, once again, an example of that phenomenon commented on above, whereby a conquered people takes what pleases it from the culture of the conquerors while retaining its own political identity. Many of these Muslim Arabs and Arabo-Berbers who acquired a French education, and who became fully at home in French social circles, were to be the leaders of the Algerian independence movement.

The other development of this period, to which the system of *bureaux arabes* certainly contributed, was the growth of a tendency among French military officers and civilian administrators that became known as *royaume arabe.* It was an Arabophile movement that favoured integration with the North African Arabs in a Franco–Arab commonwealth, arising out of the attraction these admirable French soldiers – a class that frequently had much closer human relations with the Arabs than the politicians – and certain civil administrators experienced to Islamic culture. In many ways the mirror image of the process by which certain Arabs became seduced by French culture, it may have had its roots in Napoleon I's well-known infatuation with Egyptian Islam, to the extent that many Muslims of his day confidently believed he had adopted Islam.

This Arabophile party was influential in the court of Napoleon III, who at one time espoused its ideas. Catholics were, however, fiercely hostile to it and their view prevailed. Yet *royaume arabe* was a humane and civilised manifestation of tolerance and cultural synthesis born out of the daily experience of soldiers and colonial administrators, whose lives brought them into constant contact with the Muslims, not of the lucubrations of distant intellectuals. It created among the French strong ties of affection with *Algérie française* and was largely responsible for the concept of *France d'outre mer*. It is an aspect of French colonial history it may be more profitable to dwell on than the alleged eagerness of certain individual French soldiers to try out their new weapons on their Algerian opponents.

Algeria to independence

Despite the tendency among many Algerians to adopt French culture, there remained a huge majority of Muslims for whom such dallyings with the perceived infidel oppressor seemed simple treachery. Moreover, the pervasive influence of French culture – in architecture, education, language, commerce and in all the most conspicuous aspects of daily life – appeared to them no more than a constant threat to, and humiliation for Islam. An embittered opposition had begun to develop in the immediate wake of the Amīr ʿAbd al-Qādir's defeat, growing in strength and intensity between 1918 and 1939.

The French defeat in the Second World War sounded the death knell for all her colonial administrations. While some Algerians had rallied to the French side, perhaps fearing that a German colonial occupation would be even less acceptable than that of the French, whom they knew, most saw France's difficulties as an opportunity to seize independence. The Allied landings in North Africa gave added impetus to this since the independence movement was favoured by the Allies, especially by the Americans, for obvious historical and ideological reasons. From 1945 onwards, unrest against continued French rule increased, and was held down with increasing difficulty by the French. By 1948 the Algerian resistance had gone underground where it took the form of agitation and civil disobedience. The situation continued to deteriorate until by 1954 open warfare had broken out between the Algerian *Front de libération nationale* (FLN) and the French Army. In 1962, and after the gallant but unsuccessful 'Insurrection of the Generals', who opposed what seemed to them De Gaulle's abject policy of capitulation, Algerian independence was granted.

Independence did not result in the re-establishment of an Islamic state in Algeria. On the contrary, what emerged was thirty-odd years of one-party socialist-style government under a series of secularist political leaders: Ahmed Ben Bella (1962–5), Houari Boumedienne (1965–78) and Chedli Benjedid (1978–92), that has proved just as objectionable to Muslim radicals as the colonial administration which it replaced.

Tunisia to independence

The administration that the French set up in Tunisia was remarkably similar to the later British colonial model, known as 'indirect rule' for the formula agreed by the French with the *bey* allowed him absolute power, subject only to oversight by French ministers for foreign affairs, and a Resident General. Local administration remained in the hands of *qā'ids,* Muslim officials representing the traditional Tunisian establishment, assisted by subordinates known as *khalīfas* and *kāhiyas*. Despite the initial freedom allowed to the *bey*, his position became gradually more formal, resembling that of a constitutional monarch, who reigns but does not rule. The French, the other hand, abrogated steadily greater powers to themselves by a process of increasing centralisation.

As in Algeria, so in Tunisia, there was a policy of encouraging European immigration – in the Tunisian case mainly by Italians and Maltese rather than by French nationals – by favourable land laws and other inducements. Without a doubt, this policy did much to repair the ailing Tunisian economy by the commercial and agricultural skills of these people but, inevitably, it incurred the growing hostility of the Muslim Tunisians, who felt threatened by this alien, non-Muslim influx.

By 1908 an organised opposition had emerged. It was known as the 'Young Tunisians'. In 1919 these Young Tunisians founded a new opposition party, based on their demands for a Tunisian constitution (Arabic, *dustūr*) that would give them greater control over their own affairs although they did not yet demand full independence. This association became known as the 'Destour Party' and was opposed by the *colons*, who feared they might suffer discrimination under such a constitution. By 1934 the Destour Party had become the 'Neo-Destour Party', under the leadership of Habib Bourguiba (a Gallicised form of the Tunisian Arabic Bū Ruqayba). It presented new demands that went beyond those of the original Destour, in that it aimed for a wholly independent Tunisia. Even so, this was to be completed by a treaty of friendship and unity with the French Republic.

Up to this point the Tunisian opposition to the French had certainly been less acrimonious than that in Algeria, due it would seem to the greater economic prosperity of the country perhaps arising from the predominance of Italians and Maltese among the *colons*. These people, and especially the Maltese, whose language had evolved under the strong influence of Arabic, were somewhat closer in their life-style to the indigenous Tunisians than were the French settlers.

The fall of France in 1940, the occupation of Tunisia by the Axis and the subsequent Allied landings, all contributed to weakening the French hold, though it is notable that they did not prevent Habib Bourguiba, whom the French had earlier imprisoned, from siding with the Free French in their fight against the Axis. None the less, violent clashes occurred between 1943 and 1956, although outright civil war, such as had broken out in Algeria, was avoided. In 1956, France conceded full independence to Tunisia. The *beylik*, commonly referred to as 'the monarchy', was abolished by Bourguiba in 1957 and Tunisia was declared a republic.

Morocco to independence

The treaty of protection which the French signed with the Moroccan sultan in March, 1912 issued in practice in a somewhat less direct form of government than that imposed in Algeria and Tunisia. This was partly due to the fact that the administration of this territory was placed in the hands of the well-known Marshall Lyautey, a man of great talent who was probably influenced by the ideas of *royaume arabe,* discussed above. But despite Lyautey's best efforts, Muslim discontent was never stilled. There was organised military resistance to the French occupation from its inception, especially in the mountainous tribal areas, the Middle Atlas and the Rif. From here a certain ʿAbd el-Krim (ʿAbd al-Karīm) led a revolt that, while not on the scale of ʿAbd al-Qādir's movement in Algeria, none the less gave the French, and the neighbouring Spanish in Spanish Morocco, considerable trouble. It was not finally subdued until 1934. Meanwhile, the introduction of French law, in the teeth of the predictable opposition of the religious classes, the activities of Christian missionaries, the celebration of French national holidays and Christian feast days and so on, angered the Muslims. By 1937 a nationalist party and a popular movement were both demanding independence. The Allied landings in the Second World War enabled the Sultan of Morocco to defy the Vichy French President; he was backed up in this by the Allies, particularly the Americans, whose understanding of the situation was minimal but whose sympathy for the Moroccan cause was, for historical reasons, boundless. Led by the *Istiqlāl* (Independence) Party, and strongly opposed by the Free French Committee of National Liberation, the Moroccans finally achieved independence in 1956, under King Muhammad V who, despite this appellation, ruled as a traditional Muslim sultan.

Of the three North African states to gain independence from the French, Morocco has perhaps retained its links with the Islamic past to a greater extent than either Algeria or Tunisia. None the less, it has incurred the profound dissatisfaction of Muslim radicals, for policies and attitudes that seem to these people to betray that past.

ISLAM IN NORTH AFRICA FROM THE FIRST/SEVENTH CENTURY: BELIEFS AND ATTITUDES

Early developments

The first manifestations of Islam as brought by the Arab invaders to North Africa were of the primitive *Sunnī* persuasion. By the end of the second/eighth century this had found expression in the Mālikī *madhhab*, named after the jurist Mālik b. Anas, one of the four classical codifiers of the law. A scholarly, somewhat literalist interpretation, it placed great emphasis on written texts and regarded the expression of Islam as essentially both literate and legalistic. It was assailed in the second/eighth century by Berber Kharijism, a levelling tendency that challenged the elitism of the Arab Mālikīs. This failed to take substantial root, though its tendrils survived in subsequent outbursts of popular egalitarianism; and in small Ibadite communities that clung on until the eight/fourteenth century along the Saharan caravan routes and in the Sudanic kingdoms.

Malikism was also challenged briefly in the third/ninth century by Shiʿism. This was a flash in the pan. Except perhaps architecturally, Shiʿism has disappeared from North Africa without trace.

The next significant development in the evolution of North African Islam was the appearance of the Almoravids. Their doctrines represent *Sunnī*, Mālikī Islam of the founding *ʿulamāʾ à outrance*. Indeed, the ideas espoused by the Almoravids differ very little, if at all, from those of the Wahhābīs and the Muslim Brotherhood of the present day.

The following Almohad dynasty was undoubtedly a milestone in the elaboration of Islamic ideology. While retaining the full orthopraxis of *Sunnī* Islam, the Almohads added to this a metaphysical and gnostic dimension. They did not create Sufism but they certainly popularised it in North Africa and nourished its growth. Their era witnessed the establishment of the Qādiriyya and the Shādhiliyya *Ṣūfī ṭuruq*, the mystic 'ways' or orders. But lest it be thought that the rationalist opposition to Sufism, discussed below (pp. 40–2), is some new thing, it is well to remember that the intellectually daring Ibn Rushd (Averroes) was expelled from Marrākūsh in the second half of the sixth/twelfth century for the same kind of rationalist scepticism for which, *mutatis mutandis*, such modern reformers as al-Afghānī and Muḥammad ʿAbduh were excoriated by the traditionalists 700 years later. It is doubtful whether there is ever anything new under Islam's crescent moon!

The structures of Sufism and maraboutism

The 'respectable' Sufism of the Almohads was quickly joined by what some consider the disreputable popular Sufism or 'maraboutism' of the peasants and the urban masses. This was an accretional, thaumaturgic industry that called to its aid astrology, amulets, veneration of the tombs of the *awliyā'*, 'holy men', Koranic incantation, divination by Koranic squares (*ʿilm al-awfāq*) and so on. It has thrived up to the present day.

The *ṭuruq* and these marabouts, or popular *awliyā'*, were not overtly political but neither were they apolitical for Islam encompasses the whole of political life. Furthermore, the *ṭuruq* were organised. There was a *shaykh* or *quṭb* ('Axis'), usually the founder, around whom all revolved. He in turn had his disciples, the *muqaddam*s who lived as a community in a *zāwiya, a Ṣūfī* seminary and hostel. The *ṭarīqa* members, the *ikhwān* 'brothers; or *aḥbāb*, 'beloved', formed a tight fellowship that cut across tribal and family links. They met at frequent intervals for communal prayer, led by the *shaykh* or his *muqaddam*, 'deputy', then for the *dhikr*, 'remembrance' circle, in which they incessantly intoned the Names of Allah in unison, in such a manner as to produce liminal states. The more impressionable *ikhwān* experienced visions in the course of these proceedings, serving to cement them and their companions more firmly into the *ṭarīqa*. Sometimes a particular charismatic individual would emerge, to become *al-shaykh al-murshid*, the 'guiding shaykh', who would found a sub-sect, loosely linked to the mother *zāwiya*; and would set up a *zāwiya* of his own. Thus the *ṭuruq* proliferated.

Clearly, such organisations were physically and psychologically immediately adaptable to political purposes; and to becoming quasi-military bodies apt to fight *jihād*, 'Holy War', against the infidel who constantly threatened the North African coastline. The dividing line between such organised *ṭuruq* and the marabouts of the countryside and their credulous clients, was imprecise. In consequence, the *ṭuruq* leaders were always able to recruit immediate additional manpower from the Muslim peasants and villages, as well as from the urban masses. Such levies were the mainstay of resistance to the Christians and the Turks, especially during the early colonial era, when the Janissaries and other regular troops of the sultans, *pasha*s and *bey*s had been stood down or had passed under European control. They helped to form the armies of such resistance leaders as the Amīr ʿAbd al-Qādir.

The thaumaturgic dimension to the North African political process succeeded, in the tenth/sixteenth century, in setting up its own symbols of legitimacy, which recur again and again, in the dynastic history of the area. The Sharifian Saʿdids gained power, and held it, because they were *shurafā'*, members of a hereditary noble clan who claimed to be able to trace their descent back to the Prophet's tribe of Quraysh. This gave them *baraka*, the power to confer blessing; their claim received the immediate endorsement of the *ṭuruq* and the marabouts; thus was the Sharifian empire born. It successfully renewed itself in the 'Alawids, who also claimed *baraka*. Innumerable aspirants to power during the period of hegemony of the Turkish *beys* and *pashas*, and the usurping *deys*, made the same claim, with varying degrees of success. Similarly, the early leaders of the resistance to the European intruders annexed to themselves the blessed genealogy, without which their initiatives would probably not have carried conviction with the Muslim commonality.

Some Ṣūfī techniques and beliefs

What did these *Ṣūfīs* and their maraboutic associates believe, that inspired them to their endeavours?

All the early *ṭuruq* such as the Shādhiliyya, stem from the Qādiriyya, founded by 'Abd al-Qādir al-Jīlānī (or Kaylānī) in the fifth–sixth/eleventh–twelfth century. The process involved the granting of an *ijāza*, a mystic pedigree, sometimes *silsila*, 'chain', from the master to the postulant, together with the master's *wird*, 'litany'. At the same time the postulant received instruction in reciting the litany, in contemplative and ascetic practices (*zuhd*), known collectively as *khalwa*, designed to bring about *fanā'*, 'annihilation [of self in Allah]'. This led ultimately to *baqā'*, 'union [with Allah]'. The reward for success in this gnostic process was *wajd*, 'religious ecstasy'. After al-Ghazālī the search for such *ma'rifa*, 'gnosis', was not thought incompatible with scholarly theology, that is *'ilm*, but rather as complementing it. Moreover, the practice of such Sufism was at first performed on an individual basis. Later, communal practices became increasingly popular, postulated upon such Koran verses as 23:31, 'and turn altogether to Allah, O Believers, that you may prosper'. It was at this point that the *ṭuruq* began to emerge as hierarchical organisations.

The apotheosis of the Prophet

At first it was believed that *fanā'* was to be achieved by the postulant's own efforts, or perhaps through the intercession of the angels, but gradually the idea evolved that it was possible only through the intercession of the Prophet Muḥammad. At this point there began the apotheosis of the Prophet, who became *al-Insān al-Kāmil*, 'The Perfect Man' and *Afḍal al-Khalq*, 'The Most Excellent of Creation'. This development was always inherent in Islam, for it has its roots in

Koran 94:4, 'Have We not exalted for thee thy mention?' That it became salient at this point is usually attributed to the influence of the seventh/twelfth to thirteenth-century Hispano-Arab mystic, Muhyī al-Dīn b. al-'Arabī, who was certainly in touch with North African Muslims during the formative period of *Sūfī* thought (the heyday of the Almohads) having studied in Ceuta and Tunis. Yet the elaborate nature of his ideas bespeaks a long period of gestation perhaps going back to the very beginning of Islam and having many independent lines of development.

Also in the seventh/thirteenth century there flourished the Moroccan poet and mystic, al-Fāzāzī (d. 627/1229–30). He composed his long, ardent and very popular praise poem to the Prophet, known as 'The Twenties', in reference to its verse structure. It is made up of such adulatory sentiments as:

> He is not to be compared with the full moon which reaches
> only half way through the month,
> For it increases in lustre only as long as time prolongs
> its life [but he increases in lustre for ever].[12]

But, more specifically, what al-Fāzāzī did was to take the Koran-based story of the Prophet's *isrā*, his miraculous 'night journey' from Mecca to Temple Mount in Jerusalem, on the fabulous al-Burāqa, a winged riding beast that was half woman and half mare or jenny, adorned with a peacock's tail; and his subsequent *mi'rāj*, 'ascension', in the company of Jibrīl (Gabriel), through the celestial spheres to the Throne of Allah at the summit of the Seventh Heaven, and turn it into a mystical rationale for the apotheosis. That story, which blossomed into the greatest religious romance in all Islam, and has been told and retold in all Islamic tongues, arises from two brief visionary references in the Koran:

> Glory to Him Who carried His servant by night from the Sacred Mosque [Mecca] to the Remote Mosque [Jerusalem], whose precincts We blessed, that We might show him Our signs. ...(17:1)

and 58:8–9:

> Then he drew near, drew nearer yet,
> So he was the measure of two bows or closer still ...

These are taken to refer to the climax of the *mi'rāj* when, in Jibrīl's company, the Prophet reaches the summit of Paradise and approaches to within two bow lengths – or some say bow shots – of the Divine Throne. Here, so the story goes, he received various instructions from Allah, such as the institution of the five quotidian prayers, as well as an assurance of salvation for all true Believers. Al-Fāzāzī, with this as his text, asks rhetorically,

> And is there, after his journey to his Lord, a goal?

He continues:

> I bear witness that God sent His servant on a night journey
> From the farthest mosque, ascending to the Throne.

And, most significantly for the *Ṣūfīs*:

> Leave all other work to praise Muhammad,
> for he is the road to salvation and its source.

Such ideas as these, repeated again and again by writers of *madīḥ*, 'Prophetic panegyric', who were contemporaries of al-Fāzāzī and who followed after him in North Africa and in nearby Egypt, were the germ of the notion that the Prophet, and not the angels, was the true intermediary to Allah.

Another poet who helped foster this notion of the Prophet's quasi-divinity was the seventh/thirteenth-fourteenth century Sharaf al-Dīn Muḥammad al-Buṣīrī. His *al-Burdah*, 'The Cloak', in reference to the garment in which the Prophet wrapped himself when receiving revelation, is a recitation of the Prophet's evidentiary miracles contained in his *Sīrah*, 'Biography'. Al-Buṣīrī, a Berber, dwells upon these according to his muse, to demonstrate the Prophet's perfection. Like al-Fāzāzī's work, the *Burdah* spread its influence all over Islamic Africa.

This *madīḥ* nourished the development of a new kind of *Ṣūfī ṭarīqa* which, for obvious reasons, became known as 'Muḥammadī'. In the opinion of their critics, who will be discussed below (p. 40), such *Ṣūfī ṭuruq* came near to deifying the Prophet to the exclusion of Allah. Muḥammadī *ṭuruq* multiplied from *c.* 700/1300 onwards, their teachings becoming ever more esoteric. They reached their metaphysical apogee with the Tijāniyya, founded by Aḥmad al-Tijānī (1150/1737–1230/1815), whose *zāwiya* was at ʿAyn Māḍī, in Algeria. His movement, carried by numerous *khalīfas* and *muqaddams*, subsequently spread to Senegal and from there deep into the western Sudan.

The ḥaḍrāt and other Tijānī doctrines

Al-Tijānī himself is not known to have left any written work. He is believed, however, to have dictated his teachings to a certain Shaykh ʿAlī Harāzim, who subsequently published them under the title *Jawāhir al-maʿānī*, 'Jewels of Hidden Meanings'. This ponderous tome seems to depend largely on ideas traceable ultimately to the seventh/twelfth to thirteenth-century Muhyī al-Dīn b. al-ʿArabī, mentioned above.[14]

Central to al-Tijānī's teaching was the notion of the *ḥaḍrāt*, the mystical celestial architecture which in turn arose out of the *miʿrāj* story. The core of the notion is as follows, although it should be understood that individual *Ṣūfīs* will offer their own imaginative renderings and there is probably no fixed and final text. The dictionary meaning of the word *ḥaḍrā* (plural *ḥaḍrāt*) is 'presence'. In the *Ṣūfī* lexicon it appears to mean both the stages of the metaphysical cosmos and the 'presence' of the Prophet Muḥammad at each one of them. Sometimes, it can also mean the stages by which the *murīd*, the *Ṣūfī* postulant, is led, through *tarbiyya*, 'esoteric initiation', to *fanā'*, 'absorption in the Divine Essence'. There are five *hadrāt* in the metaphysical cosmos, the lowest of which is Nāsūt, the stage of material existence, then Malakūt, the stage of Divine Light which is also the world of incorporeal things, and of the planets. Then comes Jabarūt which is the stage of the Divine Secrets and the world of the angels after which is Lāhūt, in which the Names of Allah and His Divine Attributes become manifest and finally, there is the summit, Hāhūt, the stage of the Divine Essence. It is hardly necessary to draw attention to the clear Neoplatonic origins of the idea up to this point, though equally clearly it has passed through what may be thought of as a Koranic filter. Indeed, these names are based on certain letters that have special significance in the Koran.

Each of these *ḥaḍrāt* is intimately associated with the elevation of the Prophet, celebrated by the writers of *madīḥ*. Thus the highest *ḥaḍrā*, Hāhūt, is that of the Prophet's knowledge of the Divine Secrets; the second, Lāhūt, is that of his immortal spirit; the third, Jabarūt, is that of his intellect; the fourth, Malakūt, is that of his heart, which has a special significance for Muslims since it was purified by Allah; while the fifth and lowest *ḥaḍrā*, Nāsūt, is that of his carnal nature.

Interlaced with all this is also the Islamic *'ilm al-ḥurūf*, the 'science of the letters', which attributes occult significance to the letters of the Koranic alphabet. The 'science of letters' is in turn applied to a gnostic interpretation of the letters of the Prophet's name, which are then referred back to the *ḥaḍrāt*.

From all of this emerges the concept of *al-nūr al-muḥammadī*. 'The Muḥammadī Light', best rendered into English as 'The Light of Muḥammad', behind which lies a metaphysical structure in which the celestial architecture of the *ḥaḍrāt* is suffused with Divine Luminance, made up of *ma'rifa*, 'gnosis', *fayḍa*, 'grace', *baraka*, 'blessing' and so on. Because of its divine source, this light is too intense for mere mortal man to gaze on directly since it would destroy him. He can only do so through the intermediacy of Muḥammad who, uniquely among mortals, is able to sustain its brilliance and pass it on to the rest of mankind as 'The Light of Muḥammad'. It is surely at this point that the apotheosis of Muḥammad reaches its most extreme development.

While, as far as I know, no systematic study of the antecedents and development of Tijānī gnostic theory has yet been undertaken, it seems reasonably clear that what is set out above represents a corpus of ideas that had circulated in North Africa, no doubt changing from time to time in detail and emphases, ever since the Muḥammadī *ṭuruq* began to emerge under the influence of Muhyī al-Dīn b. al-ʿArabī and the writers of *madīḥ*, in the eighth/fourteenth century.

The Tijānīs also require of their *ikhwān* that they hold to the following main precepts and obligations which indicate a general trend among the Muḥammadī *ṭuruq,* though not necessarily their precise emphases. The adept must believe that it is possible to invoke the blessing of the Prophet, the *awliyā*ʾ (holy men) and the *shaykhs* of the brotherhood; that the Prophet will intercede for true Believers on the Last Day and that they will enter Paradise without the judgement; that it is obligatory to visit the graves of holy men and pray there, as well as visiting living *shaykhs* to seek their blessing; that the recitation of the special litanies of the Tijānī *shaykhs* and certain other holy men is peculiarly efficacious; that the holy men and *shaykhs* are literally capable of performing miracles; that Koranic amulets do afford protection from evil; that it is obligatory to remove the shoes in the presence of pious and learned men; that there is an obligation to give alms and offer supplicatory prayers for deceased Muslims; that the use of the Islamic rosary is obligatory; that the celebration of the Prophet's birthday is obligatory; that it is possible to experience true visions of the Prophet both when asleep and when awake and that such experiences are facilitated by the Tijānī *dhikr* (recitation of the Names of Allah); that the vision of the Essence of Allah (though apparently not of Allah Himself) is possible and that it is for this that the postulant should strive.

In addition to these precepts the Tijānīs celebrate *fayḍa*, held to be appropriate only to the fully initiated. This is explained in *Jawāhir al-maʿānī* as an emanation from the *ḥaḍrā* known as *Lāhūt.* Its literal meaning is 'overflow'. In the sense in which the *Ṣūfīs* use it, it approximates to 'an infusion of grace'. It comes from the Light of Muḥammad but can be transmitted through the *murshid*, the 'rightly guiding' *shaykh,* to individual *ikhwān* or *ṭarīqa* members, hence the great influence wielded by these persons.

Such were the ideas, the notion of man's place in the cosmos, his relationship with the divine, the purpose of life and death and the strict disciplinary code that suffused North African Muslims in the days of the Almohads, that helped to inspire them to elevate the Sharifian Saʿdids; to die at the battle of al-Qaṣr al-Kabīr, to fight the

Turk, 'to knock on the head so many brave Englishmen' and finally to join the army of the Amīr ʿAbd al-Qādir in his holy war against the infidel invader.

The opposition to Sufism

Sufism has had its critics – most of them fierce – within North Africa and beyond from the days of the Almoravids who, it will be remembered, burned the works of al-Ghazālī in a gesture of disgust and revulsion at ideas that so affronted their own notion of an anthropomorphic deity firmly ensconced in the literal text of the Koran. Despite the enormous momentum that Sufism gained over the centuries, such opposition was never entirely overcome. It simply remained in the background, awaiting its day.

By the end of the twelfth/eighteenth century, a tendency, known as the Wahhābiyya, after its founder Muḥammad b. ʿAbd al-Wahhāb, had emerged in Arabia, to become from that point on the spearhead of opposition to the *Ṣūfīs*. By *c.* 1225/1810 it numbered among its adherents the Moroccan sultan Mawlāy Sulaymān. He took a firm stand against both the Darqāwī order and that of the Wazzāniyya as a consequence of which these *ṭuruq*, which were largely Berber in membership, revolted against him, though with only limited success.

The Wahhābīs argue that all these *Ṣūfī* beliefs and practices are *bid'a*, 'blameworthy innovations', that are contrary to the Koran. But above all – and this is the gravamen of their objections – they contend that the *Ṣūfī* apotheosis of the Prophet – and especially the Light of Muhammad – goes too far, to the extent that the *Ṣūfīs* venerate him more than Allah Himself. They are strongly disapproving of the *madīh*, the panegyric verse, which proliferated in North Africa and elsewhere in the Islamic world, in the centuries that followed al-Fāzāzī. Finally, according to the Wahhābīs, the *Ṣūfī* notion of salvation through the intermediacy of *shaykhs, murshids* and so on, let alone the Prophet himself (for the Wahhābīs regard Muḥammad are solely and exclusively a human messenger and no more) is wholly unsupported by the Koran and even by the Prophet's own *Sunna.*

Ijtihād and the Salafiyya

Out of this argument between the *Ṣūfis* and their opponents there developed in Islam in the course of the late twelfth/eighteenth century and onwards, a tendency known as *ijtihād*, 'personal inter-pretation', originally a traditional legal tool that permitted a degree of individual interpretation to legists and became, in Choueiri's deft expression, 'recast to stand for freedom of thought'.[15] It was applied to issues of secular reform and modernism, as well as to the specific issue of Sufism and maraboutism. Most importantly, it was seen as a means of halting Islam's decline as a consequence of the collapse of the Ottoman empire and European colonial encroachment. Thus the trend against Sufism became caught up in a wider tide of modernism and even rationalism that flowed across the Islamic world as the inevitable consequence of Western hegemony.

The *ijtihād* tendency strongly influenced the New Ottoman movement, the movement of modernist reform that arose in Turkey at this time. From Istanbul it quickly spread to Tunisia, Morocco and Algeria, where it did much to inspire the early leaders of independence movements. Out of it there developed a trend that came very near to Islamic social engineering. It aimed to penetrate the rural and tribal areas, the strongholds of maraboutism to break down tribal groupings, seen as repositories of conservative backwardness, and to replace regional autonomies with central government. It envisaged universal fiscal reform and the encouragement of western-style secular education and military reorganisation along European lines. Such attitudes and activities in the end became circular, in that they eventually met up with colonial policies. Differences thereupon became concerned with the identities of the reformers, not with the substance of policies nor the methods of implementing them.

This trend in Islam, which was born largely out of reaction against what were perceived as the excesses of Sufism and maraboutism, but quickly acquired wider horizons, became known as the *Salafiyya*, Salafism. The word derives from the Arabic root 'S L F', 'past'. It may be rendered inelegantly but accurately as 'ancestorism', though this term at first sight seems to belie its modernist emphasis. It is, however, appropriate enough when one understands that what the Salafists set out to do was to halt the decline of Islam and the advance of colonial domination by returning to the roots of early Islam and, as it were, rethinking its subsequent development in an attempt to eliminate the damaging accretions of centuries, foremost among which was Sufism.

Salafism manifest itself at many different levels, from a rather timorous reformism that sought only slow and gradual change, to the fierce iconoclasm of *al-Ikhwān al-muslimūn*, the notorious 'Muslim Brotherhood', which Choueiri regards as representing the culminating phase of this Islamic reformist tendency.[16] The Muslim Brotherhood was founded in Egypt by Hasan al-Bannā' in 1928. It is studied in detail in Chapter 2.

While Algeria was still part of the French empire, the Salafist *ʿālim*, ʿAbd al-Ḥamid Badis had founded the association of Algerian

ʿUlama in 1931. He then led the opposition to the *ṭuruq*, as well as to the French, his particular target being the quietist Tijāniyya which he accused, with some justice, of collaborating with the colonial administration. He also campaigned for a separate political identity for Algeria, though not necessarily in total dissociation from a French commonwealth. In Morocco, ʿAllāl al-Fāsī founded the *Istiqlāl* (Independence) Party *c.* 1940 on a Salafist platform. It failed, however, to prevent the emergence of an Islamic 'monarchy' in Morocco after independence. Morocco remains probably the least modernist of the three former Barbary states. In Tunis, ʿAbd al-ʿAzīz al-Thaʿālibī founded the first Destour party in 1920, also on Salafist principles.

Yet despite their modernism, these Salafist reformers never abandoned the Koranic basis of the argument in which they engaged. For instance, the notion of *shūrā*, 'consultation', which captured the conscience of the Salafist Wazīr of Tunisia, Khayr al-Dīn, who flourished *c.* 1287/1870, was based squarely on the Koran chapter of that name, *Sūrat al-shūrā* (Chapter 42). The Salafists took their stand on such verses as:

> I believe in what Allah has revealed in the Book, and
> I am commanded to do justice between you (42:15),

and:

> And those who respond to their Lord and keep up prayer,
> and whose affairs are conducted by consultation [*shūrā*]
> among themselves (42:38)

Up to this point, modernism, for all its daring, still remained firmly anchored in traditional Islam.

Islam and nationalism

Modern texts from Western sources dealing with the history of North Africa sometimes contain references to 'nationalism' and occasionally even to 'mass nationalism'.[17] It is argued that it was this sentiment that ultimately fuelled the drive for independence from colonial rule. Yet as was pointed out above, such men as ʿAbd al-Ḥamid Badis, al-Fasi, al-Thaʿalabi, and others who were the leaders of the North African independence movements, were firmly ground-ed in a Koranic hermeneutics which, if modernist, none the less fell far short of advocating the secular, pluralist nation-state.

The distinction between what is Islamic and what is nationalist is indeed uncertain, by reason of the fact that all independence movements since the *Risorgimento* – an essentially European experience springing out of the Renaissance which Islam did not share – display certain common characteristics: xenophobia, a desire to be rid of foreign overrule, an ambition for political power to be centred in a particular ethnic or cultural set, for a particular cultural symbolism to be elevated and so on. Unless all of this is turned specifically towards the creation of a nation-state, however, it seems that to define such manifestations indiscriminately as 'nationalism' may be to over-simplify.

The notion of the nation-state is of course wholly alien to Islam, which aspires to a world-wide *umma*, an Islamic community, unified under a single *imām* or *khalīfa*. While individual post-Islamic secularists may, from time to time, be seduced by the notion of the nation-state, it is questionable whether the great majority of Muslims have ever thought in such terms, to an extent that warrants attributing to them 'mass nationalism'. At any rate, the radical Islamic point of view on this issue is as follows:

> The political fragmentation of the *Ummah* was achieved [by the west] by the imposition of the nation-State system. If, despite this, the disintegration has remained peripheral, it is because of the political culture of the Muslim masses, which has resisted the breakdown of their traditional societies.[18]

It is extremely doubtful whether, between 1900 and 1962, when the independence process in North Africa was finally completed, 'the Muslim masses' of the three former Barbary states had so far abandoned their traditional political culture as to think in terms that justify foisting 'mass nationalism' upon them, even if some of their leaders do appear to have been seduced by this most unIslamic notion.

That some were so seduced is no doubt true enough. But these were a small élite of French-educated North Africans who even gallicised their Arabic names; and whose own attachment to Islam, such as it was, was purely formal. There seems little doubt that these men and their immediate entourages are better described not as 'Muslims' in any traditional sense of that term, but as post-Islamic secularists who gave every impression of having turned their backs on Islam as a belief system, and who appear to have adopted secular socialism in its place.

If these men were really 'nationalists', their victory was short lived. For, as will be seen below, they did not carry the mass of their people with them. The next thirty years were to witness a long, powerful and continuous reaction against the secularist values they stood for, which surely makes it clear that 'mass nationalism' is simply a misnomer for the nationalism of a small secularist élite carried along for the time being on a tide of popular anti-colonialist xenophobia beneath which Islamic values remained as real as ever.

NORTH AFRICA FROM INDEPENDENCE TO THE PRESENT DAY

Algeria since independence

In Algeria the first fruits of independence fell to Ahmed Ben Bella, a gallicised Algerian who had abandoned the earlier Salafism of the Association of Algerian 'Ulama in favour of the secularist, socialist FLN, which he founded and as leader of which he became the first president of independent Algeria in 1962. His term of office was brief. He was ousted by an army *coup* in 1965, apparently because his support was too narrowly based upon the secularist FLN, even for his modernist colleagues. He was replaced in that year by Houari Boumedienne, another gallicised Algerian who was, however, more aware of the need to concede some recognition to Islam.

Houari Boumedienne swiftly embarked upon a programme that, in some measure, involved a return to Salafist reform in that it attempted to combine Islam and modernism. But it also bore a distinct similarity to the Marxist policies of the former Soviet Union towards its Islamic republics – that is, it involved a deliberate attempt to tame Islam, and to manipulate it to serve the requirements of the secular, socialist state. Thus an Algerian Ministry of Religious Affairs scrutinised the 'religious orientation' of mosques, paid the salaries of 2,881 officially appointed *imāms* and *mu'adhdhins* (muezzins) and placed officially appointed preachers and religious teachers on its payroll.

In 1967, the whole traditional Islamic education system was nationalised. Students in state schools ceased to receive religious education but in 1979 the FLN government began to open Koran schools with the specific aim of explaining what was alleged to be the real causes of the decline of Islam and disseminating the official doctrine that this decline could only be halted and reversed by political and social reform of the kind enshrined in the FLN programme. A five-year plan introduced in 1980 envisaged the setting up of training centres for *imāms* in the various regions, where such teaching could be spread.

The government sought to control not only the mosques and Koran schools but also all Islamic publishing. The Ministry of Religious Affairs issued its own publication, *al-Risāla*, 'The Message', which gave a view of Islam carefully edited so as to justify government policies. These policies were again supported by *fatwās*, 'religious edicts', issued by the government-appointed Islamic Supreme Council. Such sources propagated a highly modernist version of Islam, strongly influenced by socialist ideas, which none the less did represent a return in some measure to the Salafist model. Houari Boumedienne, who was responsible for initiating this programme, even sought the help of the Egyptian Muslim Brotherhood, as tutors in this endeavour, a fact that surely makes it clear that not even these post-Islamic secularists had been able to extinguish Islam and replace it with secular nationalism and all that that implies. The most that they had been able to do was to strive to manipulate it in their own interests.

More recently, President Chedli Benjedid, who succeeded Boumedienne in 1978, has gone further in the direction of reinstating traditional Islam. He has deleted all references to socialism from the present Algerian constitution, has abandoned the one-party system that obtained under his predecessors and has allowed free elections in which a number of political parties, including the Front Islamique de Salut (FIS), have participated. The result, to the apparent surprise and dismay of the ruling socialist FLN, was a resounding success for the FIS in the local elections of 1990, followed by a further success in the general election of 1991. This gave the FIS what would have been an absolute majority in the Algerian National Assembly. The ruling FLN responded to this development by alleging abuses and irregularities on the part of the FIS during the poll and demanded that the election be annulled. The results have been the resignation of President Chedli Benjedid in January 1992, the transfer of power to a five-man Council of State in the course of a *coup* that amounted to a forcible annulment of the election, and a denial to the FIS of the victory the party undoubtedly won at that time. These measures have been enforced by the Algerian army. The leader of the FIS, Abdelkader Hachani, an Islamic fundamentalist strongly influenced by the ideas and attitudes of the Iranian Revolution, has defiantly announced that:

> The FIS intends to stick to its programme, which is for an Islamic state using the code of Islamic law, the Sharia.[19]

Whatever the outcome of this tangled situation, it will surely illustrate that secular nationalism, if it ever existed at all, has had a very short life-span among Muslim Algerians.

Morocco since independence

In Morocco the *Istiqlāl*, 'Independence (party)', under ʿAllal al-Fāsī, led the independence struggle. It was responsible for inviting back the sultan, Muḥammad V, who had been exiled by the French in 1953. Thus Morocco, uniquely among the newly independent Barbary states, returned at least nominally to a traditionally Islamic form of government. This is constantly referred to in Western sources – and scornfully in some Islamic ones – as a 'monarchy'. In fact, it simply continues the traditional Moroccan sultanate, an Islamic, not a Western institution.

Istiqlāl controlled the government until 1963, after which its influence declined. In 1961, Muḥammad V died and was succeeded by

Hasan II who proved to be of a somewhat authoritarian, not to say dictatorial character, but has none the less ruled the country under a nominally multi-party system since that time. Although a number of political parties are allowed to compete in parliamentary elections, a very firm hold is kept over them by the sultan using policing methods. The latter gives deliberate prominence to Morocco's religious identity and plays a leading role in Arab and pan-Islamic affairs. Despite this, he has been strongly criticised by Islamic radicals, firstly because he allegedly encourages the secular socialists in an effort to stem the growing Islamic fundamentalist trend in Morocco and secondly, for his subservience to what is alleged to be the Saudi–United States axis.

Behind this orientation in foreign policy lies the fact that, since 1976, Morocco has been fighting a costly war in the Western Sahara, against the Polisario Liberation Movement. This conflict is said to cost Morocco some $2m daily, against which the country receives massive aid from the Saudis and the USA, as well as large credits from the latter for the purchase of military hardware. In return, the USA has been granted certain naval and air force bases in Morocco. This war, the aim of which is to establish Moroccan suzerainty over the Western Sahara, may reasonably be regarded as the revival of Sharifian imperial nostalgia.

Riots against the policies of Hasan II occurred as early as 1965 and were severely suppressed. In 1979, Shaykh Mutīʿ Abdul Krim, leader of a radical opposition group known as 'Al-Shabībah al-Islāmiyyah', 'The Islamic Youth Movement', was sentenced to death *in absentia*. Further *coup* attempts led to the death sentence being imposed, again *in absentia*, on a certain Al-Mirjawī Mustafā, head of a faction known as 'The Jihad Group', in 1983. Yet opposition to Hasan II, which comes mainly from Islamic fundamentalist groups, has so far been successfully marginalised. This appears to be due to the fact that the sultan, for all his authoritarian ways and his alienation of the Islamic far right, continues to enjoy legitimacy in the eyes of most of his subjects. This is no doubt due to his conspicuously Islamic stance, to his claimed ancestral links to the Sharifian Saʿdids and even, perhaps, to his imperial policies in the Sahara, which chime with the popular Moroccan yearning for lost grandeur.

Tunisia since independence

After gaining independence in 1956, Tunisia's Habib Bourguiba (1957–87) abolished the Tunisian sultanate in the following year and set out, among other reforms, to modernise the *Sharīʿa.* From then onwards until 1987, he governed the territory at the head of his ruling

National Front. This consisted of the Neo-Destour Party in alliance with the Tunisian trade union movement. The only other officially recognised party was that of the Tunisian communists, which Bourguiba is alleged to have tolerated as a counter to the rising Islamic tendency in Tunisia, which he feared.

Between 1970 and 1981 this Islamic tendency, which was at first diffuse and unorganised, crystallised around the leadership of Shaykh Rashid al-Ghannushi, into a movement that took the Arabic name *Harakat al-ittijāh al-islāmī*, 'the Tunisian orientation movement', frequently referred to in English sources as 'Islamic Tendency Movement' (ITM). Al-Ghannushī, a former supporter of the Egyptian Gamal Abdul Nasser, came under the influence of the Egyptian Muslim Brotherhood, although it appears that al-Ghannushi, unlike the Muslim Brotherhood, later renounced the use of violence for political ends.

Al-Ghannushi was, however, profoundly hostile to Bourguiba's policies, and especially to his pluralism, bitterly opposing the granting of the franchise, and other concessions implying equality of status, to Christians and Jews. This he felt to be inconsistent with the imperialism of the former and the Zionism of the latter. Against Bourguiba's secular liberalism, he set an uncompromising demand for a return to Islam, centred on the mosque as the focus for rallying the Muslim masses. He also opposed Bourguiba's attempts to modernise the *Sharī'a* by banning polygamous marriages, giving women the right to sue for divorce, certain rights of inheritance they had not traditionally enjoyed as well as such lesser demonstrations of modernism as discouraging the wearing of the *ḥijāb,* the Islamic face veil, in universities and other public places. Bourguiba's acceptance of substantial aid from the USA, given to him to keep him out of the clutches of Qaddafi's Libya, also antagonised the radical ITM.

Although the ITM had existed as an organised faction since 1979 at the latest, it did not openly declare itself until 1981, whereupon it issued its demand for the full implementation of traditional Islam in Tunisia. The government thereupon accused the tendency of 'obscurantism and intolerance' and in 1981 it arrested and tried seventy-seven of its leading members.[20] Shaykh Rashid al-Ghannushī, by that time the President of the ITM, and Shaykh Abd al-Fattāh Morou, its General Secretary, were both sentenced to eighteen years' imprisonment. Later, the sentences were much reduced and they were given freedom on the understanding that they did not attempt to politicise the mosques or carry out other subversive activities. This change of attitude on the part of Bourguiba and his ruling National Front seems to have arisen for two reasons: firstly, the suppression of the ITM provoked widespread and often violent popular protest; and secondly, it appears that Bourguiba entertained hopes of taming the ITM and using it to combat the growing influence of the left in Tunisia, thereby hoping to identify himself with what was clearly becoming an increasingly powerful Islamic resurgence. None the less, the ITM continued to be precluded from participating in Tunisian elections until Bourguiba's successor Zayn al-Abidīn b. ʿAli allowed them greater freedom in his coming to power in 1987.

Libya

This is the name given by the Italians to the extreme eastern stretch of historical Ifrīqiya, lying between Tunis and Cyrenaica. It is alternatively known as Tripolitania, from the Arabic Tarāblus. It will be recalled that it was governed by the Hafsids until the ninth/fifteenth century, coming under Ottoman control in the tenth/fifteenth century when it was the base of the formidable corsair, Dragut. Its coastal towns, particularly Tripoli, were frequently bombarded by the European powers during the seventeenth, eighteenth and nineteenth centuries AD, in an attempt to suppress the piracy that these towns were held to patronise. In the twelfth/eighteenth century, the region came under the control of the Qaramānlī dynasty.

Unlike the rest of the Barbary states, Tripolitania never came under French rule, at least not until after the Second World War. In 1911 it fell to the Italians, who governed it as a colonial possession until their defeat in 1945. The area, by now known as Libya, then passed under joint British and French control.

In 1951 it was declared the independent kingdom of Libya under Muhammad Idrīs Al-Maḥdī Al-Sanusī. This person was a learned Muslim *ʿālim* and a noted Koran scholar. He was also the 'Grand Sanūsī' of the Sanūsiyya order of *Ṣūfīs,* founded in the thirteenth/nineteenth century and most influential in North Africa and the Sahara at that time.

In September 1969 this Sanūsī sultanate was overthrown by a certain Captain Muʿammar al-Qadhdhāfī, commonly known in the west as Gaddafi, Qaddafi and other phonetic spellings, at the head of a group of 'Free Officers', a designation that became standard among the rebellious young army officers who resorted at this time to such *coups*, not only in Libya but also in Egypt and Iraq.

Qaddafi and his Free Officers were professional soldiers, of mainly middle-class backgrounds, who had been trained in western military academies and appeared to have known very little about traditional Islam. None the less, Qaddafi now issued his 'Third Universal Theory', a confused manifesto consisting largely of pan-Arab socialism of a highly autocratic kind that had little to do with Islam though he loudly proclaimed that the ideology of his 'September Revolution' stemmed from the eternal message of Islam. At the same time he ordered the suppression of the Sanūsiyya *Ṣūfī* order, upon which the authority of the deposed Muḥammad Al-Sanūsī had rested. Its *zāwiyas* were placed under strict state supervision. Its *ikhwān* were persecuted when their views or behaviour appeared in any way hostile to the revolutionary regime. The Islamic Koran schools and *madrasa*s were, in effect, nationalised and turned into propaganda organs for the regime, while the Sanusi Islamic University was absorbed into a state-run university. Qaddafi then set up a network of subservient *ʿulamā'* who were prepared to support the policies of the revolutionary government and in 1970 appointed his own man, a certain Shaykh Zahr al-Zawi, as Grand Mufti, that is the person responsible for the administration of Islamic law.

While engaged in these oppressive policies towards the former Sanūsī establishment, he also inaugurated an extremely strict Islamic puritanical regimen: it involved the banning of alcohol, the closing of bars, restrictive measures against the tiny Christian minority in Libya, the declaration of Arabic as the official language and the adoption of the Islamic calendar. He also announced the incorporation of the Islamic *Sharīʿa* into the existing Libyan legal system.

At first he gained some acclaim among the religious classes for these measures. But he subsequently emerged as both confused and inconsistent as he increasingly mixed Marxism, socialism and references to 'democracy' – which meant no more than what pleased his own band of revolutionary followers – with his Islamic rhetoric; while his persecution of the traditional *ʿulamā'* provoked hostility.

Among his somewhat disordered aspirations was a passionate attachment to pan-Arabism; he attempted to set up unions based on a common Arab identity, with Egypt, Syria and Morocco. These were disapproved of by Islamic radicals throughout Islam, who regarded such unions as secular nationalism. They came to nought.

Qaddafi began to incur yet deeper hostility by what were seen by many Muslims both within and beyond Libya as his arrogant attempt to interfere in Islamic theology. For instance he began to question the validity of the Islamic *Sunna*, on the ground that some of the Prophetic traditions on which it is largely based were forged and used this as an excuse to marginalise the traditional *ʿulamā'* in matters involving the administration of the law. He even attempted to change the ancient Islamic calendar, claiming it should begin from AD 632, the year of the Prophet Muhammad's death, and not AD 622, the received date of the Prophet's *hijra*, 'migration', from Mecca to Madina. Latterly, he copied the Tunisians and the Algerians in attempting to ban the wearing of the *ḥijāb*, the face veil, and in other modernist gestures.

Mounting opposition to his regime has resulted in eleven apparent attempts on his life since 1982. The most serious of these was a bungled assault in May 1984, when a group of Muslim Brothers tried to assassinate him in his tent just outside Tripoli. However, it has to be said that his constant escapes from these recurrent attacks have been so remarkable that there is reason to believe that some of them may have been stage-managed. So, despite this radical Islamic disapproval, Qaddafi has survived. This has to be attributed, in part, to the popularity of his consistently anti-Western stance, for which, it seems, the Muslim masses are willing to forgive much else. But it must also be attributed to his undoubted political skills and to the manner in which he has based his power on the small but ardent 'revolutionary committees'. On the other hand, since the destruction of the Sanūsī network, opposition to him has been fragmented and ill-organised.

Colonial aftermath: Muslim immigration into France

No account of France's long involvement with the Barbary states would be complete without describing how the wheel has come full circle – with the very substantial immigration into France of North Africa Muslims, who now claim the right to become French citizens.

There has always been a North African presence in France since even before the granting of independence to the three territories that were under French rule. An unexpected, and surely unintended, consequence of this development has been to set off a greatly increased flow of Muslim immigrants from these independent countries, and especially Algeria, into France. Most of these people were straightforward economic migrants, fleeing from the failing economies of the newly independent North African states, disrupted by the independence struggle and by the mass exodus of European settlers that followed independence. They had, for reasons of material self-interest, now chosen to settle permanently in the former colonial metropolis rather than in the independent homeland. There were, however, a number of genuine political and religious refugees among the economic migrants. They were Islamic radicals, pious *ʿulamāʾ* and persons identified with traditional Islam, who felt unable to live under the government of the secular socialist regimes of Algeria and Tunisia, or under the monocratic Moroccan 'Monarchy'.

As of 1979 there was a total of approximately 2,000,000 Muslims permanently domiciled in France, of whom the majority were Algerians (782,111) but with significant minorities of Tunisians (183,782) and Moroccans (399,952). The remainder comprised smaller groups of Senegalese, West Africans, Turks and others.[21]

The presence of these permanent immigrants in France has given rise to severe problems of cultural clash. There has been constant pressure from Muslim spokesmen, *imāms* and the like, for a dispensation that allows their communities to be governed not by French secular law but by their own religious law, the medieval *Sharīʿa*. There is also constant pressure from Islamic organisations for the lifting of such controls as still remain on further immigration by Muslims, and on their employment in France. There is also an insistent demand for state aid for Muslims, *qua* Muslims, for specifically Islamic education, mosque-building and the like.

There seems little disposition among these Muslim immigrants to adjust to the cultural and social norms of the secular, pluralist society which they have entered of their own free will. This is particularly noticeable in the conduct of the family where the power of the Muslim extended-family–male hierarchy over its womenfolk remains in the majority of cases absolute, despite the prevailing ethnic of feminism and equal opportunities that prevails for better or for worse, among the non-Muslim majority. These immigrant Muslims still insist, for the most part, on their right to impose arranged marriages, and the extremely strict code of premarital behaviour that goes with it, on their daughters, even though these girls have been brought up in France and have been educated in French schools where they have acquired notions of personal freedom that continue to be unacceptable to first-generation immigrant parents. Many of these girls who kick against the traces are simply sent back to Algeria and other North African countries, where they lose whatever protection French law might otherwise have afforded them, and where they are constrained into arranged marriages against their will.

Muslim fundamentalism is strong among Muslim immigrants in France, and calls from mosque pulpits are frequent for the implementation of separatist policies that would make the Muslims virtually autonomous within the French state.[22] Such cultural clashes, and the political and social demands that go with them, have given rise to considerable disquiet among the non-Muslim majority of the French people, which has inevitably been given political expression. As has been the case elsewhere in Western Europe, any individuals or organisations that have ventured to express concern over this issue of immigration have immediately been accused of 'racism' by liberal opinion.[23] No doubt some racism exists. But to offer such a blanket explanation for an ancient and deep-seated cultural incompatibility, which has been inherent in the confrontation between *dār al-islām*, the 'House of Islam', and *dār al-kufr*, the 'House of Unbelief', since the first/seventh century, will seem adequate only to those who begin by wishing to see it in that light.

NOTES

1. Braybrooke, Lord (ed.), p. 185.
2. Ibid., pp. 262–3.
3. Ibid., p. 263.
4. Ibid., p. 297.
5. Ibid., p. 95.
6. Ibid., p. 133.
7. Ibid., p. 243
8. Ibid., p. 300.
9. Ibid., p. 301.
10. Martin, B. G., p. 43.
11. Ibid., p. 51.
12. Nouschi, André, p. 306.
13. This and the other examples from the *madīḥ* poets will be found in Hiskett, 1975, pp. 43–63.
14. This work has been published in an Arabic edition, Cairo, n.d. I know of no translation into a European language.
15. Choueiri, Youssef M., op. cit., Bibl., p. 34.
16. Ibid., pp. 48ff.
17. Martin, op. cit., p. 40.
18. Ghayasuddin, M., ed. cit., Bibl. 1986, p. vii.
19. *The Daily Telegraph*, 16 January 1992.
20. Siddiqui, Kalim, (ed.), *Issues … 1981–1982*, p. 67.
21. These figures are taken from J. S. Nielsen, 'Muslims in Europe: An overview', *Research Papers*, no. 12, 1981. It is almost certain that the numbers have increased considerably since that date.
22. See for instance Gilles Kepel, 'The Teaching of Sheikh Faisal' in Nielsen, J. S. (ed.), *Research Papers*, No 29, March, 1986.
23. For instance *News of Muslims in Europe* (ed. Nielsen), Centre for the Study of Islam and Christian–Muslim Relations, Selly Oak Colleges, Birmingham, No 24, 30 January 1984, 'Marchers and Bishops against Racism in France', which claims that 'in several recent local by-elections parties with an explicitly racist platform have made significant gains'. This is in reference, particularly, to attitudes towards Algerians; see also ibid., No 32, 30 July 1985, 'Youth against Racism', which makes similar claims.

2

Egypt

EGYPT FROM 20–1/641 TO 1264/1848

Geography has linked Egypt closely to North Africa, with which it shares a Mediterranean coastline. Yet, almost as much of its coast is coterminous with that of tropical Africa down the western shore of the Red Sea, while looking eastward, that coastline confronts the Arabian desert, on the farther side of the Red Sea. It is therefore a matter of emphasis at particular points in its history whether Egypt is regarded primarily as part of Africa, or whether it pertains more closely to the Middle East. Islamic Egypt has also always exerted a profound influence over Islam in tropical Africa simply because the Nile, a channel for man's earliest river-borne communications, links it to that area.

The Arab conquest of Egypt and its early dynasties

At the dawn of Islam, Egypt, like North Africa, was a rich Byzantine possession. It therefore quickly attracted the envious eyes of the Muslim Arabs, fresh from their conquest of Palestine. In 20–1/641 the Muslim commander, ʿAmr b. al-ʿĀṣ, invaded Egypt and seized Alexandria, its major Byzantine city. Egypt thus became a province of the Islamic empire, still at that time in its expansionist phase, under the early *Rāshidūn*, the 'Rightly Guided' caliphs of the first years of Islam. At the time this Arab invasion occurred, Egypt comprised a mixed population, some of whom were of Negro descent, while others were Copts, Greeks and other Middle Eastern and Mediterranean peoples. As a consequence of the conquest, the country was rapidly and almost totally 'arabised' in terms of language. By the first/seventh century the Arabs of the northern Arabian peninsula were themselves already racially mixed, whether, therefore, they also arabised Egypt by an admixture of Semitic blood, or simply added to the existing ethnic *mélange*, may be a matter of opinion.

By 40/661 the Umayyad dynasty had become established in Damascus, Egypt being under its sway. By 133/750 the partly Persian ʿAbbāsids had replaced the Arab Umayyads as supreme rulers of the Islamic empire, including Egypt but by 235–6/850, ʿAbbāsid power had waned to the point where it was no longer able to exercise effective control over its provinces. Profiting from this, Aḥmad b. Tulūn, nominally the ʿAbbāsid governor of Egypt, took power in 254/868 and established the first independent, but short-lived, Muslim dynasty in Egypt. By 323/935, after an interregnum in which Egypt reverted to direct rule from Baghdad, a new dynasty, known as the Ikhshidids, had assumed power, though paying nominal allegiance to Baghdad.

The Fāṭimids in Egypt

Contemporary events in North Africa were, however, about to impinge upon Egypt. By 296/909 Abū ʿAbd Allāh al-Shīʿī had arrived in North Africa to set in train the events that led to the proclamation of a *Shīʿī*, Fāṭimid caliphate, challenging the right of the ʿAbbāsids, not only to Egypt, but also to their claimed lordship over all Islam. In 359/969 the Fāṭimid anti-Caliph, al-Muʿizz, conquered Egypt from the Ikhshidids. He then set up a Fāṭimid dynasty there, leaving North Africa to his turncoat vicegerents, the Sanhaja Zīrids. The Fāṭimids now ruled from al-Fuṣṭāṭ, the early Muslim camp founded by the first Muslim conquerors in 22/642, which they rebuilt and renamed al-Qāhira. It was reputedly named after the planet Mars (Arabic Al-Qāhir, 'The Conqueror') under the ascendency of which the rebuilding began. The name was corrupted as 'Cairo' and its variants in western European languages. Here the Fāṭimids founded the great university mosque known as al-Azhar, which survives as the most notable centre of learning in the *Sunnī* Islamic world to this day. Contributing much to the development of architecture, learning and civilised life in Egypt, the Fāṭimids also did their best to propagate *Shīʿī* beliefs among the Egyptian people. As in North Africa, so too in Egypt, they failed. The later Fāṭimid caliphs were feeble; their period was characterised by constant palace *coups* and assassinations. Moreover, Egypt was threatened by the Crusaders under Almaric, King of Jerusalem, who by AD 1167 was at the gates of Cairo itself.

The Ayyūbids

This situation enabled the rise to power of a certain Ṣalāh al-Dīn Ayyūb, the well-known Saladin, a military governor of the Fāṭimids, a man of Kurdish origin. He took over from the dying Fāṭimid caliph, al-ʿAdid in 567–8/1171, thereupon becoming the *de facto* ruler of Egypt and founder of the Ayyūbid dynasty. With Ṣalāh al-Dīn's accession the population of Egypt returned willingly to *Sunnī* Islam, to which the Ayyūbids adhered, and from which the Egyptian people had never wavered in conviction, despite almost 200 years of Fāṭimid hegemony.

The Ayyūbid period coincided with the height of the Crusades, against which Ṣalāh al-Dīn was Islam's great, and chivalrous, champion. In consequence, much of his energies and those of his successors were turned towards the Middle East, where they also had to resist the advance of the Mongols out of Asia. None the less, a party of Ayyūbids took Tripoli from the Almohads in the second half of the sixth/twelfth century.

The Mamlūks

The Ayyūbid dynasty endured for less than 100 years. It was distinguished in its closing years by the brief reign of the redoubtable Shajar al-Durr, the 'Tree of Pearls', a lady of some force of character, not to say ruthlessness, who assassinated her husband and briefly became sultana in an interregnum between the Ayyūbids and the Mamlūks. In 648/1250, power passed to the Mamlūks, who had originally been the slave soldiers of the Ayyūbids. There were two branches of the Mamlūks: the *Bahrī* ('Sea') or Turkish Mamlūks and, after them, the *Burjī* ('Citadel') or Circassian Mamlūks, names arising from incidents in their history too involved to be recounted here.[1] The greatest of the *Bahrī* line were Baybars (658–76/1260–77) and Qalā'ūn (678–89/1279–90). It was during the reign of Qalā'ūn's son, al-Nāṣir b. Qalā'ūn, that Mansa Mūsā, king of the Sudanic kingdom of Mali, passed through Cairo on his way to perform the Pilgrimage, thus bringing the western Sudan firmly within the Islamic orbit (see p. 94).

The Ottomans

By the end of the eighth/fourteenth century, the Circassian *Burjī* Mamlūks had replaced the *Bahrīs*, their first sultan, Barqūq, seizing power in 784/1382. The *Burjīs* ruled until 922/1517, when they were defeated by a Turkish dynasty, the Ottomans, at the battle of Raydāniyya, near Cairo. The battle is notable for the fact that the Ottomans used cannon and firearms, which the *Burjīs* had refused to adopt, considering them unmanly – or so the pleasing story goes! Other explanations have been proposed, among them the more mundane one that the *Burjīs* were incapable of forging artillery pieces! I see no reason to doubt the more picturesque explanation, since honour was centrally important for this ancient Islamic military class. The Ottomans did not drive the *Burjīs* out of Egypt, though they executed the last *Burjī* sultan; the Mamlūk system of administration was left intact. Gradually, the Mamlūks regained control of the government, although they were now vassals of the Ottoman sultan in Istanbul.

Muḥammad ʿAlī

The rule of the Mamlūks continued, largely untroubled by their Ottoman overlords, until in 1219–20/1805 an Ottoman military officer, Muḥammad ʿAlī, established himself in Cairo in the immediate aftermath of Bonaparte's invasion and brief occupation of Egypt from AD 1798 to 1801. He became virtually independent of his masters in Istanbul and established a local hereditary despotism, the Khedives, that survived beyond his death in 1264/1848. He also established Egyptian control over the Sudan – ancient Nubia – which was maintained by him and his successors until the setting up of the Anglo-Egyptian Condominion by the British in AD 1898 – and even extended his control over Yemen and Lebanon at one point. Some of his successors among the Khedives, yet another Turkish honorific from Persian *khidiv*, 'king', were able men; others were ineffective but by and large the authority and efficiency of the Egyptian government declined after Muḥammad ʿAlī.

Muḥammad ʿAlī was a Salafist of despotic inclinations. He introduced cadastral changes that antagonised longstanding landed interests, tried to bring about an Egyptian industrial revolution, set up an Egyptian army along European lines and introduced a European system of largely secular education. Indeed, in many ways he anticipated the later Ottoman programme of modernisation, known as the *Tanẓīmāt* and is consequently regarded as the founder of modern Egypt. He certainly set that country on the road to westernisation, along which it then advanced more rapidly than most other Islamic countries, with the exception of Turkey, until after the Second World War.

At one level Muḥammad ʿAlī was reacting against the French invasion and the general intrusion of the western powers into the Islamic world that became marked at this time. But at another level, his enemies were the Mamlūk *beys* and their allies, the Egyptian *ʿulamāʾ*. The former operated an oppressive system of taxation while the *ʿulamāʾ*, in Muḥammad ʿAlī's opinion, held a monopoly over an archaic system of education and waxed fat on *waqfs*, the rich religious endowments of the mosques, which they annexed to their own purposes. These domestic shortcomings, as he saw them, were surely as potent in inspiring him to modernist reform as his resentment at foreign interference.

His reformist policies were bitterly opposed by traditionalists, among whom were the *Ṣūfīs*. Such Salafist ideas challenged their charismatic hold over the Muslim masses, which they had been accustomed to exercise for many generations. Muḥammad ʿAlī's attack on the traditional *madrasa* system of education, and the setting up of a Western, secular model in its place, was particularly resented by the *ʿulamāʾ*: it not only encroached on their livelihoods, it also undermined the ancient institution of Islamic scholarship they represented. In traditional Islamic society the *'ulamā'* have always been a highly respected class; they therefore felt diminished in the measure that Muḥammad 'Alī's modernising policies were pushed ahead. Egyptian society polarised, with the traditional *'ulamā'*, the *Ṣūfī ṭuruq* and their urban and rural followers on one side and on the other a modernist and predominantly urban middle class. During Muḥammad 'Alī's day, the *'ulamā'* remained largely leaderless and divided, not able to mount any effective opposition against him. Yet the split that occurred at that time, between a westernising and increasingly secular ruling class and a traditionalist Islamic constituency, persists to the present day. It foreshadowed the rise of the Muslim Brotherhood, which despite its own Salafist origins, may be seen in some degree as a belated reaction on the part of the traditionalists to the modernising process begun by Muḥammad 'Alī.

Islam in Egypt

Early Islam in Egypt was *Sunnī* and pristine, since its planting took place barely twenty years after the *Hijra*. By the fourth/tenth century a tussle had developed for supremacy between this *Sunnī* Islam, the heritage of the conquerors and early dynasties, and the *Shī'a*, represented by the Fāṭimid hegemony which endured from the fourth/tenth century to the sixth/twelfth century. As was pointed out above, *Sunnī* Islam won the day and, apart from the architecture and literature of the Fāṭimid period and certain aspects of court ceremonial, Egypt has retained little trace of the *Shī'ī* interlude.

Yet this period up to the fall of the Fāṭimids did make a substantial contribution to cultural life. Ṭulūnid architecture, and especially the great mosque of Ibn Ṭulūn, reflects a style already by this time established in Iraq, the home of the 'Abbāsids; Egyptian culture during this epoch developed under predominantly Mesopotamian influences, largely extinguishing its earlier Byzantine patina.

The Fāṭimids created the Azhar, undoubtedly the greatest centre of learning in the *Sunnī* Islamic world, even though its early *Shī'ī* curriculum was later replaced by that of the *Sunnī* Ayyubids. It continued to thrive as a centre of *Sunnī* learning.

It was under the Mamlūks, however, that Egypt achieved what was probably its greatest cultural influence in the Islamic world, especially as regards its influence on tropical Africa.

Despite the fact that, like the North Africans, the Egyptians adhered firmly to the *Sunnī* form of Islam, they differed from the North Africans in one respect. Whereas the North Africans, led by the *'ulamā'* of Qayrawān, were unbending followers of the Mālikī *madhhab*, the *'ulamā'* of the Azhar and other Egyptian centres of learning were more liberal. Thus, in Egypt, a pluralist Islamic system obtained, in which all of the four legal rites: the Mālikī, the Shāfiʿī, the Ḥanafī and the Ḥanbalī, were accommodated. This meant that Egyptian scholarship enjoyed wider horizons that stretched beyond the rather limited vision of the North African *ʿulamāʾ*. Egyptian scholars were more accustomed to tolerating differences of opinion, provided these remained within the broad consensus of the *Sunna*. Apart from the period of the Crusades, there was in Egypt on the whole, less of the militant zeal that called for a *jihād* of the sword at every opportunity.

The early Mamlūks were munificent builders of schools and institutions of higher learning. It was under them, and their Ottoman successors, that the two-tiered system of Islamic education became institutionalised, which was based on the *katātīb* (singular, *kuttāb*), primary schools. Here young boys were taught memorisation and recitation of the Koran and with it literacy in the Arabic script. These institutions were known to western observers as 'Koran schools'. Above the *katātīb* ranked the *madāris* (singular *madrasa*, from the Arabic root 'D R S', 'study'). These were schools of higher Islamic learning where students of all ages – from youths to octogenarians – attended to study such aspects of the Islamic curriculum as jurisprudence (*fiqh*), grammar (*nahw*), prosody (*ʿurūd*), theology (*ʿilm al-tawhīd*) and so on. At the summit of the system, which became widespread across *Sunnī* Islam, stood the great teaching mosques, such as the Azhar in Egypt, the Zaytūna teaching mosque in Tunis, a Ḥafṣid foundation, and the Sankore mosque in Timbuktu (see Chapter 4 below). Many consider that these great teaching mosques and others like them, exercised some influence over the development of the university in Christian Europe, as a result, perhaps, of Crusader contacts with Islam during the Middle Ages, as well as Christian contacts with Muslim Spain and Sicily and wider trading contacts with the Islamic world.

Islamic literature in Egypt

Egyptian literature during the Mamlūk period and beyond became extremely elaborate in form. Word play and verbal prestidigitation, the skill of the composer of *takhmīs*, the pentastich, who takes his master's couplet and interweaves this with three hemistichs of his own, and that of the glossist who expands upon an original text, all tended to assume greater importance than originality of content. Such literature profoundly influenced the development of other Islamic literatures elsewhere in Africa, as will become clear from Chapter 7 below.

Mamlūk Cairo was a venue for Islamic story-tellers. Thus such well-known Islamic folkloric themes as the *Sīrat Iskandar*, the Alexander cycle, *Sīrat ʿAntar*, the 'Life of ʿAntar', the *Sīrat Abī Zayd* and *Sīrat Sayf b. Dhī Yazan*, as well as the well-known *Alf Layla Wa Layla*, the 'Thousand and One Nights', were told and re-told in Cairene streets, cafés and market places where they were picked up by pilgrims from tropical Africa and carried home to become incorporated, often in localised forms, into the African vernacular literatures, both written and oral.

Sufism in Egypt

Sufism flourished in Egypt. The earliest *ṭarīqa*, the Rifāʿiyya, was founded during the Ayyūbid period, by Aḥmad al-Rifāʿī (d. 578/1183) and was given to extreme thaumaturgic practices that came near to conjuring. Arberry attributes these tendencies to the influence of Shamanism, stemming from the Mongol occupation of Mesopotamia at this time.[2] It is this sect that also contributed to the well-known 'Dervish' form of *Ṣūfī* practice. By the thirteenth/nineteenth century at least nineteen distinct *Ṣūfī ṭuruq* were active in Egypt.

Under the Mamlūks, right up until the advent of Muḥammad ʿAlī, whose reforms they opposed, the *ṭuruq* were a recognised institution of the state and enjoyed many privileges. Yet Sufism had its enemies in Egypt, as elsewhere in the Islamic world. The centre of Wahhabism at this time, that is between *c.* 1160/1747 and 1227/1812, was still in Arabia and its main message was opposition to Sufism and all that it stood for. The Wahhābīs won many converts, especially among pilgrims visiting Mecca, who picked up anti-*Ṣūfī* attitudes which they then carried back to their countries of origin, including Egypt. This growing opposition to Sufism provoked a strong reaction from the Egyptian *Ṣūfīs*, which reached a climax during the second half of the twelfth/eighteenth century in the Azhar. The Khalwatiyya *ṭarīqa* led the movement, drawing in the ancient Qādiriyya, which now acquired a new militancy. It also inspired the founding of the Tijāniyya, in North Africa, which then spread rapidly across the western Islamic world. Sufism and popular maraboutism, though increasingly challenged by the Wahhābīs, remained influential at the spiritual level in Egypt, among the illiterate and semi-literate masses, right up until the outbreak of the Second World War. Only under the attack from the Muslim Brotherhood on the one hand and rising secularism on the other, has it recently begun to fade, part of the wider decline of Sufism generally over the past thirty years.

FROM THE AGE OF THE KHEDIVES TO *C.* 1991

Muḥammad ʿAlī died in AD 1848. His successors, the Khedives, pursued increasingly ill-advised policies, to be summed up as extravagance, financed by exorbitant taxation of the peasants. The European powers, in consequence and especially Britain and France, became increasingly drawn into Egyptian affairs, mainly because of involvement in Egyptian debt. This had a progressive impact on the Egyptian economy. The building of the Suez Canal, undertaken between AD 1859 and 1869, further involved the European powers in that faltering economy. In AD 1875, Khedive Ismā'īl sold his shares in the Canal to the British government; in AD 1876, the Egyptian government was forced to agree to foreign supervision of its finances. A period of economic and political confusion followed, culminating in the British military occupation of Egypt in 1882.

Egypt as a British protectorate

During the First World War, Egypt was declared a British protectorate. The Sudan, annexed to Egypt by Muḥammad ʿAlī early in the nineteenth century AD, had been established as a joint Anglo-Egyptian condominion in 1898 in which, however, Egypt played an increasingly minor part. In 1922, a form of independence was granted to Egypt, which became a kingdom under Fouad I. None the less, British troops continued in occupation up to the outbreak of the Second World War.

During the Second World War, relations between the British and the Egyptians became increasingly taut, owing largely to the escalating activities of *al-Ikhwān al-muslimūn*, The 'Muslim Brotherhood', founded by Ḥasan al-Bannā'. He had created a secret organisation, the purpose of which was to infiltrate the police and armed forces and also set up youth organisations modelled on the Nazi Brown Shirts and Black Shirts. The *Ikhwān* were alleged to have been responsible for a number of political assassinations, including that of the Egyptian Prime Minister, Mahmūd al-Nuqrashī, in 1948. In consequence, the *Ikhwān* were for the time being suppressed. Ḥasan al-Bannā' was himself assassinated in 1949, as a result of an internal squabble within the Brotherhood.

Egyptian hostility to foreign occupation, however, was in some measure restrained by fear of jumping out of the Allied frying pan into the Axis fire. Moreover, American involvement on the Allied side, and the material benefits this brought to the Egyptian economy, helped to contain Egyptian discontent until the end of the war.

When the war ended, the discontent could no longer be held back.

The Muslim Brotherhood rallied again, under the leadership of Sayyid al-Qutb. In 1952, General Muḥammad Neguib, at the head of a Free Officers' *coup*, ousted the posturing but ineffective King Farouk. Neguib was shortly replaced by Colonel Gamal Abdul Nasser, in 1954 and British troops left the Canal Zone in the same year. The Suez crisis followed in 1956 at which point British colonial involvement in Egypt came to a humiliating end. From now on independent Egypt became an increasingly influential player in the drama of Islam's interaction with the non-Islamic West. In this role it has exercised a powerful influence on tropical Africa.

Independent Egypt

Since becoming an independent republic in 1953, Egypt has been governed briefly by General Muhammad Neguib and then by Gamal Abdul Nasser (1954–70), by Anwar al-Sadat (1970–81) and by Husni Mubarak (1981–), each of whom has ruled as President with a People's Assembly and a Consultative Council.

Gamal Abdul Nasser began his career as an army officer. Like many of his colleagues he became dissatisfied with what he regarded as the corruption of the Farouk regime and in consequence he became involved in the military *coup* of the so-called 'Free Officers' in 1952. Rising to a position of influence among them, he assumed the premiership of Egypt in 1954 and then presidential powers in the same year, deposing General Muhammad Neguib. In 1956 he nationalised the Suez Canal, leading to the Israeli invasion of Sinai and the intervention of the Anglo-French forces in what became known as the Suez war. Nasser's aim was to create a united Arab state and in 1958 he set up a federation with Syria known as the United Arab Republic. This was dissolved by the Syrians in 1961. The heavy losses sustained by Egypt in the six-day Arab-Israeli war of 1967 led to his resignation but he was persuaded to stay on and died in office in 1970.

Nasser, although nominally a Muslim, had little real interest in Islam. He tried to combine socialism, Arab nationalism and popular democracy based on a one-party system. Islam was subordinated to development, economic and social planning and nation building in a manner that quickly stripped it of its universality and reduced it to no more than an aspect of Arab nationalism. The union with Syria represented the high point of Nasser's pan-Arab efforts. When this broke up in 1961, be became increasingly concerned to establish his own interpretation of scientific socialism in Egypt. In May 1962 he presented his National Charter. This was a programme of sweeping political, social and economic reform in which traditional Islamic values were largely ignored. It involved an attempt to rewrite nineteenth-century and twentieth-century Egyptian history in the light of new socialist concepts and it rejected the achievements of the Khedives and even anti-British politicians such as Saʿd Zaghul who had led a revolt against the British in 1919, but it lionised Muḥammad ʿAlī. The Charter very largely ignored the ideal of the world-wide Islamic *umma* and concentrated on the achievements of Egypt as leader of the Arab world. Despite the fact that he flourished in an era of Islamic revivalism, it is a mistake to regard Nasser as in any way a champion of Islam. It was secular Arab nationalism and socialism, not religion, that were his guiding lights.

Nasser was followed by Anwar al-Sadat under whom the country fought the Yom Kippur war against Israel, subsequently participating in the Camp David Peace Process. Egyptian involvement in the latter aroused deep anger within the radical Muslim constituency which opposed any *rapprochement* with Israel. Anwar al-Sadat was assassinated on 6 October 1981, by an extreme wing of the Muslim Brotherhood, the *Ikhwān*, which was by this time an underground but none the less powerful organisation. An Islamic fundamentalist source, commenting on this assassination shortly after it occurred, described Sadat as 'a compulsive traitor in life and death'.[3]

Under Anwar al-Sadat's successor, President Husni Mubarak, the *Ikhwān* have been firmly held in check. Many have fled Egypt and continue to plot their fundamentalist schemes from areas, including the non-Islamic, pluralist West, that are more tolerant of such activities. Under President Husni Mubarak, Egypt has continued a pro-Western alignment, joining the American-led coalition in the Gulf war of 1991, less out of love for the West than out of an antagonism towards the Iraqi Baʿthists and, probably, economic self-interest.

Social and political change in modern Egypt

The present scene in Egypt is one in which a tenacious traditionalism, represented typically by the Muslim Brotherhood, currently held down, but by no means extinguished, struggles against the modernist and secularising pressures of a largely professional Egyptian middle class from whose ranks the government is drawn.

Since the Nasser era, successive Egyptian administrations have made considerable efforts to impose modernisation on the country, receiving some support from the powerful Coptic Christian minority. For example, in 1950 women over eighteen were given the right to vote, though it would appear that only a small number of middle-class women have ever exercised this right. Among the largely illiterate rural population it continues to be widely neglected.

Like many authoritarian regimes in the Islamic world, Egyptian administrations allow the formation of opposition parties but then withdraw that right when they become too challenging. In the Egyptian case, this happened in 1953; the right was not restored until 1983.

Like the Tunisians, the Egyptians have attempted to regulate polygamy though they have not gone so far as to abolish it. The Personal Status Laws of 1985 state that if a man wishes to marry a second wife, the first wife must be informed and has the right to ask for a divorce. While monogamy is widely adopted among the middle and professional classes, this trend has evoked little response among the rural population, where traditional polygamy and divorce still prevail. Moreover, the institution of arranged marriage and the power of the extended-family-male hierarchy, which is so solid among Algerian Muslims, is equally powerful in Egypt, despite official efforts to break it down. A recent authority comments:

> Chastity of the daughter and sister, fidelity of the wife, continence of the widowed and divorced daughter and sister are basic principles on which a family's reputation and status in the community depend.[4]

Secular Western-style education is also largely a prerogative of the middle class. There remains a very high rate of illiteracy among the rural population. Moreover, there is a powerful traditionalist opposition to women working, other than in the approved roles of housewife or agricultural labourer. The same authority remarks:

> In spite of all this [pressure from United Nations organisations for female emancipation], there are many objections against women working outside the home, with conservatives saying that a woman's main duty is as a housewife and mother, and that women should devote their efforts to their husbands and children.[5]

There is a 'Women's Liberation Movement' in Egypt, which has considerable influence among the middle classes. It is interesting to note that not even these feminists – surely the shock troops of modernisation – reject Islam outright. On the contrary, they attempt to rationalise it by arguing that it was the Ottomans who were responsible for the suppression of womens' rights, and for other social aspects perceived as reactionary. Islam prior to the Ottoman period is idealised and great efforts are made by these feminists to find precedents in pre-Ottoman Islam that seem to support their own ideological assumptions. For instance, the persona of Shajar al-Durr, mentioned above, is elevated to the status of the first Muslim Egyptian feminist. Although the historical relevance of her life to present-day feminism is far fetched, none the less Shajar al-Durr has become a symbol and a rallying cry for some Egyptian feminists illustrating the way in which even such a radical modernist tendency as feminism will often seek to establish an Islamic legitimacy when it arises among those who are culturally Muslims.

The main opponent of these and similar manifestations of modernism and secularism in Egypt and the government programme of modernisation pursued with increasing determination since independence are the Muslim Brotherhood. The organisation was founded in Egypt, in 1928, by Hasan al-Bannā', a Muslim *'ālim* of a rather theocratic turn of mind who was politicised by his experiences in Palestine during the British Mandate, which he perceived as favouring Zionism. Apart from its opposition to Zionism, his movement has much in common with the early Wahhābīs: it advocates the re-establishment of the universal Islamic caliphate, and insists on the veiling of women and on the Koranic penalties for adultery, theft and drunkenness. Some of its members, including it appears the founder himself, were also attracted to international socialism and to the model of German National Socialism. It still displays strongly authoritarian attitudes.[6]

The stance of the Brotherhood toward Gamal Abdul Nasser and his ruling group of 'Free Officers' was ambiguous. It approved their overthrow of King Farouk, and their anti-western stand but disliked their modernising inclinations. It also took particular exception to the Anglo-Egyptian Agreement that Nasser concluded with the British in 1954 leading to an assassination attempt upon him by certain extremist *Ikhwān* that year. Nasser responded by arresting a number of leading *Ikhwān* and imprisoning them; the Brotherhood then went underground and was sustained by only a small group of radical Muslim intellectuals, until it resurfaced in 1970.

Among those arrested in 1954 was a certain Sayyid al-Quṭb, who had been one of Nasser's familiars but later quarrelled with him because Nasser and his Free Officers favoured a plural constitution while Quṭb wanted an exclusively Islamic form of government based on the Brotherhood's theocratic principles. Quṭb remained in prison almost continuously until 1966, when he was hanged on the orders of Nasser, apparently on the ground that his writings, which he had diligently pursued during his imprisonment and which were then smuggled out and published, were seditious. He has become a hero of the Islamic fundamentalists, who have given him the posthumous title, *shahīd*, 'Martyr'.

His ideas, set out in a number of works but most comprehensively in his *Fī ẓilāl al-Qur'ān*, 'In the shade of the Koran' and his *Ma'ālim fī 'l-ṭarīq*, 'Milestones along the road', were prolific as well as somewhat confused. They have been the subject of an excellent study by Choueiri.[7] Sayyid al-Quṭb believed that the forces opposing Islam have always been a continuum from its beginning to the present day. Thus, he perceived present-day 'imperialism' and 'neo-colonialism' as no more than a continuation, under a different guise, of the Crusades, and even of early Christian opposition to the Prophet during his lifetime whose true purpose is not even material exploitation, which is incidental, but rather the destruction of Islam and its beliefs. In a similar way, modern Zionism has been continuously and directly linked back to Jewish scheming against the Prophet in first/seventh-century Mecca and Madina. He considered such secular leaders as Ben Bella and Bourguiba, who had won independence from the imperial powers, not as fighters against imperialism, which was surely the Third World consensus in their day, but as dupes of the imperial masters, deliberately educated by them in secularism and placed in positions of power to carry out the task of destroying Islam. According to his teaching, all of nationalism, the nation-state, socialism, communism, democracy and capitalism are no more than aspects of the essential anti-Islamic force, *kufr*, 'unbelief' or in modern parlance 'atheism'. Quṭb eventually arrived at the conclusion that Islam no longer exists; it therefore has to be created anew. Although his programme for achieving this became somewhat confused and self-contradictory, it consisted essentially of the subordination of human reason to the strictly literal interpretation of the Koran. At the root of his ideas was the total conviction that the Koran is, quite simply, the direct revealed Word of Allāh, together with an intense frustration that it could not be made to prevail.

These ideas of Sayyid al-Quṭb, as expounded by the Muslim Brotherhood, played a central part in fuelling the rise of Islamic radicalism in Egypt and North Africa during the 1960s and 1970s. As will be seen below, they have played a similar part in the rise of this radicalism in the Nilotic Sudan and elsewhere in Africa.

Sadat's assassination led to further government measures such as arrests and imprisonment against the *Ikhwān*. The movement survived under the leadership of a certain 'Umar Tilmisanī, who denounced the murderers of Sadat and publicly expressed the opinion that they deserved the dealth penalty. His somewhat ambivalent stance appeared to be that armed struggle to enforce the *Ikhwāns*' programme was justified – but not yet! Al-Tilmisanī died in 1986 leaving behind a Brotherhood somewhat less virulent than that nurtured by Hasan al-Bannā' and Sayyid al-Quṭb and somewhat compromised by the suspicion that it had been tamed by Husni Mubarak's administration, to the extent that in common with certain secularist political parties it has now been allowed some freedom to engage in political activities. Nevertheless, the Egyptian *Ikhwān* still have very considerable support among the rural and urban masses: the tendency is a reservoir of fundamentalist ardour that may overflow again at any time.

NOTES

1. These incidents are recorded in Lewis's fascinating account of Egypt in Holt, P. M., et al. (eds), 1A, pp. 209 and 219.
2. Ibid., 2B, pp. 621–2.
3. Siddiqui (ed.), *Issues* ... 1981–1982, p. 110.
4. Effat, Rajia, loc. cit., Bibl.
5. Ibid.
6. Youssef M. Choueiri, op. cit., Bibl., pp. 48–52, gives a detailed account of the rise of Hasan al-Banna and the Muslim Brotherhood. See also articles by M. Forstner, Mir Zuhair Husain and K. A. Magd listed in the Bibliography.
7. Op. cit., p. 150 and passim.

Ibn Baṭṭūṭa's probable view of Africa, c. 756/1355: *based on Idrīsī's World Map of 549/1154*

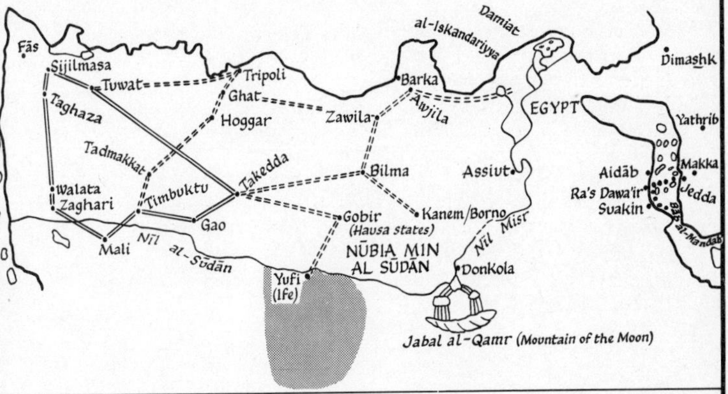

Caravan routes actually travelled by Ibn Baṭṭūṭa in 753/1352

Other caravan routes believed to have been in use at this time

Country of the Līmīs

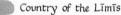

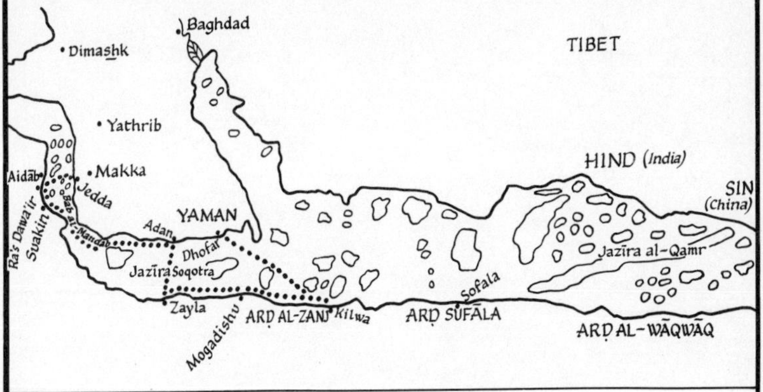

Ibn Baṭṭūṭa's sea routes *circa* 732/1331

This map is necessarily conjectural and not to scale

Main Trade Communications of Muslim Africa c. 906/1500

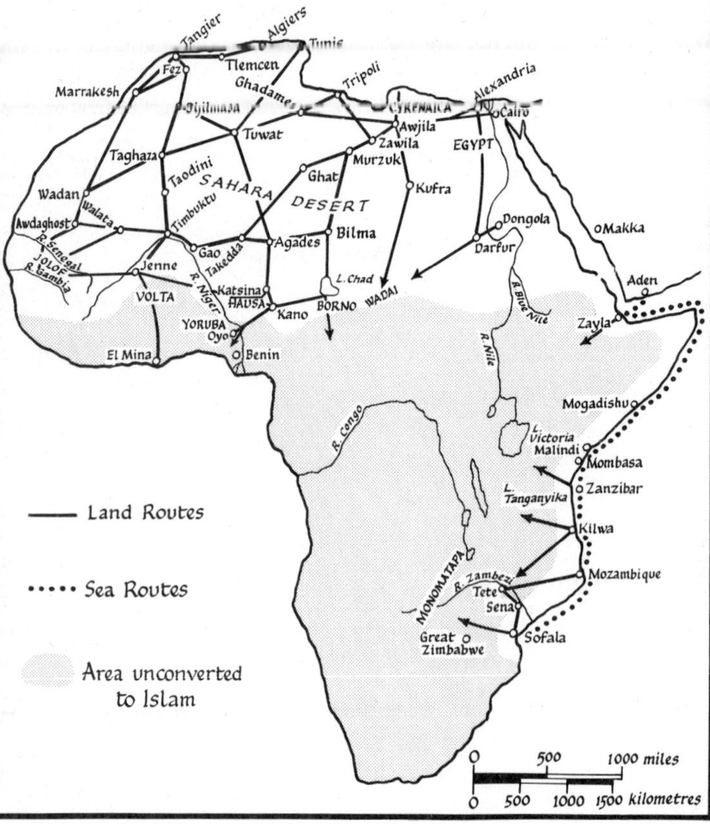

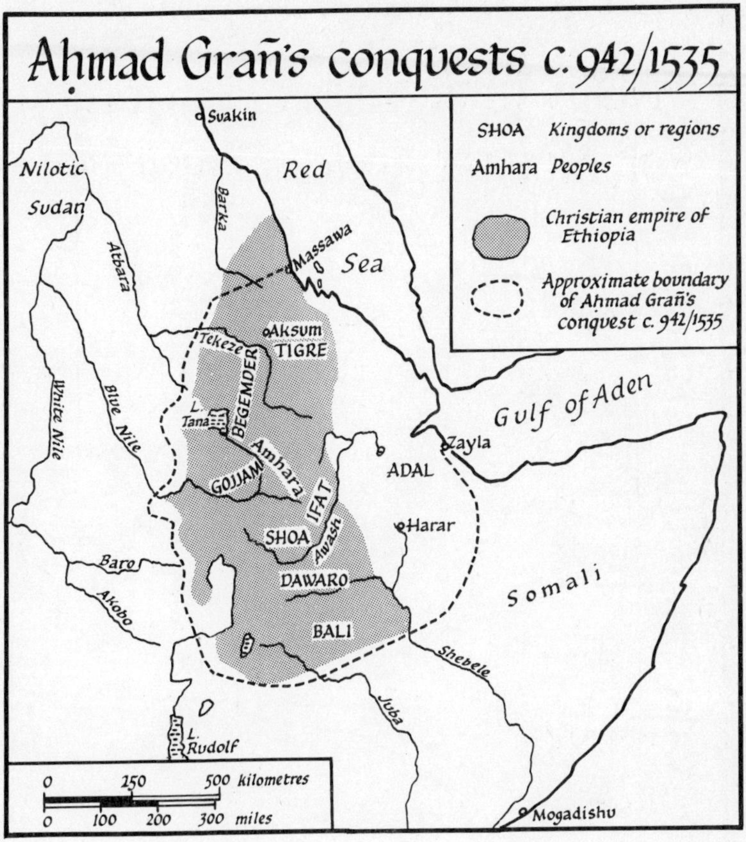
Aḥmad Grañ's conquests c. 942/1535
SHOA Kingdoms or regions
Amhara Peoples
Christian empire of Ethiopia
Approximate boundary of Aḥmad Grañ's conquest c. 942/1535
Suakin
Red Sea
Nilotic Sudan
Barka
Atbara
Massawa
Aksum
TIGRE
Tekeze
BEGEMDER
L. Tana
White Nile
Blue Nile
GOJJAM
Amhara
IFAT
ADAL
Zayla
Gulf of Aden
Harar
SHOA
Awash
Baro
Akobo
DAWARO
BALI
Somali
Shebele
Juba
L. Rudolf
Mogadishu
0 250 500 kilometres
0 100 200 300 miles

North Africa and the Sudan c. 1009/1600

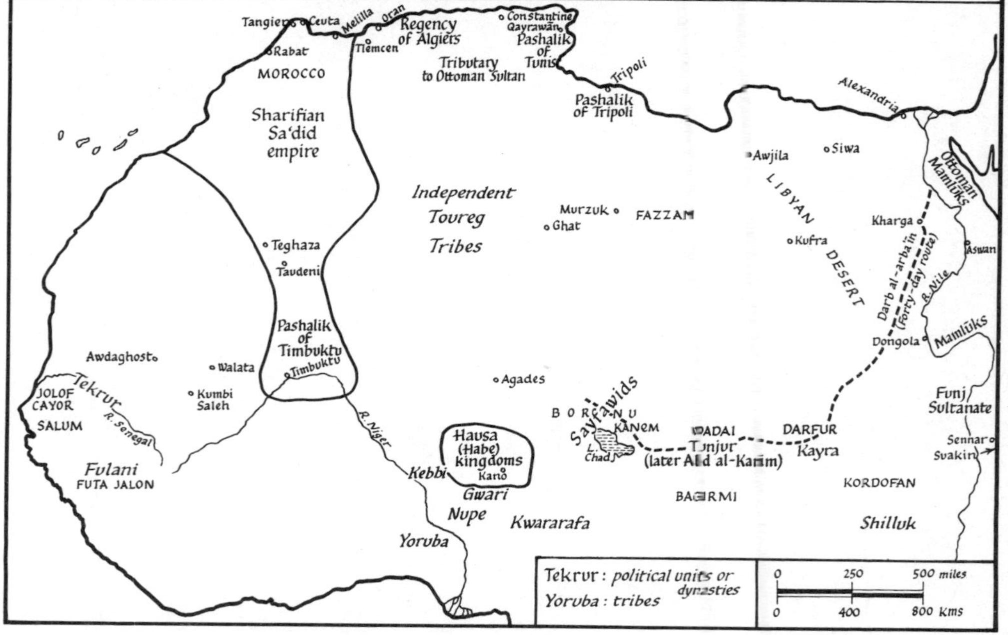

Colonial Africa, 1923

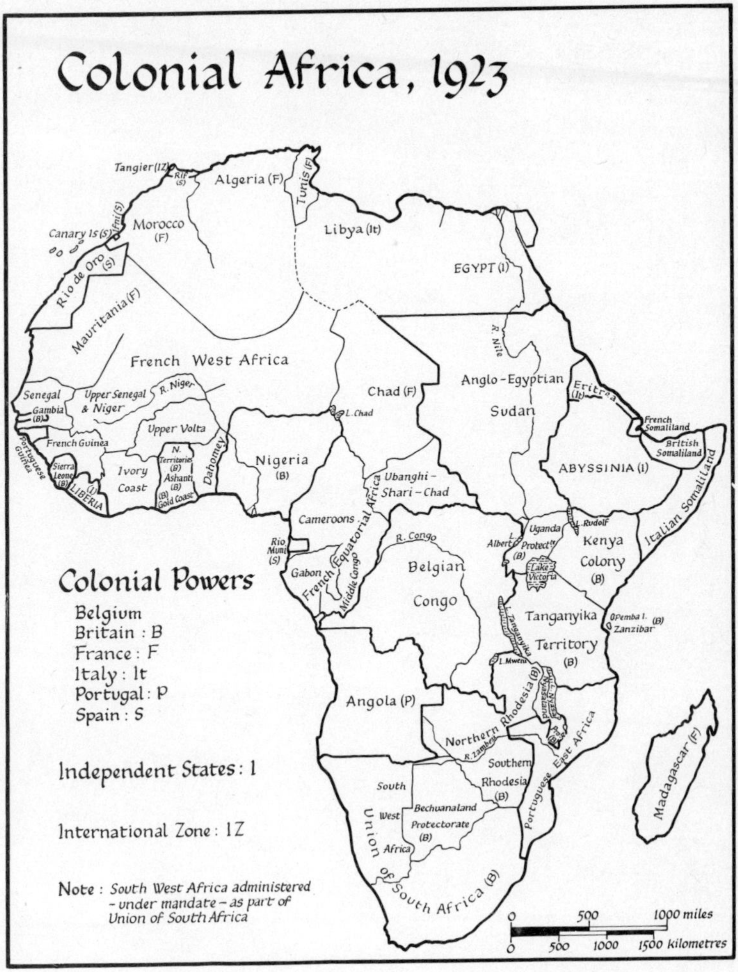

Tangier (IZ)
Rif (S)
Algeria (F)
Tunis (F)
Ifni (S)
Canary Is (S)
Morocco (F)
Libya (It)
EGYPT (I)
Rio de Oro (S)
Mauritania (F)
R. Nile
French West Africa
Anglo-Egyptian Sudan
Senegal
Gambia (B)
Upper Senegal & Niger
R. Niger
Chad (F)
L. Chad
Eritrea (It)
French Somaliland
British Somaliland
Upper Volta
French Guinea
Portuguese Guinea
Sierra Leone (B)
(I) LIBERIA
Ivory Coast
N. Territories (B)
Ashanti (B)
(B) Gold Coast
Dahomey
Nigeria (B)
Ubanghi-Shari-Chad
ABYSSINIA (I)
Italian Somaliland
Cameroons
French Equatorial Africa
Rio Muni (S)
Gabon
Middle Congo
R. Congo
Belgian Congo
L. Albert
Uganda Protect[te] (B)
L. Rudolf
Kenya Colony (B)
Lake Victoria
L. Tanganyika
Tanganyika Territory (B)
Pemba I. (B)
Zanzibar
L. Mweru
Northern Rhodesia (B)
Nyasaland
Angola (P)
R. Zambezi
Southern Rhodesia (B)
Portuguese East Africa
Madagascar (F)
South West Africa
Bechuanaland Protectorate (B)
Union of South Africa (B)
0 500 1000 miles
0 500 1000 1500 kilometres
Colonial Powers
Belgium
Britain : B
France : F
Italy : It
Portugal : P
Spain : S
Independent States : I
International Zone : IZ
Note : South West Africa administered – under mandate – as part of Union of South Africa

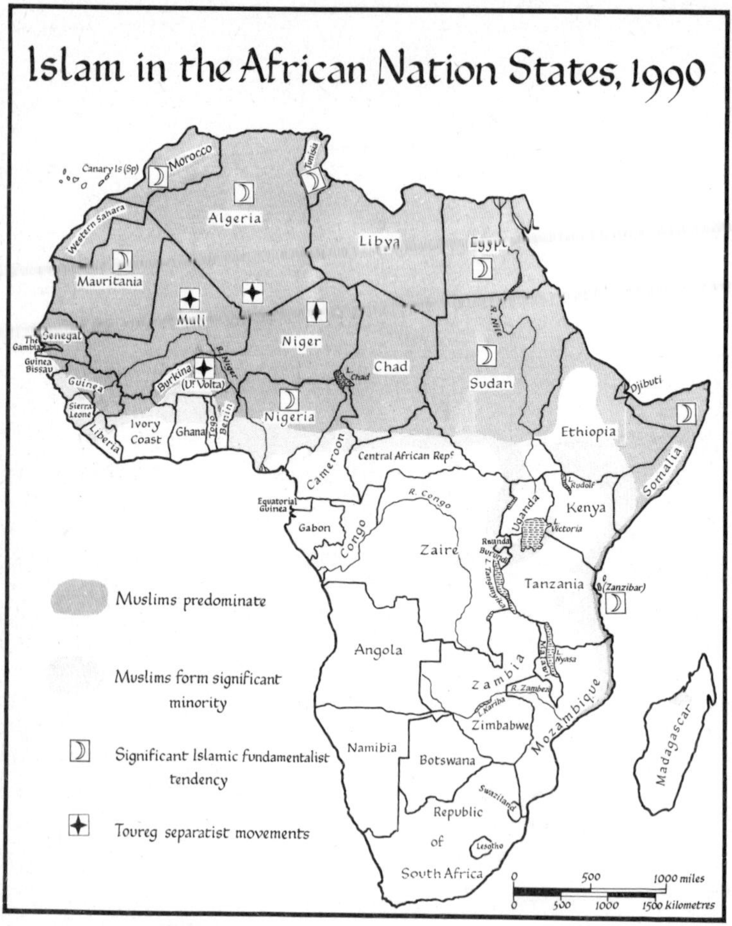
Islam in the African Nation States, 1990
Canary Is (Sp)
Morocco
Tunisia
Algeria
Libya
Egypt
Western Sahara
Mauritania
Mali
Niger
Chad
Sudan
R. Nile
Senegal
The Gambia
Guinea Bissau
Guinea
Burkina (Ur Volta)
R. Niger
Sierra Leone
Liberia
Ivory Coast
Ghana
Togo
Benin
Nigeria
L. Chad
Djibuti
Ethiopia
Somalia
Cameroon
Central African Repc
Equatorial Guinea
Gabon
Congo
R. Congo
Zaire
Uganda
L. Rudolf
Kenya
L. Victoria
Rwanda
Burundi
L. Tanganyika
Tanzania
(Zanzibar)
Angola
Zambia
Malawi
L. Nyasa
R. Zambezi
L. Kariba
Zimbabwe
Mozambique
Madagascar
Namibia
Botswana
Swaziland
Republic of South Africa
Lesotho
Muslims predominate
Muslims form significant minority
Significant Islamic fundamentalist tendency
Toureg separatist movements
0 500 1000 miles
0 500 1000 1500 kilometres

3

The Nilotic Sudan

FROM FIRST CONTACTS WITH ISLAM TO *C.* 1215/1800

The southern boundary of Egypt had, since ancient times, lain at the First Cataract of the Nile, approximately at Aswan. South of this lay Nubia (Nobatia), a Christian state from the sixth century AD, heir to ancient Kush, occupying the area from the First Cataract, south as far as present Khartoum. Its central province was known as Makuria, which perhaps gave rise to the later Arabic al-Maqurra, the name by which the Muslim Arabs referred to Nubia. Its capital was Meroe, a name also associated with ancient Kush. Beyond Makuria lay ʿAlwa (Alodia), apparently an independent kingdom with its capital Soba (Sūba). South-east of ʿAlwa and beyond the Nile Valley lay Axum, on the Red Sea coast. It was a trading station founded by a mixed population of Greeks and Semites at the beginning of the Christian era. It later became the nucleus not of an Arab Muslim state but of the kingdom of Ethiopia trading with Nubia and ʿAlwa. Such was the extent of organised statehood south of the First Cataract at the revelation of Islam. South of ʿAlwa lay vast expanses of savannah and riverain country roamed over by stateless, Hamitic-speaking, nomadic cattle grazers known as the Beja. They probably supplied slaves, ivory and other tropical products to Axum, ʿAlwa and Nubia but did not fall under the political or, it would seem, the cultural sway of any of these early kingdoms.

Early Arab migrants and traders

The Nilotic kingdoms had become converted to Christianity by the sixth century AD; Nubia appears to have paid tribute to Byzantium in the pre-Islamic period. These kingdoms became known to the Muslim Arabs shortly after their conquest of Egypt though contacts at this time appear to have been limited to raids by the Muslims that were easily beaten back. A trade in slaves between the early Muslims and the Nubians may have arisen shortly after the conquest of Egypt but none the less, for the next three centuries, these Christian Nilotic kingdoms formed a geographic and cultural barrier to the organised advance of Islam.

In the third/ninth century, however, a development gathered pace that resembled that of the Hilalian invasions of North Africa 200 years later. Indeed, it may have been an earlier manifestation of the same phenomenon. Nomadic Arab tribes, the Rabīʿa and the Juhayna, acting independently of any Islamic government, began to migrate into Nubia in increasing numbers, probably attracted by the gold mines located south of Aswan at al-Wādī al-ʿAllāqī, in Nubia. Arab tribes continued to press from north to south, towards the grasslands of the Upper Nile, until well into the ninth/fifteenth century. They adopted – or were given – a variety of names. These Arabs gradually intermingled with the Nubians, and with the Beja on their fringes, to create a people of mixed blood speaking Arabic as a mother tongue who were gradually drawn into the Islamic cultural orbit. Tomb inscriptions testify to the settlement of Arabs in Nubia as from the second half of the fourth/tenth century.[1] These Arabs became known as the Jaʿaliyyūn, after an ancestor who, it was claimed, was an ʿAbbāsid from Baghdad. One may suppose this to be yet another example of what Holt aptly calls 'genealogical sophistication', by which non-Arab peoples adopting Islam seek to confer a retrospective ethnic and religious respectability upon what they have come to regard as their own less meritorious origins.[2] Arab Muslim traders, engaged in the slave trade, and the gold trade from the Wādī al-ʿAllāqī mines, may also have functioned, in addition to the nomadic migrants, as Islamic missionaries among the Nubians at this early period. Perhaps theirs are the bones that lie beneath the tombstones.

The Banū Kanz

Despite these influences, no substantial Islamic political entity was established south of Aswan until well into the Fāṭimid period. Then, *c.* 394–5/1004, a mixed-blood group of Nubians and Arabs emerged, probably created by marriage or concubinage between Arab nomads and Nubian women, given to these Arabs as a form of tribute by the Nubian incumbents. Its members rendered service to the Fāṭimid caliph, al-Ḥākim. They were given the sonorous Arabic title *Kanz al-dawla*, the 'Treasure of the Dynasty'. In consequence they became known as the Banū Kanz. With Fāṭimid approval they established an Islamic principality in the area of Aswan. Throughout the Ayyūbid period, which followed that of the Fāṭimids, these Banū Kanz were sometimes at loggerheads with the Ayyūbids, who sought to establish their own hegemony south of Aswan. At other times they co-operated with them. By and large, they extended their own control, and at the same time pushed Islam and its way of life slowly southwards, helped by Baybars's conquest of Nubia.

The Mamlūks

In 674–5/1276 the Mamlūk sultan Baybars sent an expedition into Nubia that finally defeated the Nubian army. In consequence, al-Māris, the northern part of al-Maqurra, as the Arabs now termed Nubia, became a Mamlūk possession. In about 716–17/1317 the Christian cathedral at Dongola (Dunqula) was taken over as a mosque. Christianity in Nubia was still not entirely stifled by these events but it suffered a setback that adversely affected the position of the Christian minority under Islamic government in Egypt. They now lacked the protection of what had formerly been a powerful Christian neighbour. Christianity in Nubia henceforth slowly faded in the course of succeeding generations. Another consequence of the Mamlūk conquest was to increase the migratory pressure from the Arab tribes moving into Nubia, and further upstream. By *c.* 906/1500 the Nilotic Nubian kingdom of antiquity, stretching from Aswan to Karri (the site of present Khartoum) had become a single Mamlūk possession, governed for the most part by Nubian Muslim governors owing allegiance to the Mamlūk sultans.

The ʿAbdallab and the Funj

As for the kingdom of ʿAlwa, the most southerly of the ancient Nilotic kingdoms, with its capital at Soba (Sūba), less is known of its early history. It existed as an independent kingdom early in the seventh/thirteenth century, probably succumbing to a confederation of Arab tribes known as the ʿAbdallab, at some point between the seventh/thirteenth century and the end of the ninth/fifteenth century. By *c.* 906/1500 it had disappeared.

Involved in this ʿAbdallab confederacy was an ethnic element known as the Funj, of African, not Arab origin. As Holt points out, 'Their remoter origins, which are obscure, have given rise to luxuriant speculation'.[3] What does seem clear is that at the point at which they emerged into recorded history they were not yet Muslims. By the beginning of the tenth/sixteenth century these Funj had established domination over the rest of the ʿAbdallab and at the same time had adopted Islam under the influence of teachers who resembled the North African marabouts – the Sudanese *fakīs*. Later, in accordance with the established convention among non-Arab converts to Islam, the Funj adopted a contrived genealogy, linking them to the Umayyads. Sennar, south of Soba, became the capital of what has been referred to as the 'Funj sultanate'.[4] The Funj extended their influence southwards and westwards to the White Nile and into the country of the Shilluk, powerful animists living in the area of present-day Malakal, though the Shilluk were never converted to Islam in any substantial numbers.

The Funj appear to have remained out of the Mamlūks' reach. They were at their height *c.* 1060/1550 but continued to dominate the surrounding tribal groups and to practise slave-raiding in the Nubian hills until they declined in the course of the twelfth/eighteenth century. Their decline happened under the onslaught of marauding Arabs, among whom there were almost certainly arabised Nubians. They called themselves Jaʿaliyyūn, in the line of the ancient inventors of the ʿAbbāsid genealogy, and were centred on Shendi, above the Sixth Cataract, north-east of present-day Khartoum. None the less, an entity known as the Funj sultanate lingered on until 1236–7/1821, when its last representative recognised the suzerainty of Muḥammad ʿAlī of Egypt.

Frontier areas

Meanwhile, to the west, Darfur became increasingly open to Arab and Islamic influences as a result of long-term pressures from nomadic Arabs entering the Sudan from both east and west and infiltrating constantly towards the grasslands of the Upper Nile and also from traffic along the *Ḍarb al-arbaʿīn*, the 'Forty-days' Route'. This passed from Wadai, through Darfur, to the Kharga Oasis and on to middle Egypt. Darfu's first known rulers were the Daju, a faintly arabised group from the east, who flourished in the seventh/thirteenth century while another arabised people known as the Tunjur, took over from them *c.* 751/1350. These people claimed to have come from Tunis and may also have been a distant ripple of the great Hilalian invasions of the fifth/eleventh century. About the middle of the ninth/fifteenth century the Tunjur gave way to a dynasty known as the Kayra, again probably the product of marriage, or more probably concubinage, between Muslim Arabs and local animist women. All of these Darfur dynasties boasted Islamic names from time to time yet it seems that the hold of Islam over them was sometimes tenuous. Darfur and Kordofan, to the south east of Darfur, represented over many generations an indeterminate frontier area, where the nomadic and often only faintly Islamic culture and way of life of infiltrating Arab migrants interacted with that of local African animists. Islam consequently coloured the existing social structures and belief systems but failed to win an overall, decisive hold, at least until the early thirteenth/nineteenth century. By this time Darfur had emerged as a powerful and prosperous Islamic sultanate.

FROM THE TURCO-EGYPTIANS TO SUDANESE INDEPENDENCE (AD 1956)

In 922–3/1517 – the year of the battle of Raydāniyya – Mamlūk suzerainty over the Nilotic Sudan passed in theory to the Ottomans, although in fact the Mamlūk *beys* continued to exercise authority there. Indeed, by 1226/1811 Dongola had become a centre for dissident Mamlūks, driven to seek refuge from Muḥammad ʿAlī's impetuous social engineering.

The Turco-Egyptian hegemony

In 1236–7/1821 Muḥammad ʿAlī dispatched the first of several expeditions into the Nilotic Sudan, with the aim of bringing it fully under Egyptian control. Thus began a period of Turco-Egyptian overrule during the early thirteenth/nineteenth century more unified and complete than anything that had gone before it. As a result, the area of the Upper Nile was opened up to Ottoman and European traders seeking ivory and, in the case of the former, slaves – although the dimensions of the slave trade have probably been somewhat exaggerated. In many ways the rampant ivory trade was more disruptive. Darfur and Kordofan now came under Egyptian administration. This widening of Egyptian control was made possible largely by the employment, in the khedival service, of a number of Europeans and some Americans, part of whose task was to suppress the slave traffic in the area. Among these officials was the British General Gordon, appointed Governor-General of the Sudan in AD 1877. Also prominent at this time was the notorious Zubayr Pasha, infamous as a slave trader, although in fact his main interest was ivory. The slaves were somewhat incidental to the ivory trade in that they were required in the first instance to transport it to the coast. Once there, they were usually sold off. Zubayr Pasha achieved considerable political influence in the area known as Bahr al-Ghazal, of which he was appointed governor by the Khedive Ismāʾīl in 1290/1873. But his activities in this capacity brought him into conflict with the khedival authorities; after certain adventures, he ended up under house arrest in Cairo, where he was held until 1317/1899.

The Mahdiyya

The Sudan was too vast for the khedives, Muḥammad ʿAlī's successors, to hold down, even with European assistance. The foreign intrusion, the interference with ancient patterns of trade and social structures and the dislike of the khedival establishment for the *fakīs*, the Sudanese equivalents of the marabouts, all combined to arouse deep discontents among the Muslims of the Sudan. They had long been conditioned by the *fakīs* to a form of *Ṣūfī* Islam that was highly susceptible to messianic excitements and expectations. In 1298/June 1881, one claiming to be the Expected *Mahdī* became manifest among them in the person of Muḥammad Aḥmad b. ʿAbd Allāh, a *fakī* from Dongola. With a following of tribesmen from the hills of Kordofan, he captured al-Ubayyid (El Obeid) in 1300/1883 and defeated a Turco-Egyptian expedition commanded by Hicks Pasha, a British soldier in the khedival service, in the same year. He then besieged Khartoum, hopelessly defended by the brave but theatrical General Gordon, who perished in the siege.

The *Mahdī* now set up a typical, stark Islamic theocracy, modelled on early Prophetic precedents, even to the extent of casting his lieutenants in the role of the Prophet's Companions, while his followers became the *Anṣār*, the 'Helpers'. It seems he had expectations beyond the Nilotic Sudan, hoping his *mahdiyya* would ignite the whole Islamic *umma* in righteous, xenophobic wrath against the infidel intruders and against the sacrilegious dismantling of the values and habits of the traditional Muslim community he and his followers believed to reflect the will of Allah. It is necessary to bear this angry heritage in mind for it flares and smoulders still in present-day Islam among the Sudanese, with a heat that may be more intense than is to be met with elsewhere in black Africa.

When the *Mahdī* died in Omdurman, which had become his centre after the fall of Khartoum in 1302/1885, he was succeeded by one of his lieutenants, ʿAbd Allāh b. Muḥammad, as *Khalīfa*, 'vicegerent'. ʿAbd Allāh at once declared *jihād* against the surrounding tribes who had not adopted Islam. Despite a defeat at the hands of the Egyptians when he tried to extend his *jihād* into Egypt, and some internal dissension among his own supporters, the *Khalīfa* was able to consolidate his theocracy. It remained undisturbed until, for political reasons that had little directly to do with the Sudan, it was attacked and overthrown by the British, under Lord Kitchener, at the battle of Omdurman, in AD 1898. The *Khalīfa* himself was killed in battle shortly after in 1317/1899.

The Anglo-Egyptian Condominion

The British intervention against the *Khalīfa* was inspired partly by a desire to avenge Gordon, a national hero whose death had aroused great anger in Britain and partly by a wish to secure the British position in Egypt and also to forestall certain other European powers who were already jockeying for influence in the Sudan, and thus over Egypt. It inaugurated what became the Anglo-Egyptian Condominion of the Sudan.

Up until the First World War this condominion was shared in

some measure between British and Egyptian officials. But from *c.* 1920 Egyptian co-operation became, for political reasons, increasingly uneasy for the Egyptians, while it proved equally unsatisfactory from the British point of view. The Sudan then became, to all intents, a British imperial possession administered by the Sudan Political Service. This highly trained and paternalistic body, composed mainly of British civilian officials, was an elitist corps, even by the standards of the British Colonial Service, or Overseas Civil Service as it later euphemistically became under the influence of shamefaced liberal, post-imperial embarrassment. One of the requirements for its entrants was that they should acquire fluency in Arabic. The Political Service was also uniformed and was in some aspects more autocratic than the more timid British colonial civil services elsewhere in tropical Africa. There is no doubt that at a material level, the devoted members of the Sudan Civil Service conferred considerable benefits upon the Sudan by way of communications, improved agriculture and development in general.

In particular, the British-run Sudan education service conscientiously endeavoured to educate the Sudanese for eventual independence – which was always recognised as the ultimate outcome of the condominion – by a programme of secular, Western-style studies while at the same time making every reasonable effort to involve traditional Islamic education with these studies. Steady progress in this was made up to the Second World War. During the post-war period, and especially in the years immediately preceding independence, however, the Sudanese department of education fell into the hands of some who were, perhaps, over-excited by the liberal progressivism of those years. Some observers of this period – including the present writer – considered, rightly or wrongly, that education in the Sudan at that time came near to being out of step with the more measured approach to Sudanese independence favoured by the political cadres. Such progressivist influences – perpetuated, perhaps, from Oxford cloisters after independence had been conceded – may have adumbrated certain leftist *coup* attempts and other manifestations of European-style left-wing activism that bedevilled the early years of Sudanese independence. Some of these had ugly consequences – from which their cloistered sympathisers had the advantage of being safely removed. Moreover, the cleavage that subsequently developed between secularists and radical Muslims, described below in this chapter, while it was to some extent, no doubt, an inevitable consequence of the times, may also fairly be attributed to a Western-style education – sometimes informal and extra-mural – that exhibited markedly liberal emphases, which many of these young Sudanese leftists imbibed. Of course, it would also be fair to point out that many Sudanese students trained in Egypt and elsewhere in the Islamic world, received indoctrination of a different kind, which may have been no less confrontational.

But whatever may be said for or against the British administration in the Sudan – and it was graced by many deep and long-lasting personal friendships that may in the end have been more important than the political friction – the issue of the southern Sudan was a constant source of tension. The Muslim Sudanese felt that the British victory at Omdurman had robbed them of eventual control of the southern Sudan, which they continue to regard as their proper Islamic heritage.

Sudanese 'nationalism'?

To speak of Sudanese 'nationalism' in the context of the Sudanese campaign for independence, as even so measured and careful an historian as Holt occasionally does, is to reopen the debate entered in chapter 1 above.[5] Yet it is as questionable a notion when applied to the Sudanese as it was in the case of the Algerians, Moroccans and Tunisians.

The Ashiqqa Party, founded in 1943 and led by Ismā'īl al-Azharī, at first advocated union with Egypt though it later changed its stance. In so doing it is clear that it was responding not to any onset of popular enthusiasm for a solely Sudanese 'nation-state' but rather to disgust at Nasser's modernising and secularising policies. The other main party of the pre-independence era was the Umma Party. The name is significant. It harked back to the *Mahdī*'s radical theocracy, which he had styled an *umma*, an Islamic community. The word also carries universalist connotations, implying a world-wide Islamic *oecumene*. There is little doubt that the *Mahdī* himself entertained these wider ambitions, which were reflected in the attempt by his *Khalīfa* to extend his theocracy into Egypt. The Umma Party deliberately recurred to the Mahdist ideal, although it did not envisage Egypt being involved, at any rate not in the first instance. But once again it is open to question whether this should be attributed to a straightforward sentiment for Sudanese nationhood, as some have tried to argue. The underlying ideology remained the ancient one of the pan-Islamic *umma* while the more immediate sentiment was distaste for the secularism associated with the Egyptian revolution of 1952.

If such a sentiment as modern, secular nationalism did exist among the northern Sudanese, it was surely confined to the communists and other leftists who were, for the most part, self-proclaimed secularists. Any such vision of a nation-state in the Sudan as they adhered to had nothing to do with Islam. Moreover, as subsequent events were to prove, they were insufficiently representative of the people at large for their ideology to be labelled 'Sudanese'.

But perhaps the most weighty objection to any notion of 'Sudanese nationalism' arises from the question, 'Who were the Sudanese to be nationalists?' There were northern Sudanese, who were united in their desire to see the backs of the British and in their resentment at the continuing resistance of Christian and animist southern Sudanese to absorption into a greater Sudanese polity which most hoped would be Islamic. Beyond that, they were divided into secular leftists and Muslim radicals or traditionalists: *Ṣūfīs* and the like.

Then there were the southern Sudanese, whose intellectual middle class, not inconsiderable after a century or so of Christian missionary education, were ardently Christian, fearful of and hostile to the Muslims, of whose expansionist ambitions they were fully aware. Beyond them were large congeries of illiterate or semi-literate Nilotic animists, for whom the turbanned, white-robed Muslims from the north were merciless slavers, held in check for the time being only by the British, but all too eager to resume the role of conquerors only temporarily suspended on the day the *Khalīfa* died.

There was thus scant reason, on any count, to postulate 'Sudanese nationalism' as the salient sentiment among these diverse groups that competed for hegemony in an independent Sudan. On the contrary, and as will surely become clear as this account proceeds, the predominant attitude in the north was overwhelmingly Islamic, which must exclude secular nationalism; while in the south it was fear of being incorporated into an Islamic theocracy and a desire for secular, federalist autonomy. Whether that deserves to be labelled 'nationalism' is no doubt a matter of opinion.

THE DEMOCRATIC REPUBLIC OF THE SUDAN

In the years immediately preceding the granting of independence, two main parties, the Umma Party and the Ashiqqa Party, became rivals for power. In the parliamentary election of 1953, Ismā'īl al-Azharī, leader of Ashiqqa, won a majority of seats and became Prime Minister. On 1 January 1956, independence was declared. The whole of what had been the Condominion became the 'Democratic Republic of the Sudan'. The title was not entirely felicitous for 'democracy', at any rate in the Western, let alone the 'Westminster' meaning of that term – that is multi-party politics issuing in government elected by universal adult franchise and answerable to an electorate, not to God – was precisely what a very large number of northern Muslim Sudanese regarded as wholly objectionable, as the future was to show. Moreover, the country was far from united. Almost as soon as independence was declared – indeed somewhat before it – the hostility between the Muslim north and the non-Muslim south erupted into what was to become a long and bloody civil war.

Party politicians, military strongmen and Islamic radicals

Independence was now followed by two years of government by party politicians in which first Ismāʿīl al-Azharī, and then ʿAbdallāh Khalīl held the office of Prime Minister at the head of a Council of State. This proved to be a most unstable period, plagued by inter-party squabbling and tension between the communists and other leftist secularists on the one hand and the *Ikhwān*, the Sudanese Muslim Brotherhood and their religious allies, the *Ṣūfīs* and certain *ʿulamāʾ*, on the other. The latter grouping began, from the moment of independence, to press for a fully Islamic theocracy to replace the distasteful 'Westminster' structure inherited from the British and has continued to do so ever since. Much civil unrest ensued and the country became increasingly unmanageable. Finally, in 1958, ʿAbdallāh Khalīl, at that time both Prime Minister and Minister for Defence, ordered General Ibrahim Abboud, Commander-in-Chief of the Armed Forces, to take power in order to forestall what he foresaw as an attempt to overthrow his own government. This inaugurated some six years of rule by a military junta. The period witnessed growing discontent, part of which arose from dissatisfaction at the junta's suppression of all opposition and part also from growing frustration at its failure to implement an Islamic constitution, not to mention its members' own, often conspicuous moral turpitude – or what the strict Muslims regarded as such. In fact this appears to have been, in many cases, no more than a robust way of life picked up in the jovial sociability of British Army officers' messes but it horrified the *fakīs* and the *Ikhwān*. The discontent culminated in massive street protests, a general strike, mass resignations of civil servants and university staff and popular withdrawal of support from the junta orchestrated by the increasingly influential *Ikhwān*. On October 1964 the junta was overthrown. It was replaced by a Council of Sovereignty with Sir al-Khatim al-Khalifa, a modernist who installed a cabinet dominated by communists, as Prime Minister. This further fuelled the ardour of the Islamic factions, led by the *Ikhwān*, who now came out with their 'Islamic Charter'. In consequence the Islamic grouping was known as the 'Islamic Charter Front' (ICF). Under such pressure, Sir al-Khatim al-Khalifa resigned and was replaced by Muhammad Ahmad Mahjūb (1965–6), followed by Ṣadīq al-Mahdī (1966–7) who was in turn replaced by Muhammad Ahmad Mahjub from 1967 to

1969. Meanwhile, Ismā'īl al-Azharī, an old-style politician, leader of the Ashiqqa Party and an anti-communist, remained Head of State through 1965 to 1969. Throughout this period the government was torn by a power struggle between the communists and secularists on the one hand and the Islamic Charter Front, headed by the *Ikhwān*, that pressed with increasing insistence for an Islamic constitution, on the other.

The Numeiri years

This situation, in which governments rose and fell like ninepins, and in which there seemed to be no resolution of the conflict between the secularists and the Islamic radicals, culminated in the *coup* of 25 May 1969, largely engineered by the communists and other leftists. It resulted in the installation of Colonel Ja'far Muhammad al-Numeiri (Numayrī) as Head of State. At first Numeiri surrounded himself with communists, thus incurring the hostility not only of the *Ikhwān* but also of the Mahdist traditionalists, the *Anṣār*, together with *Ṣūfīs* and *'ulamā'*, who were, moreover, shocked by Numeiri's conspicuously un-Islamic life-style. It seems the communists simply regarded Numeiri as a stepping stone for their own transition to power, for in July 1971, they, together with other discontented elements, staged a *coup* against him, as a result of which he was temporarily toppled. This gave rise to widespread anti-communist riots and Numeiri – who was popular at this time with the masses who disliked the rule of the politicians – was reinstated. There are several versions as to how this came about. Spokesmen for the International Islamic Movement, a world-wide organisation dedicated to the Islamc fundamentalist cause, which disapproved of Numeiri, claimed it was brought about by the machinations of Western intelligence. This satanic interest is held to have preferred the secularism which Numeiri favoured at that time, to the return to Islamic theocracy demanded by the *Ikhwān*. Others saw the hand of Numeiri's friend, Colonel Qaddafi of Libya, behind his rescue. Some have even contrived to persuade themselves that the two agencies were one and the same![6]

Be that as it may – and conspiracy theory has always been the stuff of Islamic politics – this experience seems to have convinced Numeiri of two things: firstly, of the unreliability of his communist and leftist allies and secondly, of the strength of the pro-Islamic, anti-communist sentiment among the ordinary people that was revealed in the course of the demonstrations that followed his overthrow. Furthermore, his personal experiences at this time – which appear to have been somewhat traumatic – seem to have triggered in the man an access of personal piety which, despite his previously markedly irreligious way of life, may well have been genuine.

Numeiri now reversed his secularist, pro-communist stance and embarked upon what became known as the 'Islamisation Programme'. First, he dismissed all communists from his government and replaced them, largely with men of a *Ṣūfī* background, *ṭarīqa* leaders and the like. He accomanied this with favourable treatment for the *ṭuruq* – government grants to build mosques and *zāwiyas* – while the Sudanese media, or sections of it, began to portray him as a devout *Ṣūfī*.

Yet this was not enough to stifle all opposition to him. The former politicians, especially Ṣadīq al-Mahdī, who had briefly tasted the delights of the Premiership from 1966 to 1967 and who still had unsatisfied ambitions, were discontented at their exclusion from power while the *Ikhwān* were divided between those prepared to co-operate with Numeiri and those who felt his conversion to Islam was no more than a tactical move that lacked conviction. After much popular protest in the universities and on the streets over the period 1973 to 1975, another *coup* was attempted against him in 1976. It failed. What did result was a meeting between Numeiri and the former Prime Minister and leader of the *Anṣār* group, Ṣadīq al-Mahdī, in 1977. This led to the declaration of a 'National Reconciliation' which, in fact, was a substantial victory for Numeiri. Under persuasion from one faction of the *Ikhwān*, led by Dr Ḥassan al-Turābī, Numeiri in 1983 issued decrees promulgating the *Sharīʿa* law as the legal code of the Sudan. These were known in Arabic as *Taṭbīq al-sharīʿa*, 'Application of the Sharīʿa'. Numeiri is reported to have said at the time that his action was designed to prevent the Iranian experiment being repeated in the Sudan and that it was necessary for the Sudan to solve the problems caused by the demand for an Islamic constitution in its own way.[7] This displeased some Muslim radicals, for whom the ayatollahs' revolution had become the admired exemplar.

Numeiri's *Taṭbīq* was, however, less than complete. It applied only to the criminal and legal sides of the law, not to social and political aspects and therefore alienated the secularists while leaving the Islamic radicals less than fully satisfied. Needless to say, it was received with horror by the southern Sudanese. It was accompanied by a five-month state of emergency during which Draconian measures were used to suppress opposition. These included the setting up of special courts to enforce observance of the *Sharīʿa*, which despite the new legislation, continued to be widely ignored by the secularists. These courts were staffed largely by *Ikhwān*, who took their task very seriously indeed.

Despite the opposition to it, the *Taṭbīq al-Sharīʿa* of 1983 represented a victory for the Islamic factions in what must be seen, retrospectively, as the steady advance of Islam in the struggle between it and secularism, represented by the communists, the socialists left and certain middle-class interests, that had underlain Sudanese politics since the moment of independence. It also gave the *Ikhwān* their first real taste of power.

The *Ikhwān* now became increasingly self-confident and began to act independently of Numeiri, treating him almost with disdain. Numeiri responded by becoming savagely critical of them: he is reported to have referred to them on one occasion as *ikhwān al-shayṭān*, the 'Satanic Brotherhood'.[8] He also set about restoring opponents of the *Ikhwān* to office. A Muslim fundamentalist spokesman observed, apparently regretfully, in October 1983, 'Today, the General [Numeiri had by now promoted himself to this rank] and his army have no opposition to fear'.[9] In fact, however, from 1983 onwards, Numeiri's isolation became increasingly evident. His *Taṭbīq* had alienated not only the secularists, but also the powerful constituency of Sudanese businessmen, who objected to the Islamic banking included in this legislation on *Ikhwān* insistence. On the other hand, the *Ikhwān*, sensing that full power was within their grasp, began to see Numeiri as a half-hearted encumbrance to the full realisation of their aims. The outcome of these various discontents was the *coup* of 6 April 1985, by which Numeiri was finally overthrown.

In retrospect, it becomes clear that the real beneficiaries of this confused interlude of the Numeiri years were the *Ikhwān*. Though they did not achieve the full power they had hoped for after the *coup* of April 1985, they had demonstrated their capacity to enforce the *Taṭbīq al-Sharīʿa*, in the teeth of powerful opposition and to get rid of Numeiri when he proved less than wholehearted in bringing about the complete transition back to theocratic Islam that they desired. They had also shown that the communists and other leftists had no hope of retaining a permanent hold on power when challenged by the Islamic groupings prepared to support the *Ikhwān* in times of crisis.

Under the Transitional Military Council, set up in 1985 to replace Numeiri, the 'Application of the Sharīʿa' was frozen but not withdrawn. In June 1989, the government of Ṣadīq al-Mahdī, again Prime Minister under a Military Council, was overthrown by a *coup* led by Brigadier General ʿUmar Ḥassan al-Bashīr. In December 1990, General Al-Bashīr announced that the implementation of the full *Sharīʿa* legislation would not be long delayed.

THE SOUTHERN SUDAN (*C.* AD 1917 TO THE PRESENT DAY)

The problem of the southern Sudan has, from the beginning of the Anglo-Egyptian Condominion, been malignly involved in the matter of Islam and the Sudan.

The Muslim view

From the point of view of the northern, Muslim Sudanese, the continuous spread of Islam southwards, into the grasslands and riverine areas of the Upper Nile, was part of the ordained order of things. Had the British not interrupted the *Mahdiyya*, the *jihād* would surely have swept across the whole of what is now the Republic of the Sudan, enabling it to become a unified Islamic theocracy. Northern *'ulamā'*, who have not yet learned to moderate their traditionally blunt discourse on this issue with the more oblique, less abrasive and less honest language of their Western-trained co-religionists, are apt simply to assert that the southern Sudanese are the *mushrikūn*, the polytheists or idolaters of Koran 61:9:

> He it is Who sent His Messenger with the guidance and the true religion, that He may make it overcome the religions, all of them, even though the polytheists [*al-mushrikūn*] are averse,

and *passim*, all of which causes these *'ulamā'*, not unnaturally perhaps, to insist that the spread of Islam across the southern Sudan is neither more nor less than the Will of Allah. Thus the British policy in that territory, however well intentioned it may have been according to the pluralist values of British officials reared in a liberal democracy, was carried out in the teeth of transcendentalist opposition from these northern *'ulamā'*, many of whom made no secret of their intention to take up a *jihād* of conversion at the first opportunity.

A more blandly stated point of view – but one that in the end, boils down to the same thing – is that of A. Z. Al-Abdin, in his scholarly analysis of the 'Sudan Charter', to be discussed below in this chapter. This Muslim scholar complains that 'the Sudanese people did not have ample time to develop a homogeneous nation'.[10] But the truth is, homogeneity in this context necessarily means common adherence to Islam, or at the least, the willing submission of the southern Sudanese to the status of non-Muslim subjects of an Islamic state – the historical *dhimma* – a reality that is made very clear in the Sudan Charter itself. Both these alternatives are, of course, wholly unacceptable to the majority of the southern Sudanese.

British policy in the southern Sudan

There is now general agreement among historians that the British did encourage Christian missionary penetration into the southern Sudan and that the education they then promoted in that territory was deliberately designed to bolster southern Christianity against the Islamic influences from the north. The argument now no longer turns on whether this was, or was not, British policy; but rather on whether that policy was advisable or inadvisable, morally praiseworthy or reprehensible.

The British 'Southern Policy' was implemented with vigour from 1917 onwards. Muslim troops were ordered out of the territory in 1922 and were replaced by local levies. The whole of the south and some border areas became 'closed districts' to northern Muslims and special permits were required for entry. Grants-in-aid were made to mission schools where instruction was carried out in English, not Arabic. At one point the British administration in the south somewhat timidly urged the missionaries who ran these schools to include some Arabic in the curriculum but this was scornfully ignored. The Muslims especially resented the loss of Arabic literacy this entailed; in their view it was a deliberate spiritual deprivation as well as an intellectual loss, visited on southerners who might otherwise have adopted Islam as a result of their familiarity with the language of the Koran.

In 1930 this policy of creating what the Muslims contemptuously refer to as a 'Christian bantustan' was intensified, but after the Second World War the British, flustered by the highly indiscriminate pressure of world opinion in favour of the dismantling of colonial rule, regardless of the consequences, initiated measures to create a 'United Sudan'. In 1956 they handed over power in the south to a cadre of mainly Muslim northerners whose only qualification for the task was their somewhat elitist Western education. These people proved, in the first place, highly uncomfortable in their posts; indeed some of them had never even set foot in the southern Sudan before and did not speak the local languages and in the second place they were often both unsympathetic to, and lacking in understanding of the aspirations of their southern subjects. It was not their fault. They, the British and the southern Sudanese, were all equally the victims of an ignorant tide of world-wide liberalism that demanded the instant solution of decolonisation to intractable problems of race, culture and religion that had been seething for centuries.

In 1967 the southern Sudan erupted into open civil war.

An irresolvable crux?

It is easy to feel impatience at, and even hostility towards what seems to be the intransigence of the Muslim position, as the missionaries and many British colonial officials surely did. To do so is to ignore one crucial fact – that the Muslim believes implicitly that the Koran is direct, divine revelation and therefore beyond human arbitrament, while his non-Muslim critic does not. Moreover, while most Muslims would not deny that the *Mahdiyya* was a violent business, they would argue that it was necessary. If the British had not intervened, it would now all have been over; there would be no obstacle to the formation of a unified Islamic state in the Sudan. This consummation, in the Muslim view, is so desirable as to justify the means leading to it. After all, one cannot pick and choose when implementing the will of Allah. This is not to argue that the British, or the missionaries, ought to have given way to the Muslim demands. It is simply to emphasise the pitiless intractability of the 'Southern Sudan Question'.

Not all northern Sudanese openly adopt this stark view of the problem. Some prefer to argue that the *Mahdiyya* notwithstanding, they ought to have been given an equal opportunity with the Christian missionaries to proselytise among the animists of the southern Sudan. Clearly, this argument is not without substance; however, the reply to it of the British authorities of the day was that the *fakīs*, who would have been the people charged with such a mission, were often men of highly inflammatory attitudes. They would not have preached peaceable conversion to Islam, in the manner of the later Indian Ahmadis in West Africa. They would have preached *jihād*. The result would have been communal strife and bloodshed among the southern Sudanese. There is substance in that argument, too.

It is also easy, if one is so inclined, to blame the débâcle on 'British colonialism'. This ignores the reality of Muslim slave-raiding in the southern Sudan, in the days of Zubayr Pasha and his ilk, to say nothing of the *Mahdiyya* itself, all of which involved rapine, slaughter and enslavement on a vast scale. In 1917, this train of events was still fresh in the minds both of British officials and the animist Nilotic peoples over whom they had charge. It was therefore inevitable that these humane and civilised men should have adopted a protective and paternalistic stance towards those whom they regarded as their wards. What seemed to the Muslims to be the creation of a 'Christian bantustan' seemed to the British officials and to the missionaries – many of whom were Germans, Swiss, Irish, French and Americans as well as British – humane intervention to protect the southern people from a repetition of their unhappy experiences of the past.

Moreover, the Muslim Sudanese assumption that, had the British not intervened, Islam would inevitably have overlaid the animist cults of the southern Sudan, is open to question. The resistance of the Shilluk, the Dinka and other southern tribes to Islam has been impressive. Throughout the long Funj period they successfully repelled the tide of Islam that constantly lapped up against them. This resistance would surely have slowed the advance of Islam, even if no Anglo-Egyptian Condominion had been imposed. The history of Islam elsewhere in Africa has demonstrated that it quickly becomes etiolated the further it moves from its heartland. It is by no means a foregone conclusion that an untrammelled *Mahdiyya* would have achieved what the northern Sudanese have failed to achieve in the course of a long civil war.

Religion is not the only dimension to the Muslim viewpoint in this tangled affair, a more material consideration has to do with the Nile waters. Inevitably, it became more salient with Sudanese independence. The importance of the southern Sudan, both to the northern Sudan and to Egypt, lies in the fact that the territory encompasses the upper reaches of the Nile, where control over its flow could seriously interfere with the dams and irrigation systems farther downstream, in the northern Sudan and even Egypt. Thus the high Islamic rhetoric which the northern Sudanese habitually address to the southern problem may sometimes conceal more mundane anxieties.

Finally, nature has planted yet another mischievous genie in this unhappy bottle. It is now thought that the southern Sudan may be rich in commercially exploitable oil. Few developments could be more apt to inflame further an already intractable situation!

The Addis Ababa agreement and its sequel

The civil war dragged on, with much suffering, from 1967 until March 1972, when the Addis Ababa Agreement brought it to a close, for the time being. It was there agreed that there should be three southern provinces with autonomous administrations; that security was to remain in the hands of the southern government; and that no laws were to bc passed without first consulting the southern people. The agreement also allowed for complete freedom for Christian missionaries to proselytise among the southern animists but, to the chagrin of the northern Islamic factions, the Muslim north was bound not to 'move in the direction of Islam'.

Though both sides had accepted the agreement under international pressure, it satisfied neither. For the southerners it fell short of the total equality within a secularist, pluralist, democratic federation of the Sudan that they desired. For the northern Muslims it left the vision of a unified Islamic state of the Sudan unfulfilled.

The problem continued to bedevil the politics of the Sudan throughout the Numeiri years. In 1982 Numeiri announced the abandonment of plans to decentralise the south, according to the terms of the Addis Ababa Agreement. It seems clear that this decision was made under pressure from the National Islamic Front, in which the most powerful element was the Sudanese Muslim Brotherhood. The next move was predictable. Al-Abdin writes:

> in May 1983 a communist-oriented rebellion was started by an army colonel from Southern Sudan, John Garang, which is still ravaging the country causing a great deal of destruction and bloodshed.[11]

In fact, it seems that Garang's rebellion was provoked by Numeiri's failure to honour the Addis Ababa Agreement. The charge of communism probably reflects the fact that Garang sought support from all those opposed to Numeiri's 'Application of the Sharīʿa', among whom the communists were foremost.

Another Addis Ababa agreement was entered into between certain northern Sudanese elements and the Sudan People's Liberation Army (SPLA), the political organ of southern resistance, in 1988. Its main provision was a freeze on any further 'Islamisation' measures in the Sudan constitution. It was rejected by the government of the day, on the insistence of the National Islamic Front, largely controlled by the Muslim Brotherhood. Their alternative proposals for the southern Sudan were enshrined in Hassan al-Turabi's much proclaimed – or denigrated – 'Sudan Charter'. This will be discussed below under the section *The Muslim Brotherhood in the Sudan* (pp. 85–7).

ISLAM IN THE NILOTIC SUDAN: BELIEFS AND ATTITUDES

The course of Islam in the Nilotic Sudan differs in important respects from the Egyptian case. Indeed, it is more reminiscent of North Africa because of the strongly eschatological and apocalyptic emphases in its politics. Since the Banū Kanz were clients of the Fāṭimids, it would be reasonable to suppose that some *Shīʿī* influences may have reached the area at this early date. If so, they took no root. No trace of them remains and the Muslims of the Sudan have been militantly *Sunnī* certainly since the Ayyūbid period.

The role of the fakīs

While scholarly *Sunnī ʿulamā'* have been influential in the schools of Khartoum and Omdurman, especially during the present century, the *fakīs*, itinerant *Ṣūfī* holy men, have had more influence over the nomadic tribes and hill people. As was seen above, it was largely *fakīs* who converted the early Nubians to Islam. They, and not the scholarly *ʿulamā'*, carried Islam into the Nubian hills and the distant riverine areas. In the end, it was a *fakī*, Muḥammad Aḥmad, who discovered the *Mahdiyya* to a people outraged by Turco-Egyptian meddling and European intrusion into traditional ways. The virgate simplicity of the *Mahdī's umma* was far removed from the architectural and literary sophistication that was the heritage of the Mamlūks in Egypt. It has been the former, not the latter, that the Muslim Sudanese have always chosen as their exemplar.

This background – the *Mahdiyya* cut short, the southern Sudan lost to Islam and the burgeoning of Western-style secularism where once the austere ethic of the *Mahdī* reigned – has created in the Democratic Republic of the Sudan a somewhat angry Islam, that finds expression in a strong sympathy for the present-day Islamic fundamentalist tendency. The Muslim Brotherhood finds a ready recruiting ground in the northern Sudan. By and large, the Muslim Sudanese rallied to the side of the Iranian Revolution. They were willing to overlook a Shiʿism they might once have excoriated, in fellow feeling for an angry militancy that chimed with their own theocratic and xenophobic sentiments.

They rallied again to the Iraqis before and during the Gulf war of 1991. In this case an earlier history of most unIslamic modernism was forgotten in the heady excitement of Saddam Hussain's latter-day appeal to pan-Islamic solidarity. Young Sudanese Muslims enlisted in the Iraqi army in significant numbers.

The Muslim Sudanese are generally strong supporters of the Palestinian cause against the Zionists, more out of a desire to cock a snook at the pro-Zionist West than out of any love for the Levantine Palestinians. But above all, it was in the northern Sudan that *al-ikhwān al-muslimūn*, the Muslim Brotherhood, that most radical and theocratic expression of *Sunnī* Islam, found what has surely been its most fruitful recruiting ground in black Africa.

The Muslim brotherhood in the Sudan

Al-ikhwān al-muslimūn, sometimes *ikhwān al-muslimīn* is usually translated as 'The Muslim Brotherhood', though 'The Muslim Brethren' sometimes occurs. It is the same organisation that was founded by Hasan al-Bannā' and espoused by the hapless Sayyid al-Qutb in Egypt. It first came to the Sudan *c.* 1940, as a result of the activities of Sudanese students trained in Egypt and was initially a reaction against the rise of communism in the Sudan. It was also nourished by the example of the Egyptian *Ikhwān* in their struggle against the British. This example occasioned the rise, in the Sudan, of *Harakat al-tahwīr al-islāmī*, the 'Islamic Liberation Movement', in which many young Sudanese *Ikhwān* were prominent, though the movement was not at this point overtly linked to the Muslim Brotherhood. This faction not only sought the expulsion of the British, it also cherished heady visions of the world-wide revival of Islam and the setting up of a new Islamic world order that was to transcend the East–West dichotomy of the time. In this, the influence of Sayyid al-Qutb is unmistakable. At this time too, the notion of 'Islamic socialism' was bruited, and was taken up by some *Ikhwān*, though it later faded as the confrontation between the Sudanese left – an increasingly secularist grouping – and Islamic theocratic radicalism became sharper.

The Sudanese *Ikhwān* were, however, not solely concerned with the anti-colonial struggle. For, as Affendi points out, communism grew mainly among the westernised section of the Sudanese middle class and was itself a prime instrument of westernisation. Even without colonialist help – and as I have suggested above, it may be that elements in the Sudan education service in its later years did provide some encouragement to leftist stances – the 'forces of the left played an important role as transmitters of Western norms and values'.[12] Another factor that helped the growth of the *Ikhwān* tendency was increasing disgust, especially among the young Sudanese from rural backgrounds, at the perceived moral laxity of the middle classes, especially the Sudanese officer class, whose constant *coups* were to punctuate the Sudanese political process.

In 1954 these nascent *Ikhwān* came out finally under the name *al-ikhwān al-muslimūn*. They became, from that moment on, the spearhead of the drive, not just for Sudanese independence – there were several groupings, including the communists, striving for that – but for independence under a full, traditional, Islamic constitution. This at once brought them into confrontation with the left in Sudanese politics, as well as, of course, with the southern Sudanese interest, for whom an Islamic constitution was wholly unacceptable. It also brought them into conflict with Ismā'īl al-Azharī, the leader of the *Anṣār*, who at this point favoured union with Egypt. Despite their fervent pan-Islamic rhetoric, the Sudanese *Ikhwān* were cool on the specific issue of such a union, partly because of the widespread radical Islamic opposition to Nasser and his modernism, which they shared with Egyptian *Ikhwān*.

By about 1955, three main props to the *Ikhwān's* platform had become established: anti-communism, opposition to Nasser and the demand for the setting up of a fully Islamic constitution in the Sudan, based at every point – legal, criminal, personal, social, financial and political – on the Islamic *Sharī'a*. They even went so far as to advocate 'Islamic banking' – that is, a banking system that eschews the taking and giving of interest, which they held to be condemned by the Koranic ban on usury. In 1955, they formed the Islamic Front for the Constitution (IFC). It was at this point that the *Ikhwān* openly posed the question, which has remained unanswered not only in the Sudan, but right across the Islamic world: How is it possible to reconcile traditional Islam with a world that becomes increasingly secular? Or, as Affendi succinctly puts it, 'What does it entail to be a Muslim?'[13]

In November 1958, the constant squabbling of the rival civilian politicians, to say nothing of their evident nest feathering in some cases, led to the *coup* by General Ibrāhīm Abboud. The *Ikhwān* suffered some setback when one of their number, a certain Rashīd al-Ṭahīr, attempted a counter-*coup* against him and failed.

Hassan al-Turabi and the Sudan Charter

In 1962, Dr Hassan al-Turabi, a Western-educated Muslim academic, emerged to prominence. Under his leadership, the *Ikhwān* revived. His approach to the situation that prevailed in the Sudan at that time was that government by the military junta denied the Koranic principle of *shūrā*, 'consultation'; he therefore advocated a united front against the junta, whose moral laxity he also condemned, as well as their autocratic rule. He even encouraged the southern Sudanese to join the front. As was pointed out above, the mass demonstrations, strikes and protests that followed this initiative, led to the overthrow of the junta.

The role of Hassan al-Turabi throughout the Numeiri years has been briefly touched on above. He was first imprisoned by Numeiri but subsequently, regained favour and was appointed to the influential post of Attorney General in Numeiri's government, in 1979. For this he incurred some odium among the more radical *Ikhwān* who could not forgive Numeiri his early communist associations. None the less, it is clear that Turabi was instrumental in persuading Numeiri to take the momentous step of promulgating the controversial *Taṭbīq al-Sharīʿa*, the 'Application of the Sharīʿa' in September 1983.

As was described above, the resistance this provoked was partly responsible for Numeiri's fall, and in the disturbed conditions that led up to this, Turabi and other *Ikhwān* leaders came under suspicion and suffered imprisonment. From this they were honourably released by the Transitional Military Council that took over from Numeiri.

In fact the *Ikhwān* had not expected Numeiri to fall when he did. As was pointed out above, radical Islamic opinion in 1983 held that Numeiri no longer had any opposition to fear. Nor did they altogether desire his fall: they would have preferred a situation in which they could have engineered his departure to coincide with their own accession to full power, in order to complete what they regarded as his unfinished work. Even so, they did not hesitate to assume a large part of the credit for his fall. Yet there is no doubt that Numeiri's Application of the *Sharīʿa* was a victory for the *Ikhwān*, as well as a personal triumph for Hassan al-Turabi. As a result of it, the *Sharīʿa* was placed firmly on the political agenda, where it has stubbornly remained ever since.

One issue became central in the Sudanese debate over the *Sharīʿa*: that of the relationship between Islam and democracy. Most of the *Ikhwān*, together with more traditionalist groups such as the *Ṣūfīs* were opposed to secular democracy, which they regarded as essentially un-Islamic. Instead, they called for a constitution in which an Islamic élite – the *ʿulamāʾ* – dispensed guidance that would lead the people back to Islam. Turabi, on the other hand, insisted that the Koranic *shūrā*, 'consultation', which the traditionalists would have confined solely within the circle of the *ʿulamāʾ*, was rightfully the patrimony of the Muslim people at large. His argument, however, did suffer from serious inadequacies, not to say inconsistencies, among which the most troublesome was how *shūrā* was to be established on this mass scale; and, once established, how it was to be implemented in the face of unwilling minorities – more especially the non-Muslim southern Sudanese. His attempts to solve such dilemmas brought him perilously close to advocating straightforward democracy, based on universal suffrage, as his more radical critics were not slow to point out. Turabi was at one point even accused of succumbing to Western-style liberalism. For as *Crescent International*, an Islamic fundamentalist newspaper, sourly pointed out in August 1984:

> A faction of the *Ikhwān* led by Dr Ḥassan al-Turābī, joined [Numeiri's] government. A western-style 'liberal' period followed.[14]

And, yet more slightingly:

> Almost all Islamic groups (with the exception of the *Ikhwān* faction led by Turābī) opposed Numeiri's partial Islamization.[15]

Such comments, which simply imply a demand for out-and-out Islamic theocracy unrelieved by any form of compromise, illustrate the extreme difficulty of achieving any generally acceptable solution in the matter of the Sudan constitution.

At first Turabi's colleagues in the Islamic Front for the Constitution (IFC) demanded that in any Islamic government, all key posts must be occupied by Muslims. Later, however, this was reluctantly dropped in face of the difficulties it posed *vis-à-vis* the southern Sudanese, though Turabi did concede to the radicals the point that an Islamic state could under no circumstances be headed by a non-Muslim. This, of course, excluded the southern Sudanese from the highest office, unless the candidate was a Muslim (there being, of course, a few southern Sudanese who have converted to Islam).

Arguments such as these – how and whether secular democracy could be made compatible with Islamic political theory, whether and how even the minimum Islamic requirements could be made acceptable to the non-Muslim southern minority – continued back and forth among the *Ikhwān* and the other Islamic groups for several years. In the course of it Turabi became increasingly convinced that even an Islamic state could not hope to isolate itself from the non-Islamic world around it and must, therefore, seek some common ground. The outcome was the presentation by Ḥassan al-Turābī, in January 1987, of what is known as 'The Sudan Charter'. This was issued in the name of the National Islamic Front (NIF), yet another Islamic grouping to emerge out of this continuing debate. It appears to represent the extreme limit of compromise that Turabi was able to elicit from and Islamic consensus whose real objective was an Islamic state *à outrance*.

The Sudan Charter, which proposes a constitution for the whole of the Sudan, north and south alike, takes its stand on the fact that the Muslims are in a majority and

> are unitarian in their religious approach to life. As a matter of faith, they do not espouse secularism.[16]

Thus the Muslims cannot exist, as Muslims, in a surrounding secularist environment and therefore

> have a legitimate right, by virtue of their democratic weight and of natural justice, to practise their values and rules of their religion to their full range – in personal, social or political affairs.[17]

The Charter goes on to aver that 'Islamic jurisprudence shall be the general source of law' on the grounds that it is both an expression of the will of the majority and also that it in any case 'conforms to the values of all scriptural religions'. The first demand would seem to involve invoking an essentially secular democratic principle – 'the will of the majority' – to enforce an undemocratic, transcendental religious law, which non-Muslim critics of the Charter understandably regard as inconsistent. The second claim – that Islamic jurisprudence 'conforms to the values of all scriptural religions' – is most unlikely to win the concurrence of the Christian, mission-trained southern Sudanese.

The Charter does concede to non-Muslims autonomy in personal, family and social matters and goes on to advise that in cases of divergence between the Islamic code and the non-Islamic alternatives 'an attempt shall be made to give general, if parallel, effect to both'. But it then goes on to insist that in cases where this is not feasible, 'the majority option shall be determinative, with due respect to the minority expression'. Since, elsewhere, the Charter states that Muslims enjoy a majority, this is tantamount to saying that, in the final analysis, the Islamic point of view must prevail – an interpretation that, as Affendi points out, Turabi's more radical Islamic colleagues were not slow to latch onto.[18]

What the Sudan Charter appears, somewhat uncertainly, to propose, is a gradual progression to a loose federal structure over which Islam is, none the less, to remain the dominant ideology, but within which non-Muslim groups are to enjoy a degree of autonomy, so long as this does not conflict with the majority – that is the Muslim – preference. As Affendi points out, the Charter attempts to legislate for religious communities, not for individuals.[19] In this respect it is virtually indistinguishable from the old Ottoman *millet* system, where *dhimmīs*, non-Muslim subjects of the Islamic state, enjoyed a measure of local autonomy according to their own religious law, under what was none the less a clear Islamic hegemony.

The distance between what the Sudan Charter offers and what the southern non-Muslims hope for, is made clear in what Al-Abdin sets out as 'the demands of most Southerners':

> a federal system for the whole of the Sudan in which the South becomes one entity, i.e: a regional autonomy for the South; development of the South so that it reaches parity with the North.
> fair participation of Southerners in the central government and its various agencies.
> secular constitution and secular laws for the whole country, freedom of religion and non-discrimination on ethnic or religious grounds.
> protection of local cultures and local languages.[20]

It will be seen at once how this conflicts with the Charter's essential demand for a code of law based on the *Sharīʿa*, with the Muslim insistence that only a Muslim can be head of state, with the Charter's basic premise that Muslims cannot live under a secular system and, finally, with the urgent Muslim insistence that literacy in Arabic is inseparable from the Islamic state – an insistence that is most threatening to local cultures and languages.

The Sudan Charter has been criticised not only by non-Muslims, as was to be expected, but also by the more ardent of Turabi's fellow Muslim radicals. They object to it on the ground that it projects Islam as

> the interest of a particular ethnic-sectarian group rather than a universal ethical imperative,[21]

which is what these radicals uncompromisingly insist it must be.

It is not necessary to question Turabi's sincerity in seeking to achieve what Al-Abdin describes, perhaps somewhat optimistically, as 'national unity and diversity'. But what does stand out is the inflexibility of the limitations within which any such endeavour has to proceed. Nevertheless, despite objections to the Sudan Charter that arise both from the non-Muslim side and the Muslim side, it is what Brigadier General ʿUmar Hassan al-Bashīr has undertaken to implement as soon as possible. Unless some such federalist solution as the southerners desire can be worked out on the basis of a modified Sudan Charter or the Charter be abandoned altogether, it seems that the only other courses open to the northern Sudanese are to break away from the south and set up their own Islamic polity in what are indisputably Islamic areas (a course that would finally betray the *Mahdiyya* and incur the rage of the *Ikhwān* and their religious allies) or to continue with the civil war in the south in an attempt to impose an Islamic constitution on the southerners by *force majeure*. As of March 1992, the second alternative appears to be the one adopted by General ʿUmar Hassan al-Bashīr.

NOTES

1. Hrbek, Ivan, loc. cit., Bibl., p. 70.
2. Holt, et al. (eds), 2A, p. 329.
3. Ibid., 2A, p. 330.
4. Ibid., 2A, p. 329.
5. Ibid., pp. 342–3.
6. See for instance Kalim Siddiqui (ed.) *Issues in the Islamic movement 1983–1984 (1403–1404)*, pp. 93–5 and 335–7. As the title indicates, this and other volumes in this series represent the views of the Islamic Movement, an international Islamic organisation believed to be sponsored by Iran.
7. Siddiqui (ed.), *Issues ... 1983–1984*, p. 335.
8. Ibid., p. 335.
9. Ibid., p. 95.
10. Loc. cit., Bibl.
11. Ibid., p. 1.
12. Affendi, El-, Abdelwahab, op. cit., Bibl., p. 49.
13. Ibid., p. 57.
14. Siddiqui, *Issues ... 1983–1984*, p. 336.
15. Ibid., p. 337.
16. Abdin, Al-, loc. cit., Bibl., p. 4.
17. Ibid., p. 4.
18. Affendi, op. cit., p. 177.
19. Ibid., p. 177.
20. Abdin, loc. cit., pp. 1–2.
21. Affendi, op. cit., p. 177.

4

West Africa

West Africa is exposed in the west to the Atlantic Ocean; to its north lies North Africa; to its east lies Egypt. From the ocean it received the beginnings of Christianity, carried in by the Portuguese caravels during the fifteenth century AD, but by that time Islam had been established inland for at least 500 years, brought by camel caravans from the north and east.

MEDIEVAL EMPIRES OF THE SAHEL (*C.* 220/835 TO *C.* 1060/1650)

It is known that a diagonal caravan route ran in early times from the ancient empire of Ghana, via Gao on the Niger Bend, to enter Egypt, probably at the Kharga Oasis. This route may have been in operation before the dawn of Islam, perhaps even shortly after the introduction of the camel into the Sahara in the second century AD but it was abandoned in the middle of the third/ninth century, due, maybe, to a lack of security arising from nomadic incursions into the Nubian kingdoms at this time. Its existence means that Egyptians may have been in touch with the Niger Bend even before Islam.

On the North Africa side, North Africans are known to have been in contact with the western Sudan in their search for its gold, as early as 116/734. The Sudanic empire of Ghana was sufficiently familiar to the Islamic world to appear on the map of the Arab geographer, al-Khwarazmī, *c.* 220/835 or 231/846. Moreover, the North African town of Tahert was conducting a trade with the Sudan *c.* 290/902–3, while by the middle of the fourth/tenth century the Moroccan town of Sijilmasa was also involved in the gold trade from the Senegal. By *c.* 460/1068, the Saharan town of Tadmakkat linked Qayrawān, Ghadames and Tripoli in the north with the empire of Ghana and with the Niger Bend. The western Sudan was in no way isolated from the surrounding world during the early centuries of Islam.

Medieval Ghana

The Sudanic state of Ghana is generally held to have been founded by North African Berbers, under a dynasty known as the Kaya Maga, in the fourth century AD. However, the name of that dynasty, in the form it has come down to us, is not Berber but appears to be Mande. Moreover, the original site of the dynasty has been established as lying at Kumbi Saleh, west of the great bend of the Niger. The word 'Kumbi' is also Mande, meaning 'burial ground', namely a royal cemetery. Thus the better opinion may be that the Kaya Maga founders were Mandes, or Mandingos, not Berbers.

The way of life in medieval Ghana is vividly portrayed in a well-known passage from the Arab geographer, al-Bakrī, which relates to the second half of the fifth/eleventh century, by which time the state was ruled by Soninke negroes. He tells of a city built of wood and stone, not mud, and by this time divided into a Muslim and a non-Muslim quarter. The ruler was at that time a Soninke animist whose court displayed the characteristic ritual of an ancient and elaborate polytheist cult. Yet many of his ministers and advisers were Muslims, who participated in the life of the court but were excused from taking part in pagan ceremony rather following their own Islamic conventions in their relations with the ruler, in their worship and in their social life. They also lived apart from the animists, in their own quarter but appear, none the less, to have associated amicably with them. The state of Ghana at this time, and the community that lived there, had clearly achieved a relatively high level of culture, based on a prosperous involvement in the caravan trade, and especially the trade in gold, carried from southern riverine areas, through Ghana, to North Africa and Egypt. Ghana's rival was the Saharan city of Awdaghust, to its north west. This city was initially in the hands of Berbers but by the end of the fourth/tenth century the Soninkes of Ghana had established dominance over the Berbers of Awdaghust. The dominance was maintained until the city fell to the southern, desert Almoravids.[1]

The received view has until recently been that the empire of Ghana, which at its apogee controlled the great triangle formed by the river Senegal in the west and the western arm of the Niger in the east, was conquered by the Almoravids *c.* 469/1076. This view is based on the testimony of certain late Arabic writers including the eighth/fourteenth-century Ibn Khaldūn but is given scant support by examination of the works of earlier Arab writers. What seems much more likely is that the medieval Ghanaians were already partly won over to Islam by the time al-Bakrī visited them *c.* 460/1067. They were then peaceably persuaded into formal acceptance of Islam by the Almoravids, with whom they remained on friendly terms. Consequently, when the desert Almoravids withdrew northwards, to join their northern brethren in the conquest of Spain, some remained behind and soon integrated with the Soninkes of Ghana. In due course the rulership of Ghana – or part of it – passed peacefully to a dynasty of the Lamtuna Berbers, members of the Sanhaja group who made up the Almoravids. Meanwhile, at least one smaller state, Diafunu (Zāfūn of the Arabic texts) emerged out of Ghana. It appears that during the first half of the sixth/twelfth century it was still governed by Muslim Soninkes who had adopted the Almoravid way of life and enjoyed cordial relations with the Almoravid court in Marrākūsh. Undoubtedly the southern Almoravids did fight a *jihād* in the western Sudan but it seems it was against the Susu, the animist enemies of the Sonikes of Ghana, and against certain non-Muslim Berbers, rather than against the Ghanaian Soninkes themselves. By the seventh/thirteenth century, however, Ghana had succumbed to these animist Susu. The Muslims of Ghana then fled to Walata, north of Ghana, which became in consequence a new centre of trade.

The rise of Mali

As Ghana faded, so another Sudanic state grew in influence and extent in the Niger Bend. Mali, or Malal, was at one time a dependency of Ghana, later becoming independent under the Kaita, a dynasty of the Mandingo people. Islam in Mali remained tenuous until the second half of the seventh/thirteenth century when, between 658/1260 and 676/1277, that is during the reign of the Mamlūk Sultan Baybars in Egypt, Mansa Ulli of Mali performed Pilgrimage to Mecca by way of Cairo. He thereby established himself as a legitimate Islamic ruler and set up links with Egypt. During his reign Mali expanded more widely over the Sahel and he probably brought Walata, Timbuktu and Gao under his control. By 724/1324 the Malian ruler of the day, Mansa Mūsā, had performed his Pilgrimage, a grandiose affair that impressed the Cairenes greatly. So prestigious did he become in consequence that he figures regally on the Catalan map of ad 1375 (he had died in ad 1337), apparently as lord of the whole Sahara and Sudan. His reign marked the apogee of the empire of Mali, which in fact controlled a wide band of territory bounded by the Atlantic in the west, by Gao in the east, by Awdaghust and Walata in the north and by Niani in the south. The Sudanic city of Jenne and the Saharan city of Tadmakkat both fell under the jurisdiction of Mali.

The reign of Mansa Mūsā marked the high point of Malian influence. After him the empire began to decline, weakened by succession struggles and by revolts among the non-Mandingo – that is the Berber and Mossi – subjects of the Malian empire.

The rise of Songhay

The Sudanic empire of Songhay began as a kingdom of Sorka fishermen on the east bank of the Niger who at some point apparently intermarried with Berbers. By *c.* 399/1009 a dynasty claiming Yamanite descent and having the name Za, emerged in Gao. This claim to Yamanite origins is yet another example of the adopted genealogy that so often marks the conversion of a ruling house to Islam. However, not all the Songhay people converted to Islam with the *Zas*. The kingdom remained split into a Muslim and a pagan half until it came under the domination of Mali in the course of the eighth/fourteenth century. It was delivered from Malian overlordship by one Sonni ʿAlī, a nominal Muslim who conquered Timbuktu, by then in the hands of the Touregs, in 873/1468, and Jenne five years later. He thus laid the foundations for the greater Songhay empire.

Timbuktu was destined to play a central role in the subsequent intellectual and political history of the western Sudan. Beginning as a Toureg encampment in the late fifth/eleventh century, the city served the caravan trade but by the second half of the eighth/fourteenth century it had developed into a flourishing trading centre in its own right, having largely replaced Walata in that role. This was surely due to its commanding position over the Niger Bend, which Walata lacked. It became part of the empire of Mali during the reign of Mansa Uli, suffering attacks from the animist Mossi during the Malian period, although the Mali population was never finally driven out. Around 837/1433 it was taken over by Touregs and by *c.* 843/1439 the control of Mali had finally lapsed. It was some thirty years later that Timbuktu was seized by Sonni ʿAlī and made part of the Songhay empire. Although Gao remained the centre of Songhay kingship, Timbuktu from this point onwards became, increasingly, the real metropolis of the western Sudan.

On the death of Sonni ʿAlī in 898/1492, and after an interlude of civil war, a Songhay army commander known as Askiya Muḥammad, the first of the 'Askiya' dynasty, succeeded. Like his Malian predecessor, this Songhay ruler was quick to consolidate his claim to Islam by Pilgrimage, which he performed in 902/1496 or 903/1497. His procession to Cairo was, like that of Mansa Mūsā, a grand affair. On his return to Songhay with his authority firmly established, Askiya Muḥammad set about pushing outwards the boundaries of Songhay by wars of conquest, which he glossed as *jihād*. By the time he was deposed in 934/1528, blind, aged and feeble, he had incorporated what was left of Mali into his empire, and had extended it to the borders of the Hausa states to the east and to Taghaza in the north. There now followed half a century of intrigue and assassinations during which eight *askiyas* succeeded one another. Some were more able than others, and Songhay remained a power in the western Sudan until 999/1591. In that year it was conquered by the Sharifian Saʿdids.

The pashalik *of Timbuktu*

The Moroccan invasion of Timbuktu was a consequence of political pressures that bore upon the Sharifian Saʿdids during the reign of Mawlāy Aḥmad al-Manṣūr, especially his need to finance his *jihād* against the Spanish and Portuguese Christians with Sudanese gold.

The Songhay army greatly outnumbered the Moroccan force, but being armed only with traditional African weapons they were no match for the musketeers of the Pasha Jawdhar. Initially the Moroccan force, composed largely of Christian and especially Andalusian renegades to Islam armed with arquebuses, at that period an advanced form of weaponry, invested Gao but the commanding *pasha*, Jawdhar (sometimes Jūdār), quickly realised that, even though it was nominally the seat of the *askiyas*, it was of minor importance. He therefore turned on Timbuktu. In 999/1591, the Songhay army was defeated at the battle of Tondibi, near Timbuktu. The Moroccans then set up a puppet *askiya* to undertake the local administration; Timbuktu became a *pashalik* of the Moroccan Sharifian empire.

Although resistance on the part of certain Songbay *ʿulamā'* and their followers continued for a while, most of the Songhays accepted the conquest as the Will of Allah. At first the Moroccans, under Jawdhar Pasha, served Mawlāy Aḥmad al-Manṣūr loyally enough. Large quantities of gold and other wealth were sent back to Morocco whence it found its way onto the Mediterranean money exchanges, as was described in Chapter 1. The Moroccans at first left the local administration of Songhay undisturbed, recognising sensibly that the smooth functioning of the gold trade and commerce generally depended upon administrative continuity and a minimum of disturbance. To govern the growing Moroccan community that grew up in Timbuktu in the wake of the conquest, the Moroccans introduced a *makhzan,* modelled on that of Morocco. This was nominally administered by a *pasha* and *amīns*, functionaries borrowed from the Moroccan Sharifian model. However, rehearsing the situation so often described in the history of North Africa, real power quickly came to reside with the army commanders. The Pasha Jawdha, a reasonably honest and efficient administrator, was replaced by Pasha Maḥmūd Zarghūn, who was more tyrannical and less competent.

The Arma

Meanwhile, certain developments were taking place within the *pashalik* of Timbuktu. The first was the rise of a class known as the *Arma* or *Ruma*. The word is Arabic and was applied to the Moroccan musketeers. These persons quickly began to cohabit with the local

Songhay women, producing half-caste children. Their loyalty to Morocco was half-hearted and they showed an increasing tendency to set themselves up as *de facto* masters of what became, in due course, an independent *Arma* principality on the Niger Bend. This process accelerated, on the death of Mawlāy Aḥmad al-Manṣūr in 1012/1603, whereupon the customary succession struggle broke out in Morocco itself. As a consequence of this, the metropolitan Moroccan authorities increasingly lost interest in the distant Timbuktu *pashalik*; communications with it deteriorated. By the time the ʿAlawids had replaced the Sharifian Saʿdids – that is *c.* 1071/1660 – the *Arma* had become to all intents the independent rulers of the Timbuktu *pashalik*. They were not wholly incompetent. For a time they kept the trade routes open and the commerce of Timbuktu continued to function, but, like the metropolitan Moroccan officials, they were increasingly subject to rivalries, plots and *coups* such as bedevilled the history of the North African dynasties. They retained the Moroccan political culture even though they had thrown off their allegiance to the Moroccan sultan. Increasingly they competed with one another for the support of the local mercenaries – Berbers, Fulani, Bambaras and others – upon whom they had come to depend and who often seized power for themselves. Gradually central authority crumbled: Touregs and other local factions took over larger and larger tracts of what had once been a unitary Songhay empire. By *c.* 1163/1750 the authority of the *Arma* was confined to the banks of the Niger. Beyond that, rival bands of brigands fought for power or lived off raiding the caravans.

The Moroccan conquest of Songhay has reasonably been regarded as a watershed in the history of West Africa. As a result of it the ancient pattern of Sudanese empires changed. A new pattern of what some have thought of as Sudanic 'balkanisation' took its place. There is some substance in this view, as will become clear as the account proceeds.

Early Islam in the western Sudan: Sunnīs *versus* Ibāḍīs

The precise sequence of events that led to the establishment of Islam in West Africa, and the nature of its early theology, are uncertain. Yet some central facts are clear. It was trade, and particularly the gold trade, not military conquest, that established Islam in and around the Niger Bend during the first 300 years of its slow advance. Despite the possibility of early Egyptian influences along the Ghana-Gao-Kharga route, the main thrust of Islam came from Morocco and Tahert in North Africa from the early second/eighth century onwards. It increased in intensity up to the fifth/eleventh century. By this time the Almoravids had made their unmistakable entrance into the western Sudan and the Niger Bend.

Over this long period, the penetration of Islam occurred in the context of a tussle between the Ibāḍī persuasion, a residual tendency left over from the Rustāmids, Khārijīs who founded Tahert *c.* 144/761, and the *Sunnī* persuasion of the first Arab conquerors of North Africa. Tahert was an Ibāḍī centre, deeply involved in the gold trade from an early date; Sijilmasa and other Moroccan towns were equally involved in that trade, and were also predominantly Ibāḍī at this time. The emphasis carried by the early Muslims entering the western Sudan must surely have been of the Ibāḍī rather than the *Sunnī* kind. Also important as a staging point for the gold trade, and therefore as a channel for the entry of Islam, was the Saharan centre, Tadmakkat. This town, too, remained predominantly Ibāḍī until 476/1083–4 when it was conquered by the Ghanaians, by this time committed to *Sunnī* Islam. Until this date, it is therefore to be assumed that it was the Ibāḍī version of Islam that was propagated by the Tadmakkans.

Yet not all early influences were necessarily Ibāḍī. Qayrawān was not only a centre of *Sunnī* scholarship and a fortress, it was also an important trading centre linked to the Saharan and Sudanic caravan routes. *Sunnī* influences must therefore have flowed out from it, to compete with those of the Ibāḍī persuasion.

Typical of the ebb and flow of these two Islamic tendencies at this early period is the case of Malal. Malal was a dependency of Ghana destined to become the centre of a major Sudanic empire by the eighth/fourteenth century. Prior to 460/1067 this sub-kingdom of Ghana had been won over to Islam by a *Sunnī shaykh*, yet by *c.* 545/1150 there is evidence that the ruler of Malal had swung over to the Ibāḍī persuasion. Later, however, there is little doubt that the kingdom was once again predominantly *Sunnī* and Mālikī, although a small Ibāḍī community apparently survived there until the eighth/fourteenth century, according to the renowned Arab traveller of that day, Ibn Baṭṭūṭa.[2]

By 476/1083, the Ghanaians are reputed to have turned on the Ibāḍīs of Tadmakkat with the help of their Almoravid allies, conquered them and imposed *Sunnī* Mālikī Islam upon them. This date may be taken as the point at which the *Sunnī*, Mālikī *madhhab* finally emerged as dominant in the western Sudan. Ibadism was not wholly extinguished for many generations, but it ceased to present a serious challenge to the *Sunnī* mainstream.

The role of the Almoravids in planting Sunnī *Islam*

It has been customary to attribute the final consolidation of *Sunnī* Islam to the Almoravids. Yet the Almoravids were themselves but a manifestation of that *Sunnī* Islamic radicalism nourished, over many centuries, in Qayrawān, which had already overwhelmed North Africa. Even if an Almoravid splinter had not broken away from the main thrust and turned southwards into the Niger Bend, it seems likely that *Sunnī* Islam would none the less have prevailed eventually in West Africa, as it did in North Africa. The Almoravids were an important instrument in this process. But even without their intervention, intellectual and commercial forces, wider and deeper than just the Almoravids, were at work to bring it about.

The contribution of the Almohads

The Almoravids in North Africa and Spain were replaced by the Almohads. As far as is known, these sectarians made no physical attempt to extend their influence into the western Sudan but it seems probable that something of their distinctive theology found its way along the trade routes of the day. Yet Sufism, which was the peculiar contribution of the Almohads to North Africa, was slow to take root in West Africa. Although the *ṭuruq* flourished among the Saharan Berbers from the ninth/fifteenth century onwards, they did not take root in the savannah until the eleventh/seventeenth century. However, individuals claiming to be *shurafā'*, Sharīfs, that is descendants of the Prophet, found their way there somewhat earlier. This may be attributed to Almohad influences.

Islam in Mali

The era of the great Sudanic successor states to Ghana, namely Mali and Songhay, represents both a tussle and a compromise between the new culture and belief system of Islam and the ancient, tenacious animism of the western Sudan.

The Islam of Sunjata Kaita, the heroic founder of Mali, was nominal. It was his son, Mansa Ulli, who made the first of what was to become a succession of royal Pilgrimages by Malian, Songhay and Borno rulers, via Cairo, to Mecca. The significance of this was as much constitutional as devotional. These 'Pilgrim Kings' became thereby legitimate in the eyes of their subjects, including the Muslim *'ulamā'* who now began to throng their courts. They were also recognised by the great Islamic states of North Africa and Egypt that surrounded West Africa in a manner that their animist predecessors could never have hoped to achieve. Moreover, the existence of these Islamic states in the western Sudan drew in yet more Muslim *'ulamā'* from North Africa and Egypt, who functioned as constitutional and legal tutors to the Sudanic kings.

Yet the Sudanic rulers, much as they profited from the *baraka*, 'blessedness', that Pilgrimage conferred upon them, were not prepared to abandon the traditional polytheism lock, stock and barrel. Polytheist ritual and custom were too deeply embedded in Sudanic culture to permit that it be abruptly rooted out. Islam, however prestigious, remained alien. While rulers such as Mansa Mūsā were happy to apply the *Sharī'a* when it served their purpose, to have the *imām* – probably an Egyptian *'ālim* – conduct Friday prayers in their names, and to celebrate Islamic festivals, they none the less preserved much of the ancient animist ceremonial in their courts. They also applied customary law, not the *Sharī'a*, when it suited them.

What resulted from this has been described as 'mixed Islam',[3] which many of the *'ulamā'* disapproved of. They formed an Islamic opposition, apt to harangue the ruler. This opposition eventually became so importunate as to be burdensome; it cost some *'ulamā'* dear. Other *'ulamā'*, more easy-going, were prepared to tolerate a compromise that offered them a comfortable living. The situation in Mali is vividly portrayed by the Arab traveller, Ibn Baṭṭūṭa, who visited that state in 753/1352–3, during the reign of Mansa Mūsā's near-successor, Mansa Sulaymān. It was some twenty-eight years after Mansa Mūsā's spectacular Pilgrimage had established Mali's reputation as a great Islamic principality in the world of that day and after the *'ulamā'* who had made their way there had had nearly a generation in which to propagate their culture in this Sudanic society. It is clear from his account that, while some Malians were good Muslims, others remained pagans at heart. Islamic literacy, Islam's festivals and even its dress were widely accepted among them yet many other aspects of Islam – its food prohibitions, the moral deportment of females – were widely ignored. Moreover, court ceremonial, which Ibn Baṭṭūṭa describes in detail, was redolent of pagan survivals.[4]

One factor that does seem to have worked steadily in Islam's favour was trade. Not only did the incoming caravans bring both merchants and scholars who were Muslims, they also brought books that contributed to the spread of Islamic literacy. But trade did more than that. Islam has its own sophisticated code of commercial law that governs the conduct of markets, the availability of credit and similar essential matters. By 803/1400 it would probably have been impossible to conduct business between the Sudan, North Africa and Egypt without substantial reliance upon the commercial practice of the *Sharī'a*. Thus trade encouraged conversion to Islam among the trading classes.

Islam in Songhay: Sonni ʿAlī

The decline of Mali and the rise of Songhay brought the tension between Islam and African polytheism to a head. This tension was to demonstrate that, for all that worked in its favour, Islam was by no means yet finally assured of the upper hand. Sonni ʿAlī, who finally broke free from the rule of Mali, was nominally a Muslim. He has, however, gone down in the history of West African Islam as a great 'Khārijī', a word that by this time had lost any reference to particular doctrines and meant simply 'warmonger' or even just 'very wicked man'. No sooner had he broken from Malian domination than he turned on the Muslim *ʿulamā'*, especially those of Timbuktu, persecuted them and drove them out of his kingdom. At the same time he elevated the polytheists and openly flaunted his attachment to the ancestral cult. His reign was undoubtedly a setback for Islam – and a brief victory for African polytheism.

The history of Sonni ʿAlī is a prime example of one for which the Muslims have written all the books; there are no written sources of the day that tell the story from the polytheist side. Yet reading between the lines of the Arab historians, it seems probable that, by the time Sonni ʿAlī came to power, the Sanhaja *ʿulamā'* of Timbuktu had become importunate to the point where they seemed to the Sonni to challenge his proper authority. He probably felt he had to make a stand; otherwise they, not he, would become the masters.

The case for African polytheism

Some scholars have sought to bring out the contrast between Sonni ʿAlī and the more committedly Muslim rulers of the western Sudan by contrasting the 'magician king' with the 'Pilgrim king'. The counterpoint is neat. It may also be misleading to the extent that it suggests too trivial a notion of Sonni ʿAlī as some kind of genial African conjuror. This is far from the reality.[5]

At one level African polytheism, or animism, is an ugly phenomenon. It may involve human sacrifice and the use of human organs to manufacture charms and amulets. Yet there is another side to it that calls for empathy: it is deeply rooted in generations of the ancestors, with whom it represents an ancient continuity, it is immanent in the lives of the people and in the environment in which they live, it underlies all their social and moral values. Most importantly, the cult is held to dominate the supernatural forces that, in a pre-scientific society, reign in the earth, the sky, the forest and the waters. Without it, people felt insecure. They were not to be converted, overnight, by the simple assertion on the part of the *ʿulamā'* that Islam was the Will of a true God of whom they had no knowledge and no experience.

Moreover, the polytheist establishment enjoyed an inherent advantage since any natural disaster: prolonged drought, an outbreak of cattle pest, the plague, or defeat in war, could be attributed to the wrath of the ancestral gods, offended by the ruler's dallying with the new religion of Islam. If the prayers of the *'ulamā'* failed to bring rain, or otherwise put matters right, the animist commonality would at once rally to their traditional leaders. The ruler then had little recourse other than to turn against the *'ulamā'* and reinstate the chief animists. To talk of 'magicians' in this context may be to understate the complex nature of a society resting on the ancient values of animism.

Islam in Songhay: the askiyas

When Sonni 'Alī died in 898/1492 – drowned somewhat conveniently in the Niger – his death occasioned civil war between the animist and Muslim factions. A certain Muḥammad Ture, a Songhay military commander of somewhat sterner Islamic fibre than Sonni 'Alī, emerged the victor and in 898/1493, Muḥammad Ture took the title 'Askiya'. He became known to history as Askiya Muḥammad. Early in his reign, he made the Pilgrimage to Mecca by way of Cairo and thus renewed the lineaments of Islamic legitimacy torn down by Sonni 'Alī.

While in Cairo, he made contact with the well-known Egyptian scholar, Jalāl al-Dīn al-Suyūṭī, who became an adviser to him. Al-Suyūṭī gave much advice as to how to implement Islam in the Sudan. But he was on the whole pacific: he preferred to avoid resort to *jihād* and was also tolerant towards mixing.

At about the same time, Askiya Muḥammad contacted through other sources an altogether more fiery Muslim savant, Muḥammad b. 'Abd al-Karīm al-Maghīlī, a North African. Al-Maghīlī condemned Sonni 'Alī as an unbeliever, sanctioned *jihād* against the polytheists and roundly denounced those venal *'ulamā'* who tolerated mixing. Both men, al-Suyūṭī and al-Maghīlī, believed in the coming of the *Mahdī*; but whereas al-Suyūṭi interpreted this event largely at an intellectual level, al-Maghīlī believed it required '*jihād* of the sword', there and then. At the time, al-Suyūṭī's more tolerant views appear to have prevailed in the courts of the Sudanese kings; later generations of Islamic reformers were inspired by the more violent teachings of al-Maghīlī.

Despite the powerful advocacy of al-Maghīlī and the more temperate persuasion of al-Suyūṭī, Askiya Muḥammad and his successors never abandoned mixed Islam. They used *jihād* as a cover to extend the borders of the Songhay empire, smiled kindly on the resident *'ulamā'* but made sure that the necessary equilibrium between Islam and polytheism was maintained. The time was not yet ripe for al-Maghīlī's programme of wholesale Islamic reform.

The intellectual development of Timbuktu

During the second half of the eighth/fourteenth century, Timbuktu began to assume the attributes of a centre of learning. When Ibn Baṭṭūṭa visited the city in 754/1353 – that is while it was still part of the empire of Mali – he stated that 'Most of its inhabitants are of the Massufa tribe, wearers of the face-veil'.[6] The Massufa were a branch of the Sanhaja. It therefore appears that Berber scholarship was already established in Timbuktu before the decline of Mali set in.

The mosque of Sankore is thought to have been founded in Timbuktu late in the eighth/fourteenth century. It gradually developed into an institution of higher Islamic learning under the tutelage of these Sanhaja Berbers, and by the middle of the tenth/sixteenth century the mosque had reached the peak of its scholarly renown. Its *ijāzāt* ('learned genealogies', sometimes 'pedigrees') were fully equal to those of the other great Islamic centres of learning beyond the Sudan. Students from all over the Sudan, and even farther afield, came there to study higher Islamic learning.

At first the main intellectual influences on Timbuktu were North African, but by the tenth/sixteenth century these influences had begun to fade. They were replaced by those from Egypt, possibly because of the disturbed political conditions that existed in North Africa at this time, compared to the relative stability that prevailed in Egypt in the late Mamlūk period. Another factor is likely to have been the reputation throughout the western Islamic world of scholars such as al-Suyūṭī and others who flourished in Egypt during this century. Also significant may have been the general trend towards greater theological and legal pluralism in Egypt. Unlike the North African *'ulamā'*, the Egyptians did not insist on adherence to one *madhhab* alone. They permitted the individual freedom to make his choice among the four *Sunnī* rites, thus anticipating the *ijtihād* movement of subsequent centuries. Moreover, the Egyptian *'ulamā'* seem to have been more tolerant towards mixed Islam than their North African colleagues.

Mysticism in the western Sudan

The *Ṣūfī ṭuruq* did not make a substantial appearance in the western Sudan – as opposed to the Sahara where their appearance was somewhat earlier – until the middle of the eleventh/seventeenth century. Some traditions claim that al-Maghīlī was a Qādirī. If so, he made no known attempt to found an organised *ṭarīqa*, although long after his death his name was invoked by *Qādirīs* who were by then established in Hausaland. Moreover, the Arabic sources that tell of Timbuktu in the ninth/fifteenth century and the tenth/sixteenth century do not support the notion that organised *ṭuruq* existed there, as they are known to have done in North Africa. On the other hand, there is evidence that individual *'ulamā'* in Timbuktu espoused both mystic ideas and ascetic practices as early as the first half of the ninth/fifteenth century. Individual gnosticism and thaumaturgy seem to have begun to become conspicuous in Timbuktu from the middle of the ninth/fifteenth century, probably introduced from both North Africa and Egypt. The *ṭuruq* were not organised formally until about the middle of the eleventh/seventeenth century. In the Sahara, on the other hand, *shaykhs* of the Kunta were disseminating the ideas of the Qādiriyya as early as 802–3/1400; while Agallel, in Ahir, had become a centre for *Ṣūfīs* by *c.* 885/1480.

One possible explanation for this delay may have been the strength of animism in negro Sudan. Even the 'Pilgrim Kings' were adamant in their insistence that mixed Islam must be accommodated in their kingdoms. Where an ancient and established system for dealing with the supernatural already exists, and enjoys a measure of official support, there is likely to be a considerable time-lag after the introduction of a new formal religion before an alternative system can be widely accepted.

The fact is that in 906/1500, Sufism in negro Sudan was not in evidence. By *c.* 1060/1650 it was thriving, at which time Timbuktu was an *Arma pashalik*.

KANEM-BORNO (467/1075 TO *C.* AD 1900)

The involved dynastic history of this area to the east of present-day Nigeria can only be summarised here. The indigenous possessors of the land were the Zaghawa. Around 467/1075 a dynasty known as the Sayfawids seized power, its members ruling until *c.* 1223/1808. Then, as an indirect consequence of the Fulani *jihād* in Hausaland (see below in this chapter), a dynasty known as that of the Shehus, founded by an Islamic reformer called Shaykh (Shehu) Muḥammad al-Amīn al-Kānamī, replaced the last of the Sayfawids. This dynasty continued until the end of the fourteenth/nineteenth century, when it was overthrown by the Sudanese adventurer, Rābiḥ b. Faḍl Allāh, but was restored by the British at the beginning of their colonial occupation.

Islam in Kanem-Borno

Several ancient trade routes linked North Africa to the Lake Chad area as early as the third century BC. It is therefore probable that

Islamic influences found their way along these routes almost as soon as the Arabs conquered North Africa, while it is possible that even earlier whispers of Islam may have been heard there, from the Nile valley. Slaves, copper and gold were available in the Chad area *c.* AD 600; so, if the routes remained open during the Arab conquest of Egypt – and they may of course have been temporarily closed due to this event – news of the conquests must surely have reached the tribes of Chad. There is, however, no proof that this was so.

Whatever early influences did reach Kanem-Borno form North Africa will certainly have been Ibāḍī: from *c.* 132/750 the town of Zawila was under Ibāḍī control, and the Ibāḍī hegemony lasted until 571/1175–6, by which time *Sunnī* Islam seems to have become dominant in the area.

The conventional view of Islam's arrival in Borno is that if the early Zaghawa people of the area knew of it, they did not immediately accept it. Then, in 467/1075 or 477/1085, a certain Ḥummay seized power in Kanem, thus simultaneously founding the Sayfawid dynasty and establishing Islam. This 'hey-presto' tale of the arrival of Islam has, however, been questioned. In view of the probability of very early contacts with North Africa along the pre-Islamic trade routes, it does seem somewhat improbable, and it is more likely that Islam drifted in gradually, by way of the Fezzan. One alternative view is that some Zaghawa had already been won over to Islam before the rise of the Sayfawids, this event simply consolidating a trend that was already well under way.[8] Another, more daring, theory proposes that the Zaghawa, also called the Banū Dūkū, were in touch with Islam during the first/seventh century when they rejected it but, it is suggested, *c.* 459/1067 a Zaghawa ruler, not Ḥummay, converted to Islam. This conversion led to a division among the Banū Dūkū and resulted in the overthrow of that dynasty and its replacement by the Sayfawids. There is much surrounding detail to this theory that cannot be discussed here. However, insofar as it postulates very early contacts between Islamic North Africa and Kanem, and a somewhat less abrupt conversion to Islam than the received version, it is persuasive.[9]

It is not known what form of Islam – Ibāḍī or *Sunnī* – was received by the Zaghawa, or by Ḥummay. The probability is that by *c.* 747/1349 the reigning dynasty was *Sunnī* and Mālikī and remained so from then onwards. By the end of the ninth/fifteenth century the Sayfawids had clearly established Islam firmly in ruling circles: the self-styled caliph, Mai Idrīs Aloma of Borno made the Pilgrimage to Mecca, and also embarked on an ambitious programme of mosque-building and took other measures to enforce stricter observance of

Islam among his subjects. He adopted the common Islamic practice of styling his wars of conquest *'jihād'*. Moreover, his contacts with the Ottomans of Istanbul and with the Sharifian Saʿdids of Morocco meant that many aspects of Islamic civilisation and way of life became familiar in Borno as from the latter half of the tenth/sixteenth century. It seems probable that it was from Borno that some Islamic influences spread westwards into Hausaland at this time.

By the ninth/fifteenth century Sufism had become well established in Borno, having gradually become widespread there as a result of contacts with North Africa and the *Ṣūfī* communities of the Sahara. Several schools of higher Islamic learning developed at this time, the most important of which was at Kalumbardo, fifty miles north-east of the capital Birni Gazargamu. This school was at its height early in the eleventh/seventeenth century and became an important centre for the spread of the Qādiriyya order of *Ṣūfīs* in Borno. It also had links with Qādirī communities farther to the east in the Nile valley and with the Qādirī *shaykhs* of the Kuntī clan in the western Sahara.

THE VOLTA REGION (NINTH/FIFTEENTH CENTURY TO THE PRESENT DAY)

Malian influence

In the Volta region, now encompassed by Togo, Burkina Faso and modern Ghana, Islamic influences began to find their way in from the neighbouring empire of Mali, to the north-west during the medieval period. They were brought in the first instance by peaceful Dyula (Wangarawa) traders as well as, at times, by mounted Mande-speaking warriors bent on conquest. They established early Islamic states such as Dagomba and Mamprusi during the ninth/fifteenth century but in most cases, conversion to Islam was superficial and the forms of statehood that resulted from these early Islamic influences were compromises between Islamic constitutional practices and ancestral custom. The process may have begun as early as the seventh/thirteenth century and was at its most active during the eighth/fourteenth century, when the power of Mali was at its height. Later, by the tenth/sixteenth century, Hausa and Borno traders, seeking gold and subsequently kola nuts, began to make their way to the Volta country via Busa, Nikki and Salaga. In consequence, the towns along these routes were settled by Hausa and Borno *imāms*. Their Islam was more ardent, rigorous and learned than that of the faint, mixed Malian tradition. They left pockets of local Muslims behind them, which have survived to the present day.

THE SENEGAMBIA (FIFTH/ELEVENTH CENTURY TO THE THIRTEENTH/NINETEENTH CENTURY)

Takrūr

The Senegambia lies south of present-day Mauritania. It received Islam at an early date, even, it appears, before the advent of the Almoravids. An Islamic kingdom, known as Takrūr, was established there, between the river Senegal and the river Gambia, before 432/1040–1. This development is likely to have been a consequence of the influence of Muslim traders, moving along a route that led from North Africa, through Mauritania, to the gold-bearing regions of the Senegambia.

The Wolof and Denianke kingdoms

From the old kingdom of Takrūr there emerged a number of separate dynasties of the Wolof and Denianke, in Jolof and neighbouring Futa Toro and Futa Jalon. Certain Muslim savants, known as 'Azanaghi' (Sanhaja), frequented their courts, but none the less Islam at this time was very imperfectly observed. Conversions to Christianity brought about by visiting Portuguese were not uncommon – a situation that would not have occurred in the more solidly Islamic interior.

From the eleventh/seventeenth century to the end of the twelfth/eighteenth century, a series of *jihāds*, arising out of Islamic reform movements led by certain ardent *'ulamā'* and *Ṣūfī* leaders, took place in the Senegambia. They enjoyed some brief successes but were small-scale affairs that did not result in the establishment of truly Islamic states. This had to wait for the great *jihād* of al-Ḥajj 'Umar al-Fūtī, in the thirteenth/nineteenth century (see pp. 112–13).

MEDIEVAL HAUSALAND AND ITS NEIGHBOURS (FOURTH/TENTH CENTURY TO THE THIRTEENTH/NINETEENTH CENTURY)

Hausaland, with Borno, now forms northern Nigeria. Lying due west of Borno and due south of Ahir, in the Sahara, it is that part of modern West Africa that is now most solidly Muslim, though Islam has spread in a macular fashion farther south.

The origin of the Hausa people

The most persuasive theory of the origin of the Hausa people is that the area was originally thinly populated by speakers of the Benue–Congo group of languages who lived in village and clan groups and were probably agriculturalists who practised an Iron Age culture. Subsequently, people from the east, from the direction of Lake Chad, who were cattle-grazers and speakers of languages of the Chadic group of African tongues, moved into Hausaland. They drove out some of the Benue–Congo speakers and mixed with the rest, to produce the ancestors of the present Hausa people. When this movement took place is problematic. Some place it in the fourth/tenth century; but linguistic evidence, namely that Hausa now has very few Benue–Congo survivals, suggests it may have been much earlier.

The Hausas' own tales of origin, which postulate an ancestry from incoming people from the north, are shot through with echoes of the Hilalian invasions, with implicit claims to Yamanite origins and Umayyad genealogies, with iterations of the Prophetic *sīra* (biography) and asservations of descent from the Arab conquerors of North Africa. They surely arise from the Hausas' early contacts with Islam through trade. They reflect their deep pride in their Islam but are otherwise unreliable.

The coming of the Wangarawa and the formation of the Hausa kingdoms

What is based on persuasive evidence is that from the eighth/fourteenth century onwards, Wangarawa, that is Dyula, from the west began to move into Hausaland. They were Muslims, probably from Mali, possibly also from the Volta region and, by the ninth/fifteenth century even from Songhay. To their influence is attributed the first formations of Islamic states in Hausaland. Kano is believed to have responded to this Islamic influence in the eighth/fourteenth century, Katsina followed a century later as, too, did Zaria. What seems clear is that this influx of Muslim Wangarawa (the word is simply a Hausa alternative to Mande Dyula) was a consequence of the trade in gold from the Volta region, which by this time had set up a complex network linking that region via the Niger Bend and Hausaland, to North Africa and Borno.

With the trade came the spread of Islamic ideas; conversions to Islam resulted, perhaps sometimes no more than nominal, of individual rulers encouraged no doubt by the commercial advantages thereby accruing to them; walled towns were built that became city states conforming broadly to the Islamic model; elements from the Islamic Sharīʿa were adopted and the increasing 'arabisation' of the Hausa language occurred. Modern Hausa has a Chadic grammatical structure as well as a basic vocabulary that is clearly Chadic, but it also displays a layered Arabic lexicon suggesting several chronological levels of Arabic influence representing early contacts with North Africa, Borno and later contacts with Arab traders and visiting *ʿulamāʾ*.

Yet the conversion of the Hausas to Islam was far from complete: the nobility converted nominally and staffed their courts with some expatriate Muslim literates, but, beyond this, Islam among the common people was tenuous or often non-existent. Traditional animism continued to thrive, and the rulers simply accepted this. For example Muhamman Rumfa, who ruled the medieval principality of Kano from 867/1463 to 904/1499, and who was host to al-Maghīlī, is celebrated among the Hausas as a true Muslim ruler. After his reign Hausaland supposedly lapsed back into its pagan ways. Yet even he is said to have married 1,000 wives and to have persisted in other pagan practices. Throughout the Middle Ages, however, there steadily developed a class of indigenous Hausa Muslim literates known as the *malams*. It was their growing influence that really consolidated Islam among the Hausa people.

The 'Bastard Seven'

The Hausas refer to themselves as the *Hausa Bakwai*, the 'Hausa Seven', that is seven original kingdoms of pure Hausa descent, who pride themselves on their early Islam. They also distinguish a further *Banza Bakwai*, the 'Bastard Seven', non-Hausas, whose Islam came later, supposedly as a result of conversion by the Hausas. These non-Hausas are also alleged to have adopted the Hausa tongue as a result of conversion to Islam, but in fact it seems they adopted it as a trade language. Their conversion to Islam, in so far as it occurred, came as a result of early contacts with Mali and then as a result of the successful Fulani *jihād* in Hausaland of the thirteenth/nineteenth century. Some, such as the Kwararafas, have never accepted Islam at all. The traditional 'Bastard Seven' include the Kebbis, the Yorubas, the Nupes, the Gwaris and the Kwararafas.

THE AGE OF THE GREAT *JIHĀDS* (1200/1785 TO *C.* 1316/1898)

The old empires of the Sahel, which had offered some semblance of Islamic statehood, were in ruins by 1112/1700. The Hausa chiefs were ambiguous in their Islam. Tension between peasants and nomads over grazing was endemic. Since the chiefs usually favoured the tax-paying peasants, the nomads became ready recruits for Islamic revolution. Such a situation presented an affront and an opportunity to certain literate Muslims, convinced that the imminent overthrow of 'unbelief' and its replacement by Islamic theocracy was the will of Allah.

Moreover, the western Sudan was not immune from intellectual and spiritual currents in the Islamic world beyond the Sudan. Pilgrimage ensured that. Powerful among these currents was the rise of Wahhabism and the reaction to it, the *Ṣūfī* revival in the Azhar. All of this created a climate of expectancy among these Muslim reformers, which predisposed them to believe that the Expected *Mahdī* might be near at hand and that they were called to prepare the way for him.

The jihād *in Hausaland*

By the second half of the twelfth/eighteenth century the discontent of certain Fulānī in the Hausa kingdom of Gobir had reached a peak. They were an extended-family clan of Fulbe speakers, highly literate in Arabic, who had all but abandoned nomadism for the sedentary life-style of Muslim literates. They embarked on an ardent *jihād al-qawl*, a 'preaching *jihād*'. Through this they sought by admonition to change the ways of the faintly Muslim, 'mixing' *sarakuna* (Hausa 'kings') who claimed authority over them. The *sarakuna* refused to make the political and cultural surrender the Muslim reformers demanded. The leader of this reforming group, the learned 'Uthmān b. Fūdī (Hausa Shehu Usuman dan Fodio), thereupon adopted a course that led to the outbreak of hostilities. For the reformers it was Holy War.

While the Shehu Usuman dan Fodio did not claim to be the *Mahdī*, he did reveal himself as the *Mujaddid*, the 'Renewer' or precursor, of that messianic personality. It was an effective claim, for 4 November 1785 had ushered in AH 1200. It was therefore not difficult, in the turmoil of the times, to persuade this excited and disturbed following that the *Mahdī* himself was now not far behind.

The Shehu and his associates took their stand on the Koranic injunction *al-ʿamr bil-maʿrūf wa 'l-nahy ʿan al-munkar*, 'the commanding of what is approved and the forbidding of what is disapproved'. Thus they demanded the elimination from Hausa society of all *bidʿa*, 'blameworthy innovation', that is what is extraneous to the Koran. This included music, drumming, dancing and so on. They then insisted on the strict observance of the commercial law of the *Sharīʿa*, frequently disregarded by the Hausa peasants who sought to play the market in customary ways, on the deportment of women according to Koranic morality, a matter in which African peasant women, with the connivance of their menfolk, constantly fall short, on the observance of the conventions of Islamic marriage, frequently corrupted by African customary practices, on the strict administration of the *Sharīʿa* in matters relating to criminal and personal law, on the adoption of sober Islamic dress, on the observance of Islamic food prohibitions, on the observance of the Islamic principle of *iḥsān*, 'good conduct', which is supposed to regulate the individual Muslim's social and personal life, and on the guiding role of the *ʿulamāʾ* as leaders of Muslim society. Finally the reformers insisted upon the dismantling of all non-Islamic forms of government, especially the discrete African chiefdoms based on the custom of generations. They were to be replaced by the patriarchal model of the universal caliphate in the era of *al-Rāshidūn*, the 'Rightly-guided Caliphs', who immediately followed Muhammad and whose rule was unblemished by subsequent accretions.

In the event, the aims of these learned reformers were only partially fulfilled. As the caliphate, later referred to somewhat more modestly as a 'sultanate', developed, it came to resemble not so much the pristine patriarchal caliphate, but more the elaborate structure of the ʿAbbāsid caliphate, which reached its high point in the second/eighth century. Thus the administration of the Shehu's son, Muhammad Bello, who became the first caliph of Sokoto, and of his epigoni, was adorned by the office of *wazīr*, an ʿAbbasid invention that had no place in the patriarchal structure. Nor had many other late Islamic offices that the Sokoto rulers adopted, while certain customary Hausa titles were retained that were not even of Islamic origin.

None the less, the reform movement and the *jihād* achieved much. The organisation consisting of a central caliph or sultan, to whom largely autonomous emirs (*amīr*) – those of Kano, Zaria, Katsina et al. – owed allegiance, was an essentially Islamic polity. It differed in this respect from the former, wholly decentralised hotchpotch of faintly Islamic Habe (Hausa) chiefdoms.

Under this emiral system the *Sharīʿa* was applied, not with total perfection but with considerable consistency. Indeed, what the British took over in northern Nigeria *c.* 1906 could not possibly have been mistaken for anything other than an Islamic legal system.

Finally, although the way of life of the sedentary Hausa people continued to retain much that was pre-Islamic – animist magic, traditional medicine, a pre-Islamic African folklore, drumming and dance for instance – Islamic mores clearly predominated in Hausaland at the end of the nineteenth century AD. Christian missionaries such as Canon C. H. Robinson, who visited Hausaland on the eve of the colonial occupations, were in no doubt that they were among an unmistakably Muslim people.[10]

The jihāds *of Aḥmad b. Muḥammad and al-Ḥajj Maḥmūd*

In Masina, south of Timbuktu, in the present Republic of Mali, a certain Aḥmad b. Muḥammad raised a *jihād* against the chiefs of the pagan Fulānī of the area *c.* 1234/1818 and subsequently extended it against the pagan Bambara. This *jihād* was brought about by the decline in power of the *Arma* of Timbuktu and was intended to recreate a centralised Islamic state to replace the ruins of Songhay and the *pashalik* of Timbuktu that followed it. The *jihād* was successful. Like that of the Fulani in Hausaland, it achieved a closer approximation to the ideal of a centralist Islamic theocracy as opposed to the pluralist chaos created by warring factions, some Muslim, some pagan, which had recently prevailed. Aḥmad b. Muḥammad's empire, centred on the city of Ḥamdallāhī, which he founded, endured until it was overthrown by another jihadist, al-Ḥajj ʿUmar al-Fūtī.

In the Black Volta region, *c.* 1266/1850, al-Ḥajj Maḥmūd, a Dyula *ʿālim* with a Qādirī background, returned from Pilgrimage fired by a determination to impose Islam upon the family and clan people of this region, who had so far been barely touched by the Faith. He won some initial success but his attempt to set up a centralised Islamic theocracy in this area of fragmented stateless peoples soon foundered. The local merchants, mainly Dyulas, refused to support him since they did not see his violent revolution as being in the interests of their peaceful trade.

Subsequent *jihāds*, or so-called *jihāds*, took place against a background of mainly French, occasionally British colonial penetration. This has led some to see them as 'anti-colonialist' movements.[11] Such a a perception is misguided. These eruptions that were truly Islamic revolutions – and some have a questionable claim to this distinction – were continuations of a powerful Islamic revivalist and reformist initiative that was already under way a generation or more before the first colonial campaigns took place. For the leaders of such movements the presence of the colonial intruders on the peripheries of their Islamic spheres of influence was largely incidental. These militant reformers became embroiled, mainly with the French, not because they set out in the first instance to oppose colonialism, but simply because the colonialists got in their way. In some cases they even contrived a temporary *modus vivendi* with the inconvenient Europeans, until one party or the other found such arrangements incommodious.

The jihād *of al-Ḥajj ʿUmar al-Fūtī*

The first true *jihād* of this colonial period was that of al-Ḥajj ʿUmar al-Fūtī. This *ʿālim* performed Pilgrimage to Mecca *c.* 1241/1825 where he was won over to the new *Ṣūfī ṭarīqa*, the Tijānyya. On his return home to Futa Toro, he set out on missionary journeys to spread the Tijānī message in western Sudan. He had some limited success among the ruling Fulani of Sokoto. Elsewhere he was largely rebuffed.

On his return to his own people he engaged in a preaching *jihād* against the animists, the imperfect Muslims and the backsliding rulers of Futa Toro and Futa Jalon. Frustrated by his lack of success, he launched a *jihād* of the sword in 1267/1851. He thereupon came up against the French in Senegal, unwilling to contemplate the setting up of a militant Islamic state on their border. Defeated in several engagements by the French he turned eastwards, to pursue *jihād* against the Qādirī Muslims of Masina and their largely pagan Bambara subjects. At first he won spectacular victories, and by 1277/1862 was master of an empire that included Timbuktu, Masina, Ḥamdallāhī and Segu. However, al-Ḥajj 'Umar was largely dependent for his support on the Tukolors, an ethnic group who were distinguished by their own fierce imperial tradition. The non-Tukolors, largely Soninkes, now rose against al-Ḥajj 'Umar and the Tukolor domination he represented. Although he himself was defeated in 1280/1864 and killed shortly afterwards, his empire survived under his son Aḥmed b. 'Umar until it was finally conquered by the French in 1308/1891.

The jihād *of al-Ḥajj Muhammad al-Amīn*

Al-Ḥajj 'Umar's *jihād* was followed by a spate of Islamic militancy of a somewhat lesser order in Gambia and Jolof which achieved some initial success but was eventually smothered by the opposition of the French and, to a lesser extent, the British.

More substantial was the movement of a Tijānī, al-Ḥajj Muḥammad al-Amīn. On his return from Pilgrimage, he launched holy war in Senegal. At first he claimed the mantle of al-Ḥajj 'Umar but later, he quarrelled with 'Umar's successors and ended by attacking their empire. Despite his Tijānī adherence, it is questionable whether this was truly a movement of Islamic reform since Muḥammad al-Amīn's supporters were almost exclusively Soninkes. Notwithstanding his appeal to the Tijāniyya, his movement displays the characteristics of a Soninke revolt against Tukolor hegemony to a more market extent than it does those of a movement inspired by Islamic reform. In 1305/1887 al-Ḥajj Muḥammad al-Amīn was defeated and killed by the French.

Samory Ture

Between 1277/1861 and 1316/1898, Almamy (*Imām*) Samory Ture pursued a campaign of conquest in what is now northern Ghana. Although his own claim to be a Muslim was somewhat weak since he had long been associated with the pagan Kamara clan, he began by attempting to set up an Islamic theocracy in the areas that fell under his control. In the course of this he certainly built a number of mosques that still stand in northern Ghana. But he later largely abandoned this Islamic endeavour, turning instead to what became increasingly a war of outright conquest in which the Islamic emphasis became secondary, to say the least. Finally, he was captured by the French and ended his days in exile. He has more in common with the medieval *condottieri* in Europe than he does with Islamic reformers.

Results of the great jihāds

In retrospect, it becomes clear that the great *jihāds* were those of Shehu Usuman dan Fodio, Aḥmad b. Muḥammad and al-Ḥajj 'Umar al-Fūtī. The others were largely ineffective or too involved with temporal and secular motives to be regarded as truly Islamic revolutions. Of those that may thus be distinguished, their characteristic achievement was to set up centralised Islamic polities forged either out of the autonomous principalities of half-hearted Muslim chiefs prone to mixing or out of the fragmented pieces of the medieval empires of the Sahel. These new Islamic states remained substantially intact, though of diminishing vigour, until overtaken by the colonial occupations.

THE COLONIAL OCCUPATIONS IN WEST AFRICA (*C.* AD 1900 TO *C.* AD 1960)

The German colonial occupation of West African territory came to an abrupt end with her defeat in the First World War. The British and French occupations, which began in the late nineteenth century AD, lasted until the 1960s. They then gave way to forms of independence that were more thoroughgoing in the British case than in that of the French.

Islam under colonial occupation

The history of West Africa immediately before the colonial occupations had been one of constant upheaval and considerable bloodshed. Islamic *jihād* is no doubt uplifting for zealots, it is less so for the ordinary folk who become caught up in it. It is therefore not surprising that the colonial occupations were often received with quiescence and even sometimes with relief by West Africans, Muslims and non-Muslims alike. This was the case in those areas affected by the campaigns of the Almamy Samory and Rābiḥ of Borno.

Occupation was less well received in the empire of the former Sokoto caliphate. Here there was substantial initial resistance, though it was ineffective owing to the much greater fire-power of the British force, which overwhelmed the Muslims, both physically and psychologically. Their reaction was fatalistic. They assumed shortcomings on their own part, which had incurred the wrath of Allah. The 'Christians' therefore became, for many, instruments of divine punishment, and resistance was useless.

But the Sultan of Sokoto, backed by many of his people, took a more active line. After an armed resistance that proved costly and unsuccessful, he adopted the precedent established by the Amīr ʿAbd al-Qādir against the French in Algeria. He embarked on a *hijra* or emigration, out of infidel reach. His intention was to go to Mecca and take his people with him. In the event, however, just he and a few sad, bedraggled followers set out on their journey, leaving behind them the mass of their coreligionists. They had little alternative but to come to terms with the Christians, for this was how the British and indeed the French, were seen by the great majority of West African Muslims.

The Muslims of northern Nigeria now adopted the classical Islamic stance known as *taqiyya*. The word, which means 'to be faithful' or 'dutiful' and has Koranic authority behind it (19:18 and 49:13), had long been elevated to a principle of Islamic law. It enables the Muslim outwardly to accept a situation he is powerless to change, while inwardly waiting for the tide to turn. It condones dissimulation. It allows Muslims to co-operate with an infidel authority when there is no alternative, while reserving the moral right to restore Islam to its proper position of dominance when the time is ripe.

Not all Muslims followed the passive route of *taqiyya*. Some saw the disaster that had overtaken them as one of the portents that will announce the coming of the *Mahdī*. Various persons claiming to be the *Mahdī*, or his *Mujaddid*, Precursor, consequently appeared to lead the Faithful against the infidel invaders. In West Africa such incidents proved to be minor affairs, lacking the thrust and tenacity of North Africa or Nilotic Sudanese Mahdist manifestations. After the first uprisings, which were easily enough put down (though one rising in Hausaland at least was costly to the British), the Islamic areas of West Africa settled down quietly enough under the colonial dispensation.

In the British case this was by no means oppressive. The principle of indirect rule adopted by Sir Frederick Lugard, the first Governor of Nigeria, meant that a new sultan of Sokoto was appointed. His Muslim emirs and indeed the whole structure of Islamic government was then left virtually intact. The *Sharīʿa*, the Islamic legal system, continued to apply as it had before, with the exception that so-called inhumane punishments were replaced by supposedly humane alternatives. And so on. The only other restrictions the British placed upon the 'Native Rulers' lay in the field of 'foreign' policy; relations between the emirates, and emirates and pagan chiefdoms, were subject to the oversight of a British Resident or District Officer. Thus inter-emirate wars and slave-raiding in pagan areas were checked. But slavery itself was not abolished. Slaves were simply given the choice of remaining with their existing masters or becoming free. To the genuine surprise of the United Kingdom-based anti-slavery lobby – and possibly to its chagrin – the great majority of these slaves chose to remain where they were.

The administrative system that developed out of these arrangements was known as the Native Authority (NA). It was simply a somewhat more rationally organised version of what had existed under the Sokoto caliphate, retaining the traditional hierarchy of the emir's court, the *qāḍī* or Muslim magistrate and his court. It even transformed the emiral bodyguards into NA police forces. The function of British Provincial and District Officers was mainly to oversee this system, ensure it functioned with reasonable efficiency and check abuses.

There is little doubt that this broadly benign British system of indirect rule in northern Nigeria was in many ways helpful to Islam. The British presence served, in the short and medium term, to protect Islam from a tide of social and political change that might, under other circumstances, have overwhelmed the by now enfeebled Sokoto caliphate. In the longer term, however, its effect was moratory. Nothing in the end could insulate Islam from the modernity and secularism that the colonial occupations released. Present-day West African nationalists – who are by and large not Muslims – and their Western anti-colonialist sympathisers, as well as some Christian missionaries, have been especially severe in criticising the British colonial administration in Nigeria, less for overt tyranny but rather for a benign obscurantism that blocked what these critics have seen as desirable change.

There is some truth in this. For instance, it was not until 1960 that a new penal and criminal code was introduced, to replace the medieval *Sharī'a*. And it is indeed the case that once colonial overrule had been removed, the fabric of the Native Authorities – the Sokoto caliphate modified by Lugard's indirect rule – did in fact fall apart. But whether or not what has replaced it is to be regarded as desirable, may be a matter of opinion.

The French in West Africa were less committed to indirectness of rule than were the British. Their policy was to concentrate their constructive efforts on the urban centres: Dakar, Niamey, Abidjan and so on. These became fine cities that were centres of French civilisation; the countryside, on the other hand they left largely to its own devices. Insofar as they concerned themselves with Islam, they cultivated the co-operation of the *Ṣūfī* orders, in particular the Murīds of

Senegal and the Tijāniyya, both of which espoused a maraboutic form of Islam. They were not greatly concerned with Islamic reform; nor did they wish to promote any form of education other than the traditional Islamic one. Thus Islam in francophone territories remained somewhat static.

The education policies of the two colonial powers reflected their different priorities. The British made sincere, if artless, efforts to combine traditional Islamic education and secular education in a single syllabus, in the belief that this would encourage 'moderate Islam' and take the wind out of the sails of extremists. The subsequent rise of Islamic fundamentalism in Nigeria has proved this mistaken. The French were under no such liberal illusion. They neglected and sometimes positively discouraged traditional Islamic literacy. Instead, they offered an excellent secular, francophone education that made very little concession to Islam. The result was to create a largely secularised indigenous, francophone élite in the towns, that was increasingly out of touch with the traditional Islam of the countryside.

The Tijāniyya during the colonial era

By the time of the Fulānī reform movement and *jihād*, the Qādiriyya was well established in what became the Sokoto caliphate. No sooner was the *jihād* concluded than the movement of the Tijānī reformer, al-Ḥajj ʿUmar al-Fūtī, followed close behind. One consequence of this was the introduction of the Tijāniyya into the area as a new and vigorous rival to the Qādiriyya, by now identified with the ruling Fulānī élite.

By the beginning of the British occupation of Nigeria, the Tijāniyya had become powerful in Zaria and Kano, to the extent that it soon took on the characteristics of a largely Hausa opposition to the Fulānī hegemony of Sokoto. Indeed, the complaint of the African nationalists and their anti-colonial sympathisers mentioned above, that British indirect rule bolstered an Islamic structure that might otherwise have fallen to popular secular, or even Christian forces, as some missionaries fondly liked to believe, is almost certainly ill-founded. The old Fulani, Qādirī establishment might well have been toppled, had not the paternal British, themselves 'more holy than the holy Northerners', been there to prop it up. But what would surely have taken its place is not modern secularism, nor African Christianity, but a rival Islamic faction that took its legitimacy from the new and popular Tijāniyya and not from the ancient and by now elitist Qādiriyya.

By the 1940s, Kaolak, in French Senegal, had become the centre of a powerful Tijānī movement of Islamic, mystic evangelism, headed by the charismatic Shaykh Ibrāhīm Nyass (al-Anyās). This succeeded in spreading the influence of the *ṭarīqa* widely throughout the francophone territories of Niger, Senegal, the Ivory Coast, as well as the anglophone areas of Nigeria, the Gold Coast, both north and south, and the coastal territories of the Gambia and southern Nigeria. Tijānī *dhikrs*, prayer meetings, often involving large and liminal congregations, became characteristic of these areas.

Inevitably, this provoked opposition. Wahhabism now tended to spread among the more radically-minded *'ulamā'*, in the same measure that the Tijāniyya increased its hold over the common people.

The Ahmadiyya

Another Islamic tendency that gained ground in West Africa during the colonial period was the Ahmadiyya, a modern tendency of Indian origin founded by a certain Mīrzā Ghulām Ahmad (d. ad 1908). It surely represents in the first instance an Indian reaction against the ancient domination of the Arabs in Islam. It quickly assumed a strong missionary impetus and chose West Africa where it appeared *c.* 1921, as a main sphere for its activity. Its central doctrine is the belief that this Ghulām Ahmad is not just a *walī*, a holy man, but a full prophet and the equal of the Prophet Muḥammad himself. This is wholly objectionable to *Sunnī* Muslims who will have nothing to do with the Ahmadīs. Indeed the *Sunnīs* insist that the Ahmadīs are not true Muslims but miscreants: the Saudi authorities have even banned them from Pilgrimage to Mecca and the *Sunnīs* of northern Nigeria, in common with certain Yoruba Muslims of the riverine areas of Nigeria, as well as the hausaphone *Sunnīs* of Ghana, have all enthusiastically endorsed this Saudi anathema. Despite this, the Ahmadiyya flourished in certain areas of West Africa, particularly the southern Gold Coast and the area of Lagos, in Nigeria, where it first became established *c.* 1921. They also had some success in the northern Gold Coast and were able to foster an Ahmadī community in the northern town of Wa. In northern Nigeria, and in the inland areas of the Sahel generally, where *sunnī*, Mālikī Islam was entrenched, they were fiercely rejected. None the less, the obvious success of the Ahmadīs in promoting education in those areas where they did become established, provoked certain northern Nigerian and Yoruba Muslims into an attempt to offset this success by establishing schools of their own, where a sound anglophone education was offered, but in the context of *Sunnī*, not Ahmadī Islam. The result was the emergence of the *Anṣār al-Dīn*, 'Helpers of the Faith', a Muslim association that seeks to compete with both the Christian missions and the Ahmadīs in the fields of education and welfare. It achieved some success both inland

and on the coast, though its readiness to adopt Western-style education was still opposed by *Sunnī* diehards, for whom Arabic literacy alone was, and remains, acceptable.

The Northern Nigerian 'Islamisation' drive

The Muslims did not remain passive indefinitely. The power of the northern Nigerian establishment to act independently was increasingly allowed to them by the British as from the end of the Second World War, by which time Nigerian independence was clearly on the horizon. There was a northern Nigerian Muslim premier of the Northern Region, Sir Ahmadu Bello. He presided over a cabinet of northern Nigerian ministers, to whom the British acted as advisors, but over whom they no longer had powers of veto, except in extreme circumstances. One consequence of this development was the emergence, in the North, of the policy of 'Northernisation' – that is the deliberate allocation of posts both in government and commerce, to persons of northern Nigerian origin. In the great majority of cases, this meant Muslims. Furthermore, the Northern Muslim establishment was left free, within certain limits, to set up its own links with other areas of the Islamic world, even though the residual British administration often viewed such links with distaste and even alarm. The links were mainly with Wahhābī Saudi Arabia, which enjoyed a special place in the affections of Sir Ahmadu Bello, Sardauna, approximately 'Crown Prince', of Sokoto and Premier of the North at the time but also, during the Nasserite and immediate post-Nasserite period, with Egypt – a somewhat more uncomfortable situation for the embarrassed British! The overall consequence was greater Islamic activism that tended to take over from an earlier, gentlemanly quietism in which traditionally Qādirī emirs had rubbed along contentedly enough with a paternalistic and protective British administration. Yet behind this relationship there had always lurked the shadow of *taqiyya*, the Islamic principle that allows the Muslim to co-operate under duress while awaiting the opportunity to reassert his Islamic obligation.

From *c.* 1960 until his assassination in the course of a *coup* by Christian Ibo soldiers in 1966, the Sardauna of Sokoto, Sir Ahmadu Bello, who was also the premier of what was still at that time the Northern Region of Nigeria, pursued a policy of 'Islamisation'. It arose from long-pent-up discontent at the British policy of restraint on the advance of Islam among animists – the promotion of which the Muslims held to be their religious duty and their right – and was also intended to counter the continuing missionary attempts to convert the animists to Christianity. The British had always left missionaries free to go about their business in animist areas. In the colonial heyday there was little the Muslims could do about it – except fall back on *taqiyya*. But with the prospect of independence so close at hand, and the authority of the British slipping, the moment when *taqiyya* fulfils its promise was believed to have arrived. The Sardauna set out to persuade – or coerce – all indigenous northern Nigerian people who were not Muslims to accept Islam and made little attempt to disguise his ambition to extend this to Nigeria as a whole, thus greatly alarming the Christian southerners. The campaign was presented to the Muslim constituency as a 'preaching *jihād*'. It undoubtedly involved some harassment, as well as bribery, of residual animist groups such as the Dakarkaris and the Plateau people. It was regarded askance by the British, who tried to dissuade the Sardauna from pressing his campaign too far, though at this stage of constitutional development they were unable to do more than wring their hands. In the end the Sardauna's campaign did result in widespread nominal conversions to Islam. Chiefs, village heads, et al., took Islamic names in addition to their ancestral ones, which was taken as sufficient to establish the Islam of their people as a whole. Beyond that, it is questionable how deep such mass 'conversions' went, although empirical evidence suggests that the wider adoption of Islamic names and of Islamic dress that resulted from this campaign was led to the wider adoption of Islam.

The campaign had more immediate and disastrous consequences. It convinced the Christian Ibo people of the Eastern Region, many of whom had been settled for generations in the Northern Region, and especially the Ibo officer class in the Nigerian Army, that the Sardauna was preparing holy war against all non-Muslim Nigerians. Their fear became the justification for the *coup* in which the Sardauna was assassinated; and then for declaring an independent state of Biafra in the Eastern Region.

The situation bore some resemblance to that described above in the case of the Anglo-Egyptian Sudan; except that in the Sudanese case the southern Christians were isolated among primitive riverine peoples, most of whom were animists. But the Nigerian Christians were a highly educated and advanced community whose technological and political domination the more numerous but less advanced Northerners had good reason to fear, once the British departed.

In the event, the Nigerian civil war intervened.

The 'time of politics'

The period from the end of the Second World War to 1960, when Nigerian independence was granted, is known to the Hausas as *zamanin siyasa*, the 'time of politics', where 'politics' refers specifically to the exotic multi-party system and the full adult suffrage insisted upon by the British as a precondition for independence. It saw the rise of Nigerian political parties superficially resembling those of the British party system, but in fact reflecting ancient West African tribal and religious alignments and divisions. In the case of the Muslim Northern Region, the Northern Peoples' Congress (NPC) was identified with the interests of the sultanate of Sokoto, with the aristocratic Fulani emirates, with the Native Authority system and with the Qādiriyya order of *Ṣūfīs*. It advocated a modified Islamic theocracy for independent northern Nigeria, in which the sultan of Sokoto was to rehearse the role of the British constitutional monarch. Broadly, the NPC enjoyed the blessing of the British administration.

This party was challenged in the North by the Northern Elements Progressive Union (NEPU). Its rhetoric reflected many of the attitudes of the British left but it, in fact, represented the ancient antagonism of Hausa commoners towards their Fulani overlords. Despite its leftist oratory, it pursued a tradition of Islamic dissidence in which it claimed to represent the true Islam. It excoriated the NPC for betraying that Islam. The NEPU was closely linked to the Tijāniyya order of *Ṣūfīs* that, as was mentioned above, had stood for opposition to the Qādirī hegemony even during the immediate pre-colonial period.

By and large, the establishmentarian NPC got the better of the populist NEPU in local and national elections. But that success was transitory. The outbreak of the Nigerian civil war, and its sequel, shattered these old alignments and set up entirely new constitutional structures.

Islam in Ghana

In Ghana, formerly the Gold Coast, the situation as regards Islam was different from that in Nigeria. Pockets of hausaphone Muslims, mainly descendants of Hausa police and soldiers brought into the territory by the British in the early days of the occupation, were settled in the south. The large concentrations of Muslims were located in the northern territories, anciently part of the medieval empire of Mali. Their Islam was of the mixed kind associated with that empire, though more recently they had also been influenced by the all-pervasive Tijāniyya. This influence was particularly strong in the inland towns of Kumasi and Tamale but also important on the coast and in Accra, and widespread in the northern countryside. But the Islamic north was sparsely inhabited compared with the densely populated south. In 1981 the Muslims in Ghana amounted to only 15.7 per cent of the total population, as against 43 per cent of

Christians, the rest being animists.[12] Moreover, whereas the Christians of the south formed a highly educated middle class, the Muslims of the north were economically and educationally disadvantaged. They were therefore able to bring little weight to bear on Ghanaian politics, which were dominated by the secular African nationalism of leaders like Nkrumah, not by Islamic religio-political alternatives such as prevailed in northern Nigeria.

Unlike the Mande Muslims, the Hausas of Ghana were a radical lot, much attracted to Wahhabism. They conducted a fierce vendetta against the Tijāniyya, which found a rich pasturage in the former territories of the old Ashanti empire in what is now south-western Ghana.

Islam in Sierra Leone during the colonial period

Sierra Leone, a British Crown Colony, together with neighbouring Guinea, which is francophone, formed a cultural unity, linked by the Malian tradition of Islam. In Guinea the population is approximately 75 per cent Muslim, while the rest are animists. As one moves south west into Sierra Leone, this proportion is almost precisely reversed, to become 75 per cent of animists as against 25 per cent of Muslims. Islam in Sierra Leone has long been represented by several powerful Muslim Mande families and clans whose co-operation was cultivated by the British administration. None the less, against the huge animist majority the progress of Islam has been slow. This ancient Mande form of Islam lacks militancy: there were a few minor *'jihāds'* during the eighteenth century AD, while Almamy Samory's campaigns in the thirteenth/nineteenth century brought another wave of Muslims into the Sierra Leonean hinterland. On the whole, Muslims and animists coexisted peacefully in Sierra Leone during the colonial period.

The francophone territories during the colonial period

In the francophone territories of Senegal and French Sudan a somewhat different pattern emerged. The French reliance on the *Ṣūfī ṭuruq* elevated these to positions of influence. A French relationship already existed with the Tijāniyya in North Africa, and was strengthened by an alliance with a new *ṭarīqa*, the Murīdiyya, which, to serve the economic interests of its sheikhly leaders, became the most reliable ally of the French, especially during the Second World War. But such co-operation with the infidel was fiercely opposed by yet another *ṭarīqa*, the Hamaliyya, which had been founded *c.* 1920 by Shaykh Ḥamā Allāh, in the French Sudan, with the ostensible aim of reforming the Tijāniyya. In fact, its real purpose was to assert the total incompatibility of Islam and infidel rule. It quarrelled violently with the Murīds, thus causing the French some trouble before it was finally put down.

In the vast area of French Equatorial Africa, the French were thinner on the ground. Their primary concern was security. This led them to co-operate, for example in Chad, with the local sultans and emirs to a greater extent than elsewhere in their West African empire.

Cameroon was originally a German possession, part of which passed to the British after the First World War and became part of Nigeria while the rest went to France. In the Francophone area the main division was between the hegemonic Muslim Fulānī, scions of those who had fought the *jihād* in Hausaland, and the animist Kirdis of the highlands. The French, with their own economic interest in mind, encouraged these Kirdis to come down from the hills of the Cameroons and farm the lowlands. Many of them did so but in so doing, they converted in substantial numbers to Islam – surely an unintended consequence as far as the French were concerned!

A territory that presented the French with intractable ethnic and religious problems was Mauritania. They described their administration here as *l'Administration du vide.* But vast as the territory was and sparse as its population was, it gave rise to acute racial and cultural difficulties. Historically, it had been dominated by Muslim Moors who lived by caravan-raiding and slave-raiding of the pagan negroes of the south. Having pacified the region, the French then turned to overcoming the ancient hostilities that bedevilled relations between the Moors and the negroes by offering to both sides – Moors and negroes alike – a modern, francophone education that would enable them to participate in their own government. This was eagerly taken up by the negroes but scornfully rejected by the Muslim Moors. The result was that large numbers of negroes entered the French administration, thus achieving some political advantage over the Moors, while the latter, locked in their medieval Arabic literacy, began to lose ground. Far from alleviating these ancient hostilities, the well-intentioned French policy simply served to make them more intense.

In most of these territories the consequences of the French occupation has been the emergence of a francophone elite, whose Islam is nominal at best and who have widely adopted the European life-style. Behind them, in the countryside, there remain large numbers of illiterate or semi-literate Muslims who are still largely the creatures of the *Ṣūfī shaykhs*. Opposing this situation is a growing body of radical Muslims of Wahhābī inclination who call down damnation on both the westernised modernists and the *Ṣūfīs*.

Secularism: the colonialists' poisoned chalice

The colonial occupations proved, in the short and medium term, not detrimental to Islam. The pacifications undertaken by the French and the British, while they checked the slave-raiding and jihadist warfare by which Islam had attempted to spread in the past, facilitated its expansion by other means. Better and safer communications promoted the movement of people. Thus in many erstwhile pagan areas, Islam gained a hold by reason of its cultural attraction more readily than it had by force of arms. On the whole, therefore, Islam advanced more successfully during the colonial period than it had done in the immediate pre-colonial past.

But this medium-term picture of Islam profiting from the unwonted security imposed by 'Christian' intruders, conceals a deeper factor. Colonialism gradually began to work to Islam's disadvantage. Both colonial powers, the British and the French, had brought in their baggage an inescapable secular literacy that was as inseparable from their culture and purpose as was sacerdotal Arabic literacy from the culture and purpose of Islam. It proved to be a poisoned chalice that these colonialists pressed upon their unwilling Muslim subjects. For whatever the superficial advantages that might seem to accrue from the kindly British regimen of English, arithmetic, geography and science, with Arabic and Koran recitation fitted in for maybe two or three hours a week, or from the more ruthless French curriculum of out-and-out francophone secularism, the fact is, traditional Islam depends on a vast corpus of learning – its theology, its law, its literature, its Arabic language studies – without which Islam can barely exist, except, perhaps, as a highly attenuated personal belief system stripped of its institutions and its cultural environment. What is more, the acquiring of this learning, for which a fluent knowledge of classical Arabic is essential, consumes a lifetime. It is simply not possible to devise a curriculum that will cover the whole of what is required by the traditional Islamic syllabus, or even a substantial part of it, while at the same time covering a Western-style secular syllabus.

Another development also threatened Islamic literacy. The old trans-Saharan trade complex – that superb construction of the Middle Ages in which the elegant, swaying camel carried copper, gold, hides and skins, ivory and spices from the Sahel's edge, where it was brought from deeper in the Sudan by caravans of dainty donkeys, to the markets of North Africa and Egypt – also brought in the handwritten manuscripts the Sudanic *'ulamā'* needed to build up their own libraries. It carried ideas and intercourse with men for whom the latest mahdist manifestations in North Africa, or the pronouncements of the scholars of the Azhar in Egypt, were the news of the day. It brought Pilgrims to and from Mecca. It spread abroad the mercantile principles of the *Sharīʿa* without which a man could not hope to trade successfully in the old Sudan. It sustained a whole Islamic civilisation. Quite early in the colonial era the old trans-Saharan trade complex began to wither. Its place was taken by new rail systems and trunk roads that linked the Islamic hinterland not with the solidly Islamic heartlands of North Africa and Egypt but with coastal ports that increasingly reflected the European way of life.

This shift of emphasis was less immediate in the solidly Islamic northern areas for here the tradition of Islamic literacy remained somewhat impenetrable, for a time. Moreover, these areas were in fairly easy contact with North Africa and Egypt and even with the Islamic Middle East throughout the colonial period. Thus the leaven of Western secular thought was slower to spread, although the Muslims of northern Nigeria, for instance, were fully conscious of its threat from the early days of the occupation. A northern Nigerian Hausa poet, writing *c.* 1920, consigns to hellfire those of his fellow Muslims who succumb to such infidel allurements as 'shirts with buttons', 'tight trousers', 'electric torches' and even 'cabin biscuits'. In preference to these the honest Muslim should chew the hard guinea-corn porridge and thus assure his place in Paradise! One may smile. Yet this Hausa *malam* who put his forebodings in verse knew what he was talking about. The future was to show that it was precisely the adoption of such European ways, however trivial, that added up in the end to the dissolution of Islam.

In the south, along the coastal littoral of West Africa, an area of thinning Islamic presence that none the less remained significant, the contradictions involved in Islamic and Western education were more immediately obvious. By 1960 it had become clear to the people of these areas that their future lay in literacy in English or French. Literacy in Arabic, however ancestrally venerated, seemed increasingly irrelevant. The crux in which the departing colonialists now left the Muslims of West Africa was the inescapable fact, which forced itself increasingly on their awareness, that Islam's tradition of literacy was simply not compatible with the requirements of the modern world.

Part of the *raison d'être* of present-day Islamic fundamentalism is to fly angrily in the face of this unwelcome reality and thereby hope to dispel it.

ISLAM IN INDEPENDENT WEST AFRICA (C. AD 1960 TO THE PRESENT DAY)

The withdrawal of colonial rule not only faced West African Muslims with the problem of reconciling two incongruent literacies, and the cultures they represented; it also presented them with yet another poisoned chalice, this time of a stark political kind. The colonial withdrawal, whether British or French, left a commitment to forms of democratic pluralism that were incompatible with Islamic theocracy. Try as they might, the Muslims have been unable to resolve this contradiction.

The Nigerian civil war and after

In the Nigerian case, the attempt to cope with this exotic political heritage – which was just as alien to the tribal structures of the old Eastern Region, or the African imperialism of the Yorubas of the Western Region as it was to the emiral polities of the Islamic North – broke down in chaos. Ethnic divisiveness together with endemic corruption proved just as destructive to the new 'Westminster' system of party government as did the Muslim unwillingness to bow before an adult franchise that dared to treat Muslims and non-Muslims alike. This impossible situation was overtaken by the declaration of the Republic of Biafra in what had been the Eastern Region of Nigeria, and the Nigerian civil war that immediately resulted from it.

In 1970 Biafra surrendered to the Federal Republic. After a further period of military rule, a return to parliamentary government, based once again on adult suffrage and resulting in the notorious Shagari administration, took place. It proved spectacularly unsuccessful. It was cut short by a military *coup* in 1983, followed by another in 1985. The Federal Republic of Nigeria was then governed by a President with an Armed Forces' Ruling Council, which appoints a Council of Ministers. The old structure comprising three regions was wholly dismantled: it was replaced by twelve states, subsequently increased to nineteen states and finally, in 1991, to thirty states with a Federal Administrative District. It appears this progressive declension from the original three regions into an ever-increasing number of states, all enjoying a considerable degree of internal autonomy, is intended to reduce tensions between the various ethnic groups in Nigeria, which coexisted so uneasily together in the broader three-region framework. In particular, it is surely designed to avoid the looming clash between Muslims and non-Muslims, especially Christians, to which reference was made above.

The Model of the Rightly-guided khulafā'

The organisers of the military coups of 1983 and 1985 banned all party politics. What has taken their place in the Islamicareas, especially the old Northern Region, is a division between Islamic iconoclasts and 'moderates' (though one might equally well call them 'half-hearted Muslims', for that is how they appear to their more ardent fellow believers) who are prepared to live with a democratic, pluralist federation such as the military administration with its rather desperate resolution of the Federation into thirty states, is apparently trying to create. The iconoclasts want no truck with democracy or pluralism, calling for the North to return to Islamic theocracy of a rigour not envisaged by the early Northern politicians of the old NPC. Some go further, to envisage the whole of Nigeria as a single Islamic polity in which non-Muslims have rights, but only as subjects of an Islamic state. The influence of Turabi's 'Sudan Charter', discussed above, is obvious. As the Sudanese look back to the *Mahdiyya*, so these Nigerian Muslim radicals hark back to the Fulani reform movement and *jihād* as the ideological model for their present aspirations. That model is based on the works of Shaykh ʿAbd Allāh b. Fūdī (Abdullahi dan Fodio), brother of the Shehu Usuman dan Fodio and constitutional theorist of his reform movement. Thus Shehu ʿUmar Abdullahi, a present-day spokesman for this radical Muslim tendency in northern Nigeria, writes:

> The concept of secularism ... is totally alien in Islam. In the Islamic state there is no separation between the religious and worldly affairs. The two in Islam are indivisible. Both religious and worldly matters are ruled, controlled and regulated by Islamic legislation.[13]

This simply spells out in more detail the demand of certain demonstrating students on northern Nigerian campuses during the late 1970s and early 1980s. Their banners bore the slogan in Arabic, Hausa and English, 'Democracy is unbelief! We do not want a constitution! We want government by the Koran alone!'

The same author makes a number of further claims and proposals that illustrate the far-reaching nature of the Islamic revolution he and his fellow Muslim radicals wish to bring about. His advocacy may be summed up by his observation that Nigeria (he does not say just northern Nigeria) should be governed in 'strict imitation of the Companions of the Prophet especially the rightly guided *khulafā'* [the early caliphs] and the worthy ancestors'.[14]

Similar ideas are expounded in another recent work, *A Revolution in History*, by a northern Nigerian Muslim scholar, Ibraheem Sulaiman.[15] This work, which has been most influential in forming the opinions of the younger generation of Muslims in Nigeria, uses the Fuani *jihād* as a symbolic programme for present-day Islamic reform in Nigeria. In his foreword the Hausa Muslim academic, Shehu Usman M. Bugaje, takes it as his theme that the situation prior to the Fulani *jihād* of 1219/1804 'gave the preceding paganism a chance to resurface and some Muslims found it expedient to mix Islamic practices with pagan rituals'.[16] The *jihād* is held to have cured all this. But now these bad old ways are returning. He ends with a rousing call to his fellow Muslims to fight *fī sabīl Allāh*, 'In the way of God' (Koran, 5:57).

In a final section, 'The Shehu's Legacy', the author himself, that is Ibraheem Sulaiman, writes:

> In the philosophy of revolution articulated by the Shehu, the state, as much as the individual Muslim, had to commit its energy, resources and its very life to the propagation of Islam, the expansion of *dar al-Islam* [the territory of Islam], the abasement of unbelief, and ensuring that the perpetual conflict between Islam and unbelief would be resolved in favour of Islam.[17]

Such views are characteristic of the Nigerian *'Yan Izala*, a Hausa Muslim tendency that takes its name from the Koranic precept *izālat al'bid'a wa iqāmat al-sunna*, 'the withdrawing from innovation and the standing firm by the *Sunna*'. This fundamentalist tendency emerged in northern Nigeria *c.* 1970 and has grown in influence ever since, spreading widely across West Africa.

The opposition to the Islamic radicals

Against these views, which are widely propagated by the Muslim Students' Society of Nigeria and by such well-known northern Nigerian personalities as the late Shaykh Abubakar Gummi, Malam Ibrahim Zakzaky and Malam Yakubu Yahaya, whose advocacy sparked off a series of riots for which he suffered a period of imprisonment, are to be set those of certain Nigerian academics, said to include both Muslims and Christians, who appear to represent the stance of supporters of a secular, pluralist, democratic constitution for Nigeria. These moderates complain that the activities of the Muslim fundamentalists attack

> one of the foundations on which our country exists, namely the secular nature of the Nigerian state …[18]

while

> one of [the Federal government's] most fundamental responsibilities is to *protect the right of every citizen and resident to practise the religion of their choice.*[19]

But the fact is, it is precisely the secular nature of the Nigerian state that the Muslim radicals are ideologically unable to concede, while the right of citizens to practise any religion other than Islam can be conceded only if such citizens are prepared to accept the status of *dhimmīs*, non-Muslim subjects of the Islamic state.

Some have sought to draw a clear distinction between Islamic radicals and so-called Islamic moderates and have accordingly discounted in some measure the dangers of Islamic 'fundamentalism' in Nigeria. In fact, it is difficult to draw such firm distinguishing lines between these two tendencies, as the long debate over the introduction of a Federal *Sharīʿa* Court of Appeal under the Nigerian Constitution demonstrated. This debate took place with some vigour between 1977 and 1989, during which it became clear that many Nigerian Muslims who might otherwise have been classed as 'moderates' were just as emphatic as the radicals in insisting, against intense Christian opposition, that the *Sharīʿa* must be officially and firmly enshrined in that Constitution and should not remain a purely regional institution. But, for the Christians, such insistence was seen as a drive to convert Nigeria into an Islamic state. In a similar way most Muslims, whether professedly radical or less radical, argued, against equally fierce Christian opposition, that Nigeria should become a full member of the prestigious Organisation of Islamic Conference (OIC) when this was proposed in 1986. Perhaps, therefore, it is in the intensity of their rhetoric rather than in their real aims and aspirations that the Muslim radicals differ from those who think of themselves, and are seen by others, as Muslim moderates.

Despite the activism of Nigerian Muslims, it is improbable owing to divisions among the Muslims themselves that any one Islamic tendency will succeed in the foreseeable future in toppling the Nigerian Constitution and setting up an Islamic theocracy in its place. But what is a greater danger is the mounting antagonism between Christians and Muslims that such Islamic – and indeed Christian – activism engenders. Such antagonism is especially virulent in the former animist areas such as the Plateau and Bauchi, where Christians and Muslims compete for the conversion of the former animist populations. It is also acute in the former Eastern Region, among mainly Catholic Ibo Christians, whose fear of Islam and hostility to it is intense. This, rather than a specifically Islamic revolution, is most likely, in the end, to destabilise the secular pluralist Nigerian Constitution.

The Mai Tatsine affair

The Middle East imbroglio, from the rise of Khomeini to the seizure of the Meccan Grand Mosque in 1979, created great excitement in northern Nigeria. One of its consequences was the gruesome Mai Tatsine uprising led by a certain Muhammadu Marwa, of Cameroonian origin, that disturbed the former Northern Region between 1980 and 1984. The word 'Mai Tatsine' is ungrammatical 'Gwari' Hausa meaning 'the anathematiser'. It was applied to Muhammadu Marwa because of his habit of cursing all those who opposed him. This eruption was widely misunderstood at the time as just another outbreak of Iranian-style Islamic fundamentalism. Some attributed it, quite falsely, to the *'Yan Izala*; yet others saw it as a purely social and economic phenomenon to be explained in Marxian terms of a proletarian revolt against the consequences of the Nigerian oil boom. In fact it had complex origins. It is best understood as a manifestation of traditional Islamic messianism. 21 November 1979 marked the beginning of AH 1400 – a fact that, together with the unprecedented incident at the Grand Mosque, filled many Nigerian Muslims, and others, with apocalyptic expectations. But mixed with this most traditional Islamic excitement, which marks the turn of every century of the *Hijra*, there was also a powerful strand of ethnic resentment on the part of certain non-Hausa tribal groups, commonly known to the Hausas as the Gwaris, against what had long been perceived as Hausa elitism in West African Islam. Of course, there may also have been a perception that Hausas benefited excessively from the oil boom, to the disadvantage of non-Hausas. This was, however, but one strand in a complex web of ethnic and cultural resentments, woven over many generations.

Added to ethnic tension was a macabre resurgence of African animism in its nastiest aspect. The affair was bloody and involved the kidnap and slaughter of human victims by the Mai Tatsine's henchmen, apparently to procure human organs for use in animist magic: the manufacture of charms, amulets and so on. Any suggestion that this was an Islamic uprising was indignantly rejected by the *Sunnī malams*, who roundly condemned it as outright *kafirci* (Hausa 'unbelief', 'paganism'). It was most vigorously condemned by the true *'Yan Izala*, which abominated its animist manifestations. Broadly, their stance was justified. None the less, some aspects of the uprising did display corrupted Islamic influences, of which mahdism or Islamic messianism was one. Another was an attempt to interpret the Koran in a manner that was consistent with African animism and in a way that elevated the self-regard of non-Hausa groups. This produced some far-fetched glosses on the holy text that horrified the *Sunnī 'ulamā'*![20]

In the end, the rising was put down by the Nigerian Army, with some necessary severity.

Egyptians in Sierra Leone

Along the West African littoral a somewhat different pattern of Islamic reaction to independence emerged. Around 1965, the Egyptians, no doubt encouraged by the mass of African animists who appeared to be awaiting conversion to Islam once the colonial presence was removed, and also by the optimistic accounts from the small but influential Mande Muslim minority, entered Sierra Leone and elsewhere along the coast, in some numbers. They came as teachers sent by the Egyptian government, and in other welfare roles. The Egyptians were at this time in a triumphalist mood, after the Suez affair and other international diplomatic successes that had raised their status in the Islamic world. They clearly hoped to add West Africa to their ideological battle honours. However, they were quickly disappointed and the Egyptian initiative soon faded.

There were several reasons for this. The main one was the obvious irrelevance, described above, of Arabic in an area by this time firmly committed to anglophone or francophone literacy. The failed Egyptian initiative probably marked the knell of Islam as a contender for exclusive political power and dominant cultural influence on the coast of West Africa.

The present-day situation regarding the status of Islam in Sierra Leone is neatly illustrated by an otherwise unhappy incident. In April 1992 a military *coup* in that country led to the seizure of power by a military junta headed by a certain Captain Valentine Strasser. The junta then detained a number of Sierra Leonean politicians, some of ministerial rank, on charges of corruption and other misdemeanours. They included a number of names of obvious Islamic origin, namely: Salia Jusu-Sheriff, Hassan Gbassay Kanu, Abdul Karim Koroma, Dr Sheku Sesay and M. L. Sidique cheek by jowl with such clearly Christian names as Tommy Taylor-Morgan, Dr Wiltshire Johnson, J. E. Laverse, Dr Moses Dumbuya, Dr Birch Conteh, et al. There are even a few who combine Islamic and Christian elements in their names – for example Ahmed Edward Sesay and Michael Abdulai! This is typical of the weak Malian Islamic tradition that obtains in Sierrra Leone, and indeed along the coast generally, where many families may include both Christian and Muslim members. Moreover, it also illustrates a point that is applicable to all these West African countries where Islam is faint and much diluted with Christian or animist influences – that Muslims participate in politics as regional or tribal representatives on exactly the same footing as Christians and animists (though senior animist politicians are very few, owing to the widespread lack of education in their communities). They do not stand for election *qua* Muslims; nor do they form radical and specifically Islamic oppositions such as exist in the areas of deep Islam, inland.

Islam in the independent West African nation-states

The advent of independence in West Africa created a proliferation of nation-states where previously there had been a much lesser number of British and French zones. Almost all of them contain Muslims, some as majorities, others as minorities of greater or lesser political and cultural significance. It is not possible to deal with them all in detail in the space of this book. Broadly speaking, the nearer they are to the Atlantic, the fainter their Islam becomes. Moreover, those areas that were part of the medieval empire of Mali have inherited a tradition of Islam that, while tenacious and sincere at a personal level, has seldom been expansionist or militant. Sierra Leone and northern Ghana are typical of such areas. Here, present-day Islam has become reduced to a personal belief system that, at a political level, has been overlaid by more powerful ideologies such as secular African nationalism, or the military authoritarianism that has followed failed party democracy. As Sierra Leone illustrates, Muslims participate in secular politics as individuals. But, in contrast to Nigeria, there is no significant Islamic movement that seeks power as such.

In some cases, the francophone République de Guinée is an example, a highly rhetorical but wholly superficial commitment to Islam has been used to cloak what is in reality a laical, Marxist government. Other areas – Togoland for instance – were barely touched by Islam until the Hausa and Borno traders began to pass through them from the twelfth/eighteenth century onwards, seeking the trade of the Volta region. Here, tiny enclaves of Muslims remain to testify to the ardour of these bygone visitors who were also missionaries of the Faith. But the influence of such now residual Muslim communities over present-day politics is minimal.

In the West African interior, however, the Islamic heritage is more powerful and more oppressive. It continues to create apparently irresolvable problems that have all too often exploded in violence.

The present Republic of Mali encompasses Timbuktu and Gao and broadly corresponds to the medieval empire of Mali. It includes Saharan Touregs, a Muslim people with a fierce tradition of raiding and slaving against the negroes of the savannah and a profound conviction of their own religious and cultural superiority over them. They resolutely refused French secular education. The negroes and the mixed-bloods, on the other hand, accepted it with alacrity and now, in independence, they tend to dominate the Touregs, who are still locked fast in the memory of a God-given hegemony that was theirs by divine right. The result has been a militant movement of Toureg separatism, fuelled by negro revenge-taking, that is pursued with periodic violence. But the Touregs no longer raid on camels, but in armoured fighting vehicles and with modern weaponry supplied, so it is alleged, by Libya. This Toureg separatist movement afflicts not only Mali but also the Republic of Niger, Burkina Faso and, indeed, Algeria.

In post-colonial Mauritania a similar situation obtains. Here ethnic Moors, who are Muslims, are violently at loggerheads with the black Mauritanians, and those of mixed blood, many of whom are now also Muslims. The tension between them is aggravated, once again, by the imbalance caused by the Moorish refusal to accept francophone literacy, while the blacks received it eagerly. They have thus reversed their ancient subordination to their erstwhile Moorish oppressors. They have not always been gentle in exploiting this change of fortune and have discriminated against and even persecuted the Moors.

Even Senegal, the population of which is 95 per cent Muslim, is troubled by a separatist movement in its southern province of Casamance, while an attempt to achieve union with neighbouring Gambia proved abortive.

Such heritages of ethnic and religious antagonism, which have their roots far back in the Islamic history of the western Sudan, have not been resolved by independence nor by the many unhappy attempts to impose Western-style democratic pluralism on artificially created nation-states, many of whose Muslim citizens regard such a dispensation as no better than accursed unbelief.

NOTES

1. This Sudanic state is first mentioned by the Arab geographer al-Fazārī in the second/eighth century. But al-Bakrī, writing in the fifth/eleventh century, gives the first substantial description. His account will be conveniently found in Cuoq, op. cit., Bibl. What little is known about Ghana prior to al-Bakrī is set out by Nehemia Levtzion in his 'The Western Maghrib and the Sudan' in Roland Oliver (ed.), vol. 3, pp. 336 and 351. A shorter account will be found in Humphrey Fisher, 'The western and central Sudan' in Holt, et al. (eds), 2A, p. 346.
2. Gibb, H. A. R., op. cit., Bibl., p. 322.
3. Fisher, H. J., loc. cit., *Africa*, XLIII/1, 1973.
4. Gibb, H. A. R., op. cit., pp. 323–31.
5. Levtzion, Nehemia, loc. cit., Oliver (ed.), vol. 3, p. 428.
6. Gibb, H. A. R., op. cit., p. 333.
7. I have discussed the rise of Sufism in the western Sudan in greater detail than is possible in this broad survey in Hiskett, 1984, pp. 244–60.

8. Fisher, H. J., loc. cit., Oliver (ed.), vol. 3, p. 289.
9. Lange, Dierk, loc. cit., Bibl., pp. 495–513.
10. See for instance his *Specimens of Hausa literature*, Cambridge, 1896, in which he recognises the written literature of the Hausas as essentially Islamic; also his *Hausaland or Fifteen Hundred Miles through the Central Sudan*, London, 1896, passim.
11. See for example, A. S. Kanya-Forstner's essay, 'Mali-Tukulor' in Crowder (ed.), *West African Resistance*, London, 1971.
12. Percentage figures for Muslim populations here and subsequently are taken from the table in Rabiatu Ammah's 'New Light on Muslim Statistics for Africa' in Sicard (ed.), *BICMURA*, 2/1, January, 1984 unless stated otherwise.
13. Op. cit., Bibl., p. 46
14. Ibid., p. 58.
15. London and New York, 1986.
16. Sulaiman, op. cit., Bibl., p. x.
17. Ibid., p. 176.
18. 'The violent politics of religion and the survival of Nigeria' in Sicard (ed.), *BICMURA*, 6/1, January, 1988.
19. Ibid.
20. See my 'The Maitatsine Riots in Kano, 1980: An Assessment' in *Journal of Religion in Africa*, XVII, 3, 1987; also Paul M. Lubeck, 'Islamic Protest under Semi-industrial Capitalism: Yan Tatsine Explained' in *Popular Islam South of the Sahara*, edited by J. D. Y. Peel and C. C. Stewart, Manchester, 1985, who adopts the Marxian interpretation, and Allen Christelow, 'Religious Protest and Dissent in Northern Nigeria from Mahdism to Quranic Integralism' in *Journal of the Institute of Muslim Minority Affairs*, VI, 2, July, 1985.

5

Ethiopia and the Horn

Axum, on the coast of Eritrea, was founded at the beginning of the Christian era. It was ruled by a dynasty of Ethiopian kings who bore the title 'Negus' (Arabic *najūshī*). One of them, Ezana (320–50) converted to Christianity, thus founding the Christian kingdom of Ethiopia, of which Axum was the centre. From its beginnings it was always linked to the Coptic Church of Egypt, which was to prove crucial in future centuries, when the Ethiopian empire had to deal with Islam, as yet unrevealed.

PROLEGOMENA TO ISLAM IN ETHIOPIA

The ancient trade routes of the Indian Ocean

Long before the dawn of Islam, the Horn of Africa and the east coast, rich in wood, shells, ivory and other tropical produce, had attracted trade from much of the ancient world. Prior to the fifth century AD, trade routes from what is now Malaya and Sumatra had reached across the Indian Ocean, converging at Axum. A linking trade route ran down the east coast of Africa as far as ancient Menuthias, Zanzibar. But after the fifth century this trade declined, though it never ceased entirely. The decline was due in the first instance to the collapse of the western Roman empire and the unsettled conditions this catastrophe brought in its train. More immediately, an Ethiopian invasion of Arabia in the sixth century and constant warfare between Byzantium and the Sassanid empire of Persia disturbed the security of the area.

The Christian background

In the first half of the seventh century AD, Islam burst upon the ancient world. Its rapid conquests swept away the Sassanid empire. It seized the North African and oriental provinces of the Byzantine empire. That state was reduced to a rump in southern Europe and the Balkans, although it was a rump that survived for many centuries to come.

The Christian empire of Ethiopia fared less disastrously at the hands of the Muslims. By the middle of the ninth century AD, its centre had moved from Axum to the highlands of southern Eritrea, known as the Shoan Plateau. The empire thereupon entered an expansionist phase. It was, however, confronted by strong resistance, throughout the tenth century AD, from the pagan people of the Shoan

Plateau led, like certain other ancient pagan folk, by a warrior queen. It also experienced increasing pressure from Muslim newcomers who had by this time set up a significant trading presence both on the coast and in the interior.

Around AD 1150, a new Christian dynasty replaced the existing line of Amharic emperors. It was energetic and expansionist, embarking on a programme of evangelisation among the neighbouring pagan people. The dynasty, which was known as the Zagwe, lasted until *c.* AD 1270. During its heyday it set up diplomatic relations with the Ayyūbids of Egypt that appear to have been co-operative to the extent that the Ayyūbid sultan, Ṣalāḥ al-Dīn b. Ayyūb (Saladin), granted the Ethiopian Christians certain concessions in the Holy Land.

By the second half of the thirteenth century AD, the Zagwe dynasty had begun to decline, due to divisions within the hierarchy of the Ethiopian Church. A party arose, claiming that the Zagwe had usurped power, which rightly belonged only to those who could trace their descent directly from Solomon. Behind this claim to a holy genealogy – this time on the part of Christians – there lay a deeper cause, namely the polygamous habit of the Zagwe emperors. The custom gave rise to constant succession disputes: queen mothers gathered factions around them and schemed in the interests of their uterine sons.

By AD 1270, a new dynasty, known as the Solomonids, had arisen. There followed another period of Christian expansion that probably boosted the well-known medieval legend of Prester John, a Christian potentate supposed by some to reside in the interior of Africa and by others as far away as India. He was of immense wealth and would sooner or later lead the Christian world in victory against the Muslims. Prester John captured the imagination of Christians in the Middle Ages. The Ethiopian Christian emperors, constantly cast in the role of the Prester by importunate Christians in the West, proved, however, most reluctant to accept the responsibilities of the honour pressed upon them, especially that which involved leading a crusade against the Muslims![1]

The Solomonids were increasingly challenged, not this time by matriarchal pagans but by Muslims, who had by now set up powerful sultanates of their own in the Ethiopian interior. The result was a long period of bitter border warfare.

THE STRUGGLE FOR SUPREMACY FROM THE FIRST/SEVENTH CENTURY TO *C.* AD 1900

While it cannot be proven, it seems likely that Muslims were visiting Axum and the Horn from the first days of Islam, since it is clear that communications between Arabia and Ethiopia existed even before Islam was revealed. The Islamic conquests may have interrrupted them but there is no reason why they should not have been quickly resumed. Indeed, shortly before his death the Prophet had addressed a letter to the Negus of the day, inviting him to adopt Islam, which received a courteous but vague reply. This letter may well be regarded as marking the point at which the new religion of Islam gave notice of its proselytising ambitions to the Christian Negus, which were to be repeated in more violent terms again and again in the future.

Early Muslim settlements in Ethiopia

The date of the earliest permanent Muslim settlement on Ethiopian soil is not known, yet in view of the contacts described above, it seems likely that Arabians were living on the coast and offshore islands of Ethiopia during the first century of Islam, that is the seventh century AD. By the second/eighth century the island of Dahlak had been taken over by Muslims. It later developed into an important Islamic sultanate that reached its cultural apogee from the fifth/eleventh century to about 648/1250, after which it began to decline. Islam also began to spread among the nomadic people of the hinterland, although this remained substantially pagan for many generations to come. Conversion to Islam in this hinterland only became significant in the third/ninth century.

It was trade routes that carried Muslims into the interior. Two main routes developed, one in the north, from the island of Dahlak, which ran via Axum and Gondar, into the interior. Another, farther south, started at the port of Zayla and led into the country of the north-central Horn. Muslim communities began to grow up along these routes. Initially, they were tributary to the Christian empire and appear to have remained so at least until the middle of the fourth/tenth century.

By 283/896–7, Arab immigrants are recorded as having established an Islamic state on the Shoan Plateau, under a Mahzumite sultan, although it was clearly still tributary to the Christian emperor. The Arab geographer, al-Yaʿqūbī (d. 284/897), describes a thriving trade with what he calls the 'mighty cities' of the *Ḥabasha*, the Arabs' name for the Ethiopians.[2] By the end of the third/ninth century, the port of Zayla is known to have been frequented by merchants from Baghdad. Zayla began to assume major importance at this time, as a gateway to the interior, and a channel for Islamic influence, while the importance of Dahlak may have receded. By 287/900, the whole coastal strip from Zayla to the tip of the Horn had sustained sufficient Islamic influence, and its Muslim population was such, that it can reasonably be regarded as already part of *dār al-Islām*. Culturally, it has remained so ever since, despite periods of domination by non-Islamic powers such as the Portuguese, the Italians and the British.

During the first half of the fourth/tenth century, the Christian empire was troubled by the revolt of Shoan pagans, known in the Arabic texts as the *Banū al-hamwiyya*. This left the Christians unable to deal with competition from the Muslims, either regarding trade or regarding the conversion of pagans. Moreover, the Fāṭimid dynasty had now risen to power in Egypt and increasingly challenged the Ethiopians for the trade of the Red Sea. They also assumed the role of protectors of the Muslims in Ethiopia by reason of their power over the Alexandrian Patriarchate, upon which the Ethiopian Church was dependent. This situation strengthened the hand of the Muslims in Ethiopia.

The fourth/tenth century also witnessed the rise of certain influential Muslim families or clan groups in the Horn, of which the best known are those traditionally supposed to have been founded by Shaykh Darūd Ismāʿīl and Shaykh Ishāq who are said to have been Arabs who came from Arabia and married Somali women. These clans became increasingly powerful from the fourth/tenth century to the seventh/thirteenth century. Their history is really a personalised account of the spread of Islam among the Somali people by generations of biological and social mixing with immigrants from Arabia.

Yet despite the growing importance of the largely Muslim centre of Zayla during the fourth/tenth century, to which the Arab geographer al-Masʿūdī testifies,[3] it is clear that in the middle of this century the Muslim communities who lived in the lands of the *Ḥabasha* were still tributary to the indigenous inhabitants, probably to the Ethiopian Christians, though possibly in some cases to native pagan chiefs.

By 494/1100, Islamic influence had become well established in the hinterland of Zayla. It also stretched across the Somali country of the Horn and extended in a narrow corridor down the East African littoral that included Mogadishu, Mombasa, Zanzibar and Mozambique. There was also a small Arab settlement on the island of Madagascar.

In view of the growing Islamic presence along the coastal strip at this time, and the several trade routes leading inland, it seems probable that significant individual conversions to Islam will have taken place in the Ethiopian interior. Yet there is as yet no firm evidence of independent Islamic statehood there during the period 391/1000 to 494/1100.

By 502/1108, Muslim tradition tells of the conversion to Islam of an Ethiopian people called the Gbbah, thought to be the present-day

Argobba, who live in the eastern Shoan Plateau, in the Harar region. This development coincided with the rise of an Islamic sultanate in the Shoan Plateau that may by now have been independent of the Christian empire. Indeed, it may have converted the Gbbah to Islam. Be that as it may, a long struggle between the rising power of Islam and the still-powerful Ethiopian Christian empire now began, despite which trade continued to thrive.

The seventh/thirteenth century witnessed considerable activity and some change in Ethiopia. By the end of the century trade routes reaching the Ethiopian coast from the west coast of the Malay Peninsula, from southern India via Socotra and from Muskat on the east coast of Arabia, as well as from southern Arabia, were well established. Zayla and Berbera were still the main ports in the north for these external sea routes, but Mogadishu and Mombasa, south of the Horn and farther down the east coast, had begun to rival them. By the end of the century the Solomonids had replaced the Zagwe as the ruling dynasty of the Christian empire. Persian and Indian Muslims, as well as Arabs, are recorded as settling in the Muslim commercial centres of the Ethiopian seaboard.[4] The Somalis and the other local peoples of the Horn had embraced Islam in substantial numbers by 700/1300.

The sultanate of Ifat

In 684/1285, a certain Muslim emir, ʿUmar Walasma, annexed the Islamic sultanate founded earlier on the Shoan Plateau. This resulted in the rise of the Islamic state of Ifat, one of seven other Islamic sultanates of Ethiopia recorded by the Arab writer al-ʿUmarī during the first half of the eighth/fourteenth century. It therefore seems probable that the seventh/thirteenth century had witnessed a steady expansion of Islamic power, for al-ʿUmarī appears to be speaking of well-established principalities.[5] Certainly by 668/1269 a certain Abū Bakr b. Fakhr al-Dīn had set up an Islamic sultanate in Mogadishu, at the southern base of the Horn's triangle.

By 731/1331, the Arab traveller, Ibn Baṭṭūṭa, described Mogadishu as a fully Islamic state, with a Muslim ruler and an Islamic court served by *qāḍīs*, that is Muslim magistrates, and other Muslim functionaries.[6] It was also a centre of literacy in Arabic. It appears that the country traversed by the trade routes leading inland from Zayla was known to the Arabs of the day as 'the country of Zayla', a fact that suggests the political influence of Zayla, as well as its trading interests, had by now penetrated well into the interior. Zayla, too, was visited by Ibn Baṭṭūṭa. He thought little of it, on the ground of its extremely unhygienic condition:

> I took ship at ʿAden, and after four days at sea reached Zaylaʿ,

> the town of the Berberah, who are a negro people. Their land is a desert extending for two months' journey from Zaylaʿ to Maqdashaw. Zaylaʿ is a large city with a great bazaar, but it is the dirtiest, most abominable, and most stinking town in the world. The reason for the stench is the quantity of its fish and the blood of the camels that they slaughter in the streets. When we got there, we chose to spend the night at sea, in spite of its extreme roughness, rather than in the town, because of its filth.[7]

The rise of Adal

After *c.* 720/1320, frontier fighting broke out between Muslims and Christians, due to the attempts of the sultanate of Ifat to control the long-distance trade routes to the coast. This fighting developed into full-scale war. In the first half of the eighth/fourteenth century, the Christian emperor Amda-Siyon (AD 1314–44) overwhelmed Ifat, occupied it and reduced it to tributary status. In 733/1332 Ifat rebelled, led by a certain Ṣabr al-Dīn. The Christian emperor eventually defeated this revolt, owing to divisions among the rebels arising from linguistic differences and lack of fellowship between settled and nomadic Muslims.

By the last quarter of the fourteenth century AD, a new Islamic polity, headed by the descendants of ʿUmar Walasma and known as the sultanate of Adal, emerged, having absorbed Ifat. One Saʿd al-Dīn (775/1373–806/1403) now continued to lead the Muslims of Adal against the Christians, while substantial Muslim communities grew up in and around Harar, the centre of the sultanate of Adal. Frontier warfare between the Muslims and the Solomonids now followed, on and off, until it culminated in a major Islamic *jihād* in the tenth/sixteenth century.

The Solomonid emperor Yishaq (AD 1413–30) maintained Christian pressure on the Muslims of Harar. There were, however, serious divisions on the Christian side arising from conflicts over the succession. These had disturbed the Solomonid dynasty since the late thirteenth century and now created an opportunity for an Islamic revival that began *c.* 873/1468. By 885/1480, Adal was ruled by the capable Amīr Maḥfūz. An activist party, which favoured war against the Christian empire, was now in the ascendant; from the accession of Maḥfūz, Adal constantly pressed its attack against the Christian frontier provinces.

This century – the ninth/fifteenth century – also witnessed another event that was to prove fateful for Muslims and Christians alike. In AD 1499, Vasco da Gama reached Mogadishu and sailed along the east coast of Africa, thus opening up the region to the Portuguese. In 932/1517 the Portuguese landed. In that year they burnt the town of Zayla in the course of their efforts to establish their own control along the Ethiopian seaboard. In the same year the Ottomans took Cairo. From their base in Egypt they then began to challenge the Portuguese.

The jihād *of Aḥmad Grañ*

In 922/1516, the Amīr Maḥfūz had been killed in border fighting. Civil war now broke out in Adal from which the followers of the late Maḥfūz emerged victorious. After a confused interlude, a certain Aḥmad b. Ibrāhīm al-Ghāzī, known as Aḥmad Grañ, 'Aḥmad the Lefthander', arose. He quickly proved to be an effective and charismatic leader, for he succeeded in drawing the Somalis, and other peoples of the area who were hostile to the Christian empire, into the sultanate of Adal. He is said to have been miraculously appointed *imām*, 'prayer leader', thereby acquiring a religious afflatus in addition to his military and political authority as an *amīr*, 'military commander'. This religious aura enabled him successfully to declare *jihād*, 'holy war', against the Christians. His declaration was taken up enthusiastically by the Muslims of Adal and by those Somalis and others who had attached themselves to Aḥmad Grañ. At first the *jihād* took the form of border raids but later, Aḥmad Grañ was able to penetrate deep into the heart of the empire and seize its territory. He thereupon installed Muslim governors in these captured territories. In 935–6/1529 he brought the Christians to a pitched battle at Shimbra-Kure, where he decisively defeated them, his victory enabling him to occupy the Shoan Plateau. He proceeded to carve out a large empire that extended from Zayla to Massawa, along the coast and inland to include much of what was once the Christian empire of Ethiopia.

By AD 1541, the Portuguese had established themselves at Massawa and engaged Aḥmad Grañ. He called for Ottoman help which was given and Grañ initially drove the Portuguese back. Having joined hands with the Christian army of the Emperor Galawdewas, the Portuguese faced Aḥmad Grañ's army at Woina-Dega in 948/1543. Aḥmad Grañ was killed; his army was defeated and his empire of Adal rapidly fell apart. The Christians now recovered most of the territories they had lost in the *jihād*. In 965/1557, the Ottomans, reacting to the Portuguese presence on the coast, occupied Massawa. From here they attacked the Ethiopian interior, though with no decisive result, and subsequently withdrew.

By 985/1577, the centre of what was left of Adal moved north from

Harar to Aussa, to escape the counter-attacks of the vengeful Christians. From this point onwards, until the late thirteenth/eighteenth century the power of the Muslims of the interior declined. Islam was represented mainly by scattered groups of nomadic Beja, Afar and Somalis who lacked a central Islamic sultanate powerful enough to hold them together. On the coast, however, the influence of the Muslims increased owing to Ottoman sea power. At one point Christians and Muslims even co-operated together to oppose the tyrannical behaviour of the Portuguese, whose Roman Catholic missionaries persecuted Ethiopian Christians and Muslims alike.

The Ottoman hegemony

The arrival of the Portuguese set off a reaction from outside Ethiopia: it drew in the Ottoman Turks. As was pointed out above, the Ottomans did not press home their attack upon the Christian interior but they did contest the coast with the Portuguese, through their naval power in the Red Sea and through their surrogates. When the Portuguese all but withdrew from the east coast for reasons that are explained in Chapter 6, it was Ottoman influence that was left dominant. Thus Ottoman control of the Red Sea, the Horn and the East African coast remained intact throughout the twelfth/eighteenth century and well into the thirteenth/nineteenth century, though it was often exercised by surrogates such as the ʿUmānīs, the Meccan Sharīfs and, in the thirteenth/nineteenth century, by the Turco–Egyptian khedives of Egypt. Indeed, Muḥammad ʿAlī, the powerful viceroy of Egypt (1220/1805–1265/1848) and his successors, frequently acted independently, on their own accounts.

In the course of the twelfth/eighteenth century, Islam made gains among the Galla people, erstwhile pagans who had been thorns in the sides of both Christians and Muslims. The *jihād* of Aḥmad Grañ had caused many of them to embrace Islam while trade, in which the Galla were also involved, contributed further to the spread of Islam among them. So too did the influence of certain *Ṣūfī* orders, which had begun to reach Ethiopia at this time. Finally, a certain ʿAlī, a Muslim leader of obscure origin (d. 1202/1788), founded a dynasty of Muslim Galla in Begamder province. The indebtedness of these Muslim Galla to the inspiration of Aḥmad Grañ became evident when Sultan ʿAlī began the custom of pilgrimage to Grañ's tomb.

During the thirteenth/nineteenth century, Islamic fortunes again revived, not this time by *jihād* but as a consequence of several factors. First, the Turco–Egyptian conquest of the Sudan strengthened Egyptian political influence along the coast, which led in turn to some extension of Islam in the hinterland. More important was the conversion to Islam of many of the chiefs of nomadic tribes that took place at this time. Trimingham lists the Bait Asgede, the Marya, the Bilen, Mansa and Bait Juk of the northern Tigre area as having come over to Islam during this century.[8] So too did the Saho people, north-east of them, on the edge of the plateau. These conversions are attributable to the formation of 'holy families' such as the Mirghānī, arising from unions between Arabs and other non-African Muslims and the native women. The result of such unions was to create a class of local *ʿulamāʾ*, literate in Arabic, who served as a clerisy. Their influence on the tribal people among whom they lived resulted in these substantial conversions to Islam.

Finally, within the Christian empire the Solomonid dynasty largely fell apart during the nineteenth century AD. There was a period of internal strife during the reign of the Emperor Tewodros, while Muḥammad ʿAlī of Egypt harassed the empire from his base in the Nilotic Sudan, sometimes with the help of disaffected Ethiopian nobles opposed to Tewodros. The Egyptians occupied Harar in 1292/1875 and held it until 1303/1885. The Christian empire did not recover until the advent of the Emperor Menelik II, in AD 1889.

C. 1900 TO THE PRESENT DAY

The turn of the thirteenth/nineteenth century to the twentieth century AD ushered in the era of colonial conquest by non-Islamic European powers along the Red Sea coast, the Horn and East Africa. Thus the British became masters of most of northern Somaliland. The Italians took the south, as far down as Mogadishu, which they purchased from the sultan of Zanzibar in 1905, and also the area of Ethiopia known as Eritrea. The British occupied East Africa to the south-west of the Italians in Somaliland. The Germans, too, were installed in East Africa, to the south of British possessions in the hinterland of Dar-es-Salaam and Zanzibar, though their time there was cut short by defeat in the First World War. The Portuguese held Mozambique and its hinterland. Madagascar was a French possession. The long period of Ottoman hegemony on the Red Sea and in the Horn was at an end; by 1918 the Ottoman empire itself was in ruins.

Ethiopia 1889–1941

Ethiopia, or Abyssinia as it is alternatively known (thus the Arabic *habasha*) continued to be ruled by its Christian emperors, with the exception of Eritrea, which became an Italian colony. The policies of Menelik II (AD 1889–1911), who is regarded as the founder of modern Ethiopia, successfully unified the Christian empire, though not without prolonged and stubborn opposition from the Muslim sultanates within it. His campaign was carried out with substantial help from the European powers, especially Britain. The British supplied him with the modern armaments he required to subdue the several Islamic enclaves, mainly in the Harar region, that resisted this Christian initiative. The campaign was allegedly pursued with some severity. It is claimed on the Muslim side that it involved the destruction of many mosques, or their conversion into Christian churches. Muslim chiefs, so it is alleged, were coerced into accepting Christianity and many were forced to adopt Amharic names in place of their Islamic ones. Much land previously held by Muslims was distributed to newly arrived Christian settlers and to the Coptic Church. If such measures were in fact enacted, they simply repeated what the Muslims were themselves accustomed to impose on conquered territories – a no doubt regrettable but none the less inevitable tit-for-tat.[9]

This 'christianisation' campaign provoked a number of Islamic '*jihāds*' against Menelik from the end of the nineteenth century AD onwards. That of a certain Talaha lasted for five years before it was finally suppressed. Another occurred in 1902, led by one Firrasa, heir to the sultanate of Guma; another in 1916 and yet another in 1928. The latter was allegedly put down by air power acquired from European sources and used for the first time in Ethiopia on this occasion.

These Islamic revolts against what was undoubtedly a sustained attempt by Menelik II and his successors to unify Ethiopia, once and for all, as a Christian, Amharic state, were overtaken by the Italian invasion of 1935. They are also, however, to be seen as the prelude to what the Muslims regard as a war of liberation waged by various Muslim groups against the Ethiopian central government, that began again in 1962. This war is discussed below.

The independence of Ethiopia had been formally recognised by the League of Nations in 1923 but it was invaded by the Italians in 1935 and annexed as Italian East Africa from 1936 to 1941. The Emperor Haile Selassie who had come to the throne in 1930 went into exile in 1936. In 1941, following the Italian defeat in the Second World War, the emperor returned.

The jihād of Sayyid Muḥammad ʿAbd Allāh Ḥasan in Somaliland

The intrusion of the British, Italians and French into Somaliland at the turn of the century set off a reaction similar to that described above in other parts of Islamic Africa. Some Muslims, more especially certain quietist *Ṣūfīs*, together with trading interests, were inclined to co-operate with the 'Christians' or at least to accept them passively.

But this situation was by no means to the liking of all. From the very beginnings of the imperial intrusions into *dār al-Islām*, a fiercely opposing tendency had arisen. This excoriated the *Ṣūfīs* for their addiction to thaumaturgy; it despised them for their veneration of *awliyā'*, 'holy men', pilgrimage to their tombs and so on. And it damned them for a shameful passivity that led them to accept the government of 'infidels' and even to co-operate with it. This harsher or 'fundamentalist' tendency can be traced back to the Koran itself. From the twelfth/eighteenth century onwards it took its main inspiration from the puritanical Wahhābīs of inner Arabia and inspired the Salafist tendency, discussed above. It expressed itself in the formation of Islamic sodalities which organised themselves along the lines of the *Ṣūfī ṭuruq* but espoused an austere teaching of transcendence as opposed to the traditional *Ṣūfī* immanence. They put a rigorous Koranic theocracy in place of the political detachment of the quietists. A number of these new, radical fellowships sprang up in Mecca, which was the centre of the ferment of ideas in Islam that marked the twelfth/eighteenth century and the following century. They were founded by individual *'ulamā'*, reacting to the resentments and the revolutionary ideas that were seething in the Holy City at this time and drew support largely from Pilgrims who stayed on to sit at their feet after having completed the Pilgrimage.

One such affiliation established there at the end of the thirteenth/nineteenth century by a certain Muḥammad b. Ṣāliḥ al-Rashīd was known as the Ṣāliḥiyya. It quickly crossed the Red Sea to Somaliland where it proved most successful. The Ṣāliḥiyya's influence even extended to the borderlands of Kenya.

In 1310–11/1893 a certain Somali Muslim, Sayyid Muḥammad 'Abd Allāh Ḥasan, made the Pilgrimage. He then remained in Mecca for several years when he came under the influence of Muḥammad b. Ṣāliḥ al-Rashīd and was won over to the Ṣāliḥiyya. He became a *khalīfa*, vicegerent of the founder. In a manner already familiar from the careers of certain West African reformers, he was inspired by his Meccan experience. He became convinced that his mission was to bring about reform in his own land. He returned to Somaliland via Aden where he fell foul of the British in a manner that seems to have hardened his hostility towards them; and earned him the sobriquet 'The Mad Mullah'.[10] Around 1314–15/1897 he began preaching *jihād* against them and the Italians, while acquiring arms and gathering followers. In 1316–17/1899 he launched his *jihād* against the British. The difficulty of the terrain, and the inappropriateness of their tactics – they fought a slow, immobile, set-piece campaign in the open desert country of Somaliland, and the Muslim Somalis ran rings round them – hampered the British. They suffered severe defeats at the hands of the Sayyid, not because of any inadequacy on the part of British soldiers but because of the failure of the British command to adapt to the conditions of desert warfare required by the campaign. By 1905 both the British and the Italians attempted to negotiate a settlement with the Sayyid. It was known as the Illig Convention; by its terms he was given certain territory as an autonomous Islamic state under Italian protection.

The agreement of Illig quickly broke down. The Sayyid had not achieved what he had set out to do: that is to expel the infidels from Somaliland. Hostilities broke out again. The British now decided to adopt a purely defensive strategy. They withdrew to the coast. Sayyid Muḥammad ʿAbd Allāh Ḥasan built himself a fort at Taleh which became his base of operations, from where he raided the surrounding countryside.

During the First World War the British were fully occupied elsewhere. But in 1920, when that war was over, they launched an offensive against Sayyid ʿAbd Allāh Ḥasan. This time they used effective tactics. The Sayyid and his followers were subjected to heavy air strikes, followed up by a ground offensive. He was driven out of Taleh and took refuge in the Ogaden, out of reach of the British. His death in December 1920 ended hopes for an Islamic theocracy in Somaliland for the time being.

The Sayyid was far from mad. He was certainly a very violent man but he was also learned and, in an Islamic context, a conservative Islamic theocrat who was very much the creation of the ideological and theological arguments of his day. He stressed the duty of active *jihād* against unbelievers who invaded *dār al-Islām*. He advocated withdrawal, *hijra*, from the infidels, in the manner of the Algerian *amīr*, ʿAbd al-Qādir, of Shehu Usuman dan Fodio in Hausaland and so on. He refuted the arguments of the quietists that welfare, prosperity and justice could come out of co-operation with infidels. He argued that such co-operation was wholly contrary to the Koran and the *Sunna*. How, then, could it bring anything but evil? He also condemned the wearing of infidel clothing, in the manner of the Hausa poet, cited above. Many of his followers had claimed that Sayyid ʿAbd Allāh Ḥasan was the *Mahdī*. In fact, the Sayyid himself appears never to have made such a claim. He was content to be known simply as one who waged *jihād* against the infidel.[11]

Eritrea

The colonial hegemony had resulted in a rearrangement of the old Christian empire of Ethiopia, or Abyssinia as it was alternatively known, that stimulated separatist ambitions within its component parts. The area known as Eritrea is the strip of coastline north of Zayla, in north-eastern Ethiopia, with its capital at Asmara. As the preceding account of the port of Zayla indicates, it had been one of the earliest parts of the coast to sustain an Islamic influence. Seized by the Italians in AD 1882, it was then used by them as a base for their invasion of Abyssinia in 1935. The Italians were driven out of Abyssinia as a result of the British General Wavell's East African campaign of 1939–40, and the Emperor Haile Selassie was restored to power in 1941. In 1952, Eritrea was federated with Ethiopia under the auspices of the United Nations.

The Eritrean war for independence

In 1962 Haile Selassie abrogated the Federal Constitution and annexed Eritrea outright, as a province of Ethiopia. It seems this was an attempt on the part of this scion of the House of Solomon to continue the policies of his predecessor, Menelik II. It was not well received by the Muslims of Eritrea. In their view, the annexation to Ethiopia 'destroyed its Islamic heritage ... reverting it to feudal darkness and oppression'.[12] The Muslim population thereupon launched an armed struggle which 'springs from the Islamic tradition of the Eritrean people'.[13] Civil war now broke out. In the course of it, the Emperor Haile Selassie, whose conduct of the war against Eritrea was less than successful, and whose authority was weakened by a severe famine at this time, was overthrown by an army *coup* and died in captivity in 1975. His rule was replaced, after a military interregnum, by that of Mengistu Haile Mariam (1977–91), who set up a Marxist one-party state. The military regime now embarked on an all-out struggle against the Eritrean rebels. The result was to draw in Eritrean Christians as well as Muslims, on the rebel side. In due course, the 'Christians', who had in fact adopted Marxism as their revolutionary ideology, eclipsed the Muslim faction, which was made increasingly ineffective by internal rivalries and the competing interests of its international Islamic supporters. Quarrelling soon broke out between the predominantly Muslim Eritrean Liberation Front (ELF) and the Marxist Eritrean People's Liberation Front (EPLF). In 1981, EPLF together with the main Christian Tigray People's Liberation Front (TPLF) launched an attack on the Muslim ELF most of whose people fled into the neighbouring Sudan. What had begun as an Islamic war of liberation against a Christian overlord – an endeavour that must have stirred the holy bones of Aḥmad Grañ – had turned into a secular struggle between two Marxist factions – the Eritrean nationalists and the Mengistu regime. In 1991 Mengistu Haile Mariam was ousted. He was replaced by a certain Meles Zenawi.[14]

Somaliland from the Second World War to the present day

During the Second World War the southern, Italian section of Somaliland was occupied by British forces; in 1950 the United Nations returned the southern part to Italian trusteeship. When this trusteeship ended in 1960, British and Italian Somaliland were united as Somalia. From this point onwards Somalia has laid claim also to French Somaliland and parts of Ethiopia and Kenya. These irredentist claims, immediately expressed in the *Naṣr Allāh*, the 'Victory of Allah' movement launched in 1963–4, in the wake of the termination of the Italian trusteeship, surely rehearsed an Islamic militancy that dates from the *jihād* of Sayyid ʿAbd Allāh Hasan. Its objective was to recover the Ogaden and end Ethiopian domination. By 1964, Ethiopian and Somali troops were engaged in frontier fighting that was only temporarily terminated by the intervention of the Organisation of African Unity (OAU). The Somalis again invaded the Ogaden in 1977. They were driven back but the fighting between them and the Ethiopians continued throughout the 1980s.

From 1960 to 1969 Somalia was governed by a civilian United Assembly very much in the hands of a western-educated elite. Somalis had from time immemorial been governed by tribal and clan assemblies in which all adult males had the right to participate, and in which elders and more especially the *Ṣūfī shaykhs*, acted as guides and arbitrators. The society was unused to central institutions such as it inherited from the colonial powers. In addition to the inappropriate political system, the ruling modernist elite proved both corrupt and incompetent.

The result was the military *coup* of 1969, headed by Muhammad Siad Barré, a former police officer who had served under both the British and the Italians and who represented modernist opinion in Somalia. He became head of state with a Supreme Revolutionary Council and in 1980 he declared Somalia a 'Democratic Republic' with himself as President. With total disregard for democracy, all political parties and religious organisations were banned; the education system was recast in such a way as to make it an instrument of political indoctrination; and a system of security agents and secret police was instituted to suppress all opposition.

Barré was nominally a Muslim. However, he openly claimed to be an advocate of what he called 'scientific socialism' which turned out to be Marxism of a tyrannical kind that rivalled that of his neighbour, Mengistu Haile Mariam, in Ethiopia. Moreover, Barré publicly rejected parts of the Koran which he considered incompatible with his centralist socialist regime. He proclaimed that Islam was the religion of Somalia but insisted, however, that it must apply only to the spiritual side of life, denying that it had anything to do with politics. He seems to have tried to reduce Islam simply to the status of a personal faith, ignoring all its accompanying institutions such as the *Sharīʿa*.

The Somalis are 100 per cent a Muslim people. There are tendencies among them ranging from moderate Salifism to the fierce radicalism of the Muslim Brotherhood, and then the quietism of certain *Ṣūfī* mystics. But most powerful, especially among the younger *ʿulamāʾ*, is the sentiment of Islamic theocratic absolutism that harks back to the *jihād* of Sayyid ʿAbd Allāh Ḥasan at the end of the last century, who is still greatly revered. Provoked by the modernising policies of Siad Barré – and particularly by his Family Law Edict of 1975, which attempted to modernise marriage, divorce and so on, and curtail the powers over women traditionally exercised by the Muslim extended-family male hierarchy – as well as by his imprisonment and execution of a number of dissenting *ʿulamāʾ*, the opposition of the Muslim factions became increasingly intense, and was repressed with increasing severity by Barré's administration.

Eventually, three liberation movements, the Somali National Movement (SNM), the United Somali Congress (USC) and the Somali Patriotic Movement (SPM), joined forces to drive Barré out. He fled in January 1991.

No sooner was he gone than the coalition against him fell apart. Each of the various groups now claimed hegemony for itself. Thus the civil war that began to throw Barré out now continues in his absence.

As of April 1992 it is clear that the struggle is now no longer one in which Muslims fight a tyrannous secular, Marxist government. All three organisations involved in the present fighting are Muslim. There are apparently no theological or ideological disputes between them; the situation appears to arise solely out of clan and personal rivalries and ambitions of a kind that have dominated Somali society for centuries. In the past, prior to the colonial interlude, these would have been settled by the traditional arbitrament of *shaykhs* and elders, but the colonial government caused this ancient social mechanism to lapse. The westernised elite did nothing to restore it. Siad Barré's tyrannous regime finished it off – though it has to be said in his favour that much of what he tried to do was of humane intent, particularly his attempt to release women from the chains of the medieval *Sharīʿa*. It may be that there is no gentle way of dealing with Islamic radicals who insist on the divine transcendence of a social and legal system forged in the early Middle Ages. Be that as it may, the present tragedy of Somalia is that it now lacks the social and political institutions by which such inter-clan struggles as currently obtain can be peaceably resolved.

NOTES

1. Tamrat, loc. cit., Bibl., Oliver (ed.), vol. 3., pp. 179–81 gives a convenient and detailed account of the Prester John legend and the Ethiopian reaction to it. The Western, Christian pressure on the Ethiopian emperor took the form mainly of extravagant demands that he should lead a crusade against Islam, and even establish a blockade of Egypt, a policy that was certainly not in his own interest.
2. Ibid., p. 100.
3. See Chittick, loc. cit., Bibl., in Oliver (ed.), vol. 3, p. 139.
4. Tamrat, loc. cit., p. 136ff. gives a detailed account of Muslim settlement from *c.* 494/1100 to 778/1376.
5. Tamrat, p. 142.
6. Gibb, H. A. R., op. cit., Bibl., pp. 110–12.
7. Ibid., p. 110.
8. Loc. cit., Bibl., in Kritzeck and Lewis (eds), p. 28.
9. A Muslim interpretation of Menelik's campaigns against the Ethiopian Muslims will be found in Siddiqui (ed.), *Issues 1981–1982*, pp. 203–10 and *Issues 1984–1985*, pp. 66–8.
10. B. G. Martin, op. cit., Bibl., p. 181 recounts several incidents that are supposed to have led to him acquiring this nickname. One of them involved a physical attack on a British official as a result of which that person suffered a broken leg.
11. I am largely indebted to B. G. Martin, op. cit., pp. 177–201, for the information in this section.
12. Siddiqui (ed.), *Issues 1983–1984*, p. 284.
13. Ibid., p. 285.
14. The London *Daily Telegraph*, in an article of 25 February 1992, comments that the desire of 'Meles Zenawi to reach a consensus on the new political structure has resulted in drift'.

6

East and South Africa

MUSLIMS IN EAST AFRICA FROM THE SECOND/EIGHTH CENTURY TO *C.* 1255–6/1840

The east African coastline may just as well be thought of as the western seaboard of the Indian Ocean as the eastern edge of the African land mass. This has important cultural and economic implications.

Early trade contacts

From *c.* AD 60, Zanzibar, Pemba and Kilwa were being visited by Asian traders who arrived there by way of the Indian Ocean. What is now Madagascar was settled by colonists from Indonesia in the first century AD. They merged with the local Iron Age people to give rise to the Hova, founders of the pre-Islamic Imerina kingdom on that island.

By the fifth century AD this trade had declined for reasons explained above in the context of Ethiopia. Although Muslim seafarers were navigating along the east coast by the second–third/ninth century, if not earlier, the trade did not really pick up again until the fourth/tenth century. It only reached its peak in the seventh/thirteenth century.

The 'Land of the Barbar' and beyond

Ethiopia is linked to the east coast of Africa by what the Arabs thought of as the 'Land of the Barbar' (barbarians), that is the Horn. To judge from the accounts of the Arab geographers, the opening up of the east coast below the Horn to the Muslims probably marched at least a century behind the similar opening up of the east coast in Ethiopia, to the north. But there are also important differences in other respects. First, the Muslims of Arabia did not need merely to traverse the narrow – though often dangerous – stretch of the Red Sea in order to gain access to the riches of the east African coast. They had to navigate around the Horn and down a difficult coastline for there is no evidence of land-borne caravan communications in the hinterland at this early date. It appears from the records of the Arab geographers that this seaborne exploration was slow and tentative until the middle of the sixth/twelfth century. But by then the Muslims had acquired a clear, though geographically distorted picture of the east coast of Africa, built up from their own assumptions and experience.

The second major difference is political and ideological, not geographical or nautical. The Muslims in Ethiopia were confronted from the outset by an entrenched and powerful Christian empire, with which they had to come to terms before they could establish themselves within its sphere of influence and with which they subsequently engaged in constant border warfare. Farther south, below the Horn, they were faced only by pagan Zanj, most of whom were surely Bantus at this period. Although these people had set up pagan kingdoms of some pomp and circumstance, they did not present the Muslims with an obstacle such as that represented by the Ethiopian empire. Thus the Muslim settlement of the seaboard of the Indian Ocean was in the main a peaceful affair, at least until the arrival of the Portuguese at the beginning of the sixteenth century AD. The Arab geographer, al-Mas'ūdī (d. AD 956), identifies an island known to him as Qanbulu, with a partly Muslim population. He makes the somewhat startling suggestion that the Muslims conquered this island at the time when the Umayyad caliphate in Damascus gave way to the new 'Abāsid caliphate in Baghdad.[1] This would be *c.* 133/750. If this is true, it must surely represent the first significant Muslim presence on the east coast. It does seem somewhat unlikely that this was a conquest of any substance since there is no collateral evidence for it. None the less, the story may indicate that Muslim Arabs, or possibly Persians, had begun to settle permanently on Qanbulu as early as the second/eighth century. Whatever may lie behind this story is in any case obscured by the fact that the identity of Qanbulu is itself tenebrous to say the least. Chittick believes it to be Pemba island.[2] But the learned compilers of *An Historical Atlas of Islam* attach the name Qanbulu to Madagascar *c.* AD 900 (AH 287–8) although by AD 1500 (AH 905–6) they name that island al-Ḳumr.[3] However, it may well be that, in the uncertain state of knowledge prevailing in early times, these names became applied to different islands by different geographers in different centuries, according to the probably garbled information that reached them from seafarers. Be that as it may, what seems clear is that the Muslim Arabs were successfully navigating the Mozambique Channel in the fourth/tenth century, had made landfall on certain offshore islands, were involved in the trade from them and may even have formed permanent settlements there, though this is uncertain.

Al-Mas'ūdī also mentions the production of gold in Zanj.[4] This may mean that these early Muslim traders had access at second hand to the gold of the Zambezi area as early as the middle of the fourth/tenth century. If so, it must surely have been carried to the coast by the Zanj themselves since it seems improbable that Muslim traders were installed along the Zambezi at this time.

The Arabs' picture of the east African coast c. 548/1154

By this date the Arab cartographer, al-Idrīsī, had set out with some precision the Muslims' concept of the east African littoral and its immediate hinterland.[5] Like all ancient geographers, al-Idrīsī had no notion that the African continent projected so far to the south as in fact it does. In the view of al-Idrīsī, what we now know to be the north-to-south coastline on the eastern side of the African land mass ran from west to east, as a slightly more southerly but roughly parallel continuation of the Mediterranean coastline of North Africa. As late as 987/1579, when al-Sharfī's world map was compiled, the Muslims still clung, in theory, to this mistaken notion, even though Henricus Martellus's map, published in AD 1490, presented Europe with a somewhat more correct picture, based on the Columbian discoveries.

It seems probable, however, that, while the medieval Muslims paid respectful lip service to al-Idrīsī and other theoretical geographers such as al-Sharfī,[6] whose world-view was widely regarded as reflecting that of the Koran, in practice they equipped themselves with sea charts of the 'Portulan' type, acquired from the Minorcans and other Christian seafarers. These charts gave a much more accurate representation of the African coast, though only in small stretches, than the theoretical compilations of the academic geographers. Thus there seems to have been a curious disjunction between their abstract concepts, which were in some measure sacerdotal, and their obvious practical ability to navigate the real African coastline without undue difficulty.

None the less, it was to al-Idrīsī that the Muslims were mainly indebted for their picture of East Africa. From the Horn to the river Shebele (in so far as one can guess at the location of these places on these early Islamic maps), the country was known to them as the 'Land of the Barbar', which is what the Arabs dubbed the Somalis of the day. From Mogadishu to a point just south of Pemba (but east according to al-Idrīsī's projection) was the 'Land of the Zanj', their term for the Bantus, and other Africans. From 'east' (south) of Pemba to Cape Delgado was the 'Land of Sofala'. Chittick points out that Arabic *sufāla* can mean 'shoal waters', though its usual meaning is 'low-lying land'.[7] It is therefore important to understand that references to the 'Land of Sofala' before *c.* 700/1300 probably describe a whole coastline and is immediate hinterland. They do not necessarily indicate that the town of Sofala had been founded at that date. However, by 730–1/1330, Ibn Baṭṭūṭa, shortly after his noisome visit to Zayla, does refer to 'the town of Safála'.[8] It is reasonable to suppose that this settlement, which in the form that Ibn Baṭṭūṭa knew it probably dates from the late sixth/thirteenth century or maybe even from *c*. 700/1300, took its name from the descriptive Arabic term earlier applied to the coat as a whole. Beyond the 'Land of Sofala' lay an unknown country that the Arabs named *arḍ waqwaq*, 'Waqwaq Land'. This curious name may well refer to a Far Eastern people who are said to have raided the East African coast constantly during the fourth/tenth century. As Chittick points out, *waka* is one of the names for the Indonesian outrigger canoe.[9] There was in fact considerable Far Eastern interest in the east coast of Africa during the Middle Ages, until the menace of the Mongols on the northern frontier of China created other preoccupations.

Whether the early Muslims alleged to have conquered Qanbulu in the second/eighth century really were settlers on Pemba, Madagascar or some other island (Zanzibar has been suggested with some plausibility) – indeed whether they existed at all – is uncertain.

The Shirāzī

What can confidently be said is that the firm establishment of Islamic states – as opposed to Muslim merchant communities dependent on the hospitality of Zanj rulers – on the offshore islands and along the coast of East Africa dates from the sixth/twelfth century. At this time certain traders known as Shirāzī arrived from the Persian Gulf – or so the story goes in the traditions of the period. They settled in Mogadishu, Brava, and the Comores islands, Mafia, Pemba, Kilwa, Zanzibar and Madagascar, an area some regard as constituting the ancient African empire of Shungwaya, though the evidence for the existence of such an empire is tenuous. Whether they were exclusively of Persian origin is a matter concerning which one may entertain legitimate doubts, but that is how the tradition of the people of these places has it. They mixed with the Zanj, through slave concubinage, to give rise to a class of 'Afro-Shirazis'. By 596/1200 the Shirāzīs were established as the ruling dynasty on the islands of Mafia and Pemba, and at Kilwa, where the founding member, ʿAlī b. Ḥasan, is supposed to have bought land peacefully from the local Zanj. The precise date of the Shirāzīs' arrival in their various locations is uncertain. It is likely that they came in eddies over an extended period which may have been conflated in the tradition into one or two major movements. The sixth/twelfth century does, however, seem to mark the flood tide of Shirāzī settlement.[10]

By the end of the seventh/thirteenth century the first Shirāzī dynasty of Kilwa was replaced by one known as the Mahdalī dynasty, founded by a certain al-Ḥasan b. Tulūt, perhaps as a result of factional strife between Kilwa and Mafia.

In the course of several generations the Afro-Shirazi origin of these people inevitably became so attenuated as to become unreal. At the present time it is not possible to distinguish Afro-Shirazis, whose begetters were supposedly Persians, from Swahilis, whose forefathers were Arabs. None the less, although the original African element in the Afro-Shirazi ethnic fusion was almost certainly of servile status on the distaff side, the myth of Shīrāzī origin is proudly remembered among East African Muslims.

Kilwa

Kilwa was visited under the rule of the Mahdalīs by Ibn Baṭṭūṭa in 730–1/1330, or possibly early in 731/1331, at what was clearly a time of great prosperity there:

> I embarked at Maqdashaw [Mogadishu] for the Sawáhil [Swahili] country, with the object of visiting the town of Kulwá [Kilwa] in the land of the Zanj. We came to Mambasa [Mombasa], a large island two days' journey by sea from the Sawáhil country ... We stayed one night in this island, and then pursued our journey to Kulwá, which is a large town on the coast. The majority of its inhabitants are Zanj, jet black in colour, and with tattoo-marks on their faces. I was told by a merchant that the town of Sufála lies a fortnight's journey [south] from Kulwá, and that gold dust is brought to Sufála from Yúfí in the country of the Límís, which is a month's journey from it. Kulwá is a very fine and substantially built town, and all its buildings are of wood. Its inhabitants are constantly engaged in military expeditions, for their country is contiguous to the heathen Zanj ...[11]

His statement that all the buildings in Kilwa were of wood is rather surprising, since Chittick states that, according to archaeological evidence, 'Building in stone increased markedly during the early fourteenth century'.[12] Ibn Baṭṭūṭa's visit appears, however, to have been a brief one; his memory may have failed him when he came to recount his journey many years later.

Kilwa at this date controlled Mogadishu, described by Ibn Baṭṭūṭa as 'a large town'. It had its own sultan (*shaykh*), who spoke 'the Maqdishi language, though he knew Arabic'. Ibn Baṭṭūṭa's information that the inhabitants of Kilwa were constantly engaged in military expeditions against the heathen Zanj suggests that Kilwa was a centre for the slave trade at this time, for slaves must surely have been one product of these expeditions. It also seems probable that the jet-black tattooed Zanj whom Ibn Baṭṭūṭa observed within the city were the ancestors of the Afro-Shirazis referred to above. Kilwa was obviously also a centre for the gold trade, handling gold dust brought up from the Zambezi region.[13]

Ibn Baṭṭūṭa and the map of Africa

Ibn Baṭṭūṭa's reference to 'Yúfí in the country of the Límís [African cannibals] which is a month's journey from [Sofala]' is surely an error on the part of this learned *ʿālim*, which misled Gibb into postulating a cross-continental trade both in gold and in cowries between West Africa and East Africa at this time.[14] It certainly does appear, as Gibb proposes, that Ibn Baṭṭūṭa's 'Yúfí' refers either to the Nupe, a West African people living in the Niger Bend, or to Ile-Ife, a copper and gold-producing area on the left bank of the Niger, north west of Benin. Given Ibn Baṭṭūṭa's probable view of Africa, still derived from al-Idrīsī's world map of 549/1154, in which the Niger, the Nile and even the Senegal were conflated into one magnificent stream extending from Cairo to Timbuktu, apparently rising in the fabulous 'Mountain of the Moon' and known as *nīl al-sūdān*, the 'Nile of the Sudan', it may be that this *ʿālim* really did believe that the gold-bearing area of 'Yúfí' lay on the banks of that Nile of the Sudan and was thus a month's journey from Sofala. This, at any rate, is the received view,[15] though it also seems possible that his error may have been due to confusion brought about by the passage of time, for his *Travels* were not written down until 756/1355, twenty-five years after his visit to Kilwa.

By the end of the ninth/fourteenth century, Kilwa seems to have declined, while other coastal towns began to overtake it. By 700/1300, Mogadishu, Malindi, Mombasa, Pemba, Mozambique and Sofala were already linked to ocean trade routes originating in south-east Asia, southern India, via Socotra, southern Arabia and Muskat on the eastern littoral of the Arabian peninsular. Over the course of the ninth/fourteenth century these links brought increasing prosperity to the towns. Their influence therefore increased, bringing autonomy with it.

Early Muslim settlement inland

As early as *c.* 731–2/1330–1, Ibn Baṭṭūṭa had described the sultan of Mogadishu as one who 'talks in the Maqdishi language'. Since the sultan was a Berbera, he probably spoke Somali. But after a two-day voyage, Ibn Baṭṭūṭa was in country that he clearly recognised as 'Sawáhil' – that is Swahili. It was the country of the tattooed Zanj and their Arab masters. It is surely in an environment such as this – where Zanj, that is Bantus, rubbed shoulders with Muslim traders – that the Swahili people, and their language, emerged and where they began to assume their role as agents of their Arab and Persian masters.[16]

Although the Swahili–Arab sultans of the eighth/fourteenth century raided in the hinterland for booty and slaves, it appears that the Swahili-speaking Muslims they governed made little attempt to settle permanently inland, except in the area of the Zambezi where they had become established in Sena and Tete by *c.* 906/1500. These settlements, probably staffed in the first instance by Swahili agents and not by the foreign merchants themselves, arose entirely for commercial reasons. The Muslims sought direct access to the gold, perhaps at last impatient of the profits levied for centuries by Zanj middlemen. In the course of time the Swahili agents spread Islam in the neighbourhoods of these settlements, by market contacts, by the example of their own Islamic way of life and dress and by the adoption of their own Swahili tongue by the unconverted Bantus. No doubt there was a good deal of individual admonition. One can imagine turbanned Swahilis in their white gowns with several proud generations of Islam behind them chiding their tattooed and scantily clothed Zanj clients and servants for their pagan ways, scolding them with hellfire in stark Koranic imagery and teaching them to pray. But all this would have been incidental, not why the Muslim Swahilis were settled along the Zambezi. Saving of souls was a by-product of the quest for gold, albeit an effective by-product. Apart from such scattered inland settlements, the Swahili Muslims and their pure-blooded Arab and Persian masters – to say nothing of later Turks – remained, over the centuries, a coastal society steeped in Islamic ways that came to them exclusively from the Indian Ocean, not from the vast, unknown hinterland at their backs. There, animism, nomadism and the occasional but splendid drum-beating ceremonial of black African pagan empires reigned.

Sofala

As was pointed out above, Sofala, as Ibn Baṭṭūṭa knew it, was probably founded *c.* 700/1300, although there may have been earlier makeshift settlements along that coast that fell into disuse prior to 700/1300. Ibn Baṭṭūṭa mentions the town only once, in the context of the gold trade at Kilwa, noted above. Its founding probably coincided with the first penetrations of Muslims, whether pure-blooded Arabs or half-breed Swahilis, as far inland as Great Zimbabwe. This impressive stone-built ruin appears to have begun as a fourth-century AD Iron Age foundation in the Shona country of eastern Rhodesia. Its link with the Muslims of the coast can probably be dated to the founding of Sofala at the time given above. This event established a direct connection with the gold-producing areas of the Zambezi. A coin of Kilwa, minted in the name of al-Ḥasan b. Sulaymān, sultan of Kilwa and master of Sofala *c.* 720/1320 to 734/1333, has been attributed to Great Zimbabwe. This indicates contacts with Kilwa, almost certainly by way of Sofala, at this date. It does not necessarily indicate the physical presence of Muslim traders so far inland at this time, since the coin could have been dropped by a pagan Zanj – but it surely indicates this possibility.

By the tenth/sixteenth century, during the course of which the Portuguese had become established on the coast, both Muslims and Christians appear to have been in frequent attendance at the court of the Shona ruler of Uteve, near Great Zimbabwe, in the hinterland of Sofala. Some Muslims were permanently resident in the kingdom. As was their way, they coupled with the local women to father local Muslims of mixed blood. It appears the Christian Portuguese were not far behind in a similar enterprise. But the ruler of Uteve was certainly neither a Muslim nor a Christian. He was a powerful pagan able to manipulate the gold trade at his whim and to his own advantage. It is clear from the description of him and his people left behind by the Portuguese friar, João dos Santos, writing in the sixteenth century AD, that he ruled over a highly developed African state that was still triumphantly unbelieving of either of these Abrahamic religions.[17]

Mombasa appears to have been prosperous in Ibn Baṭṭūṭa's day. He describes the inhabitants approvingly as 'pious, honourable and upright, and they have well-built wooden mosques'.[18] Clearly Mombasa was more to his taste than fetid Zayla! But the sultanate was somewhat isolated. 'It possessed no territory on the mainland'; its cereal had to be brought in by mainland Swahilis. By the end of the ninth/fifteenth century, a considerable trade passed through this town. From then on it played an increasingly important commercial and political role. Zanzibar had also grown in importance by this time and was now beginning to dominate Kilwa. Sofala too, had become virtually independent of Kilwa by the time the dark shadow of the Portuguese fell across what appears to have been, hitherto, the affluent and comfortable landscape of the east African littoral.

The Portuguese

As in the case of Ethiopia, so too in that of the east African coast, the arrival of the Portuguese at the beginning of the sixteenth century AD marked the start of a new era, and a somewhat unhappy one. For almost 200 years, the Portuguese dominated the east coast and the Indian Ocean. In fact, their main interest was not in the area itself but rather to secure it as a base on the way to the Far East, and to ensure control of the Indian Ocean. Thus the Portuguese on the east coast took their orders from the Portuguese viceroy in Goa, not directly from Lisbon. Their activities were constantly conducted with the Far Eastern connection in mind.

They held the east coast not with the consent of the local Muslims, nor with the co-operation of the Africans of the hinterland, but by virtue of their superior fire-power and, probably, their better organisation. By this means they imposed tribute upon the Muslims. Provided this was forthcoming, and the Muslims did not compete too effectively for the trade of the region, they left them largely alone. All the same, this policy of demanding tribute provoked resistance which, in turn, gave rise to Portuguese reprisals. The situation increased in violence during the latter part of the tenth/sixteenth century, when the Ottomans began to challenge Portuguese hegemony along the coast. In 993/1585 a Turkish commander, ʿAlī Bey, raided along it, fomenting revolt against the Portuguese. In 996–7/1588, the Muslims of Pemba rose against the Portuguese at his instigation and massacred them. In response the Portuguese connived at the massacre of the Muslims of Mombasa by local African cannibals, the fearsome Zimbas. Finally the Portuguese defeated ʿAlī Bey, occupied Mombasa and, in 1001–2/1593, built their formidable Fort Jesus there. From it they endeavoured, successfully for a time, to consolidate their control over the northern stretch of the coast.

Despite their wider imperial concerns, the Portuguese did have a substantial interest in trade, especially in pepper, that most sought-after Renaissance luxury, as well as gold and, to a lesser extent, ivory.

At first the Portuguese tried to establish their settlements along the whole length of the coast. Later, after their clash with ʿAlī Bey, they fell back on Malindi and Mozambique and relied on Fort Jesus as a strong point from which to control the northern reaches of the coast. They held Fort Jesus for just under a century. Then, in AD 1698, this stronghold fell to the ʿUmānīs, Muslims from ʿUmān (Oman) in south-eastern Arabia who owed allegiance to the Ottoman sultan. They were invited in by the Mombasa Muslims, who by this time had come to hate the Portuguese bitterly.

With the fall of Fort Jesus to the ʿUmānīs, the Portuguese lost control of all the territory north of Cape Delgado. Their sphere of influence was reduced to Mozambique and to their settlements along the Zambezi river. This area they retained until in AD 1751, when it was declared part of Portuguese India. Late in the nineteenth century AD it became part of Portuguese East Africa. Its subsequent history will be considered below.

The Portuguese setback initiated a period of Ottoman hegemony in the Indian Ocean, exercised partly by the Turks themselves and partly by surrogates such as the ʿUmānīs. Zanzibar became at this time part of the ʿUmānī empire developing into the dominant trading centre of the Indian Ocean. In 1255–6/1840, the sultan of ʿUmān moved his capital from ʿUmān to Zanzibar. In AD 1885 the island was annexed by the Germans, one of several events at the end of the nineteenth century AD that ushered in the colonial occupations of east Africa.

THE DEVELOPMENT OF ISLAM DURING THE MEDIEVAL PERIOD

The early centuries of the Islamic presence along the east Africa coast are shrouded in some uncertainty. But what is clear is that they witnessed the beginnings of a process of ethnic mixing between Arabs and Persians on the one hand and native Bantus on the other, that gave rise to the Swahili people and their distinctive Islamic culture.

The origins of Swahili culture

During the early centuries there were three classes of people inhabiting, or frequenting, the coast of East Africa and its offshore islands. The first were Muslim Arab or Persian traders of pure blood, or at any rate immediately unmixed with that of coastal Africans.

Then there were the people of mixed blood, part-Arab or Persian, part-Zanj, arising from earlier unions between the Arabs and Persians and native Bantu women. These were the proto-Afro–Shirāzīs and the proto-Swahilis. It is, incidentally, misleading to do as some historians have done, and talk blithely about 'intermarriage' between the Muslims and the Zanj. Virtually all the Afro–Shirāzīs and the Swahilis were of slave mothers since, although Arab and Persian Muslim males coupled freely with pagan African women, as their slave concubines, the union of a freeborn Arab or Persian Muslim woman with an African male, even if he was a Muslim, was probably a rare occurrence. Later, Muslim women of mixed blood may have married according to the Islamic rites, with Arab or Persian males, as opposed to union with them as concubines. But by this time the assimilation process must have been well under way and ethnic origins became blurred in a common Swahili identity in which even the Afro–Shirāzī strain became increasingly indistinguishable. To talk of 'intermarriage' in such a context simply places a deceptive gloss on what was frank and outright slave concubinage – a universal and morally wholly acceptable institution in Islam, sanctioned by the Koran.

Finally, there were African slaves, harvested mainly in the hinterland of the Land of the Zanj. These were unconverted to Islam in the first instance but the Islamic institution of clientage, whereby slaves who adopt Islam become emancipated over the course of three generations meant that this third group was constantly absorbed into the second group. That is, they became Swahilis.

The people who emerged out of this ethnic mixing evolved, in due course, a language of their own. It retained the Bantu grammatical structure – usually the most tenacious element in any language – but it accumulated a huge lexicon of Arabic and some Persian loan words, often deeply naturalised. By the seventh/thirteenth century this language had probably replaced Arabic as the common tongue of the Muslims settled along the seaboard of the Indian Ocean, although classical Arabic still continued to be used as the liturgical and legal language of Islam. Swahili developed and spread during the course of the eighth/fourteenth century and the ninth/fifteenth century, which was the period of greatest prosperity on the coast. In due course a modified form of the Arabic script was developed, for the purpose of recording Swahili speech in writing, for by this time the language had developed an extensive and essentially Islamic literature.[19] This is studied in Chapter 7 below.

The growth of Islamic states

The Islamic states that arose along the coast and on the offshore islands had developed characteristically Islamic forms by *c.* 596/1200, by which time the first Shirāzī sultanates had been established. It seems that Islamic state formation now burgeoned, becoming characteristic of the offshore islands and the large coastal towns. By Ibn Baṭṭūṭa's day such states were the normal mode of government right along the coast. Mogadishu and Kilwa had evolved quite elaborate Islamic ruling hierarchies by this time, even to the use of Islamic state ceremonial. Ibn Baṭṭūṭa describes how the sultan of Mogadishu proceeded with his *qāḍīs* (Muslim magistrates) in attendance:

> When the 'Shaykh' [sultan] came out I greeted him and he bade me welcome. He put on his sandals, ordering the *qāḍī* and myself to do the same, and set out for his palace on foot. All the other people walked barefooted. Over his head were carried four canopies of coloured silk, each surmounted by a golden bird. After the palace ceremonies were over, all those present saluted and retired.[20]

The Islamic political structures such ceremonial adorned, and the way of life they supported, were overshadowed by the Portuguese to a greater or lesser degree in the course of their hegemony over the east coast. But they were never destroyed. Indeed, many of the Islamic sultanates seem to have flourished during the Portuguese period, despite the tribute levied upon them by their Portuguese overlords, perhaps due to the greater security imposed by the Portuguese. These Islamic sultanates survived into the Ottoman period, during which the coast was largely dominated by the 'Umānīs, who had defeated the Portuguese. When in 1256/1840 the sultan of 'Umān transferred his capital to Zanzibar, this island became part of the 'Umānī empire.

The role of the Indian Ocean

It was suggested above that from the point of view of its Islamic history, the east coast of Africa belongs as much to the Indian Ocean as it does to the African land mass. The first and most obvious reason for this conclusion is that those who brought Islam came by way of that ocean – from Arabia and from Persia – that is from east to west. They did not trek across the continent from west to east, nor did they progress down it in caravan from north to south as happened on the West Africa side.

A further reason is that, having once arrived there, most of these Muslims remained firmly and, it appears, very comfortably ensconced along the coast and on the offshore islands. Unlike their co-religionists of the western Sudan, they did not arrive during the caravanning season and return home a few months later, to repeat the process the following year. With the exception of the tenth/sixteenth-century settlements of Muslim Swahilis along the Zambezi, this Muslim settlement remained almost exclusively coastal. So it continued until the late thirteenth/nineteenth century, when the search for ivory drew the Muslim Swahilis into the hinterland and set up Muslim enclaves there. The result has been that East African Islam developed almost exclusively in the environment of the seaboard of the Indian Ocean. It gave little to the hinterland by way of culture and drew even less from it.

It is true that the Swahili language that resulted from the ethnic mixing described above remains beholden to the mainland Bantu past for its grammar – that last bastion of beleaguered speech that resists centuries of cultural change. But as for the content of its written literature and folklore, this was, as Knappert has shown (see Chapter 7 below), drawn almost exclusively from the direction of the Indian Ocean and the Red Sea. It has little in it that recalls the African veld.

A similar indebtedness to oceanic influences, not those of the veld, is to be recognised in the coastal architecture. Archeological evidence indicates that masonry building was practised on the coast as early as the eighth/fourteenth century. It continued to develop from then onwards, especially for mosques and town walls, while monumental masonry was used for funeral purposes. It hardly needs to be pointed out that the inhabitants of the coastal strip were indebted to the Middle East, to Persia and perhaps to India, for the techniques required to accomplish such constructions. The primordial culture of the veld that lay behind them had nothing to offer in this respect but daub and wattle. An exception to this may be thought to be Great Zimbabwe and elsewhere in what was eastern Rhodesia, where hill-top fortifications in stone were apparently in use during the Iron Age. Yet the presence of Chinese and Persian artefacts at the Great Zimbabwe site must raise the question as to whether the later, more elaborate stone building there was inspired by foreign influence, even though it may have been carried out by Shona-speaking African princes of the area. Be that as it may, Great Zimbabwe was certainly not the inspiration that gave rise to the masonry constructions of the coastal cities, the earliest of which can be dated to the high point of the Shīrāzī period that is the seventh/thirteenth century. These bear all the hallmarks of an Islamic origin that can only have stemmed from the ocean side.

The impact of the Portuguese on Islam

The Portuguese made very little cultural impact on the Muslim communities along the east coast and the offshore islands during the period of their sojourn there which, apart from the area south of Cape Delgado which they held until recent times, amounted to almost 200 years. They do not appear to have tried to convert the Muslims to Christianity, except spasmodically: they were interested in their tribute, not their souls. Nor is there much evidence that they pursued with any vigour a policy of converting the pagans of the interior. Around Sena and Tete on the Zambezi, they built their small stone forts to secure their lines of communication. These they garrisoned with Portuguese. Small native communities grew up around these forts, which included Christian converts; Christianity has survived there to the present day. However, the robustly pagan sixteenth-century chief of Uteve appears to have been as innocent of Christianity as he was of Islam. Any converts to Christianity along the coast north of Cape Delgado that the Portuguese may have made were surely few and far between. They must soon have lapsed back into Islam since no trace of them now remains. Nor is there any substantial evidence of Portuguese secular culture beyond that point, except perhaps, as Chittick has suggested, the bull-baiting that still takes place on Pemba island.[21] Thus Islam along the coast entered the Ottoman period virtually intact after its experience of almost two centuries of Portuguese overrule.

By the time the colonial period opened, Islam along the east

African coast – or if one prefers, along the western seaboard of the Indian Ocean – had become substantially integrated into the Ottoman sphere of influence. It displayed many of the characteristics of that late, often luxuriant and increasingly turpid civilisation. But it remained in every way essentially Islamic.

THE COLONIAL OCCUPATIONS (THE END OF THE NINETEENTH CENTURY AD TO *C.* 1961)

A new cartography

As a result of the colonial occupations that occurred at the end of the nineteenth century AD and the beginning of the twentieth century, the nameless desert and savannah that lay behind the coastal sultanates was immediately divided up by arbitrary lines drawn by the same hands that placed their scribbled names on the treaties and concords of the day. The result was that the coast and hinterland of the Horn, for centuries the 'Land of the Barbar', became almost overnight, 'Italian Somaliland' while from there southwards the Land of the Zanj, the Land of Sofala and even the remote Land of Waqwaq, coast and hinterland, were carved up as 'the British East African Protectorate', 'German East Africa', 'Portuguese East Africa', while west of them lay the 'Belgian Congo' and 'Rhodesia'. Madagascar, medieval al-Qumr, went to the French, Kilwa to the Germans and so on. As the ink dried on these new dispensations, so the world-view of al-Idrīsī and al-Sharfī, unreal but none the less beautiful and cherished by the Muslims over centuries, finally faded.

Later, as the era of independence – the next great watershed for Islam – approached, there emerged out of this first colonial map-making such now-familiar names as Kenya, Uganda, Tanganyika and then Tanzania, Mozambique, Zimbabwe, Malawi et al. These new nation-states were barely recognisable as the ancient Islamic sultanates that had graced the coast and the islands in the past. Not only had they become geographically rearranged, but they had also undergone profound cultural and political changes and depletions.

Early colonial attitudes to Islam

The security – that is the restraint on slave-raiding, tribal war and what the colonial authorities regarded as banditry brought about by more efficient policing – had the largely unintended effect in East Africa, as in West Africa, of facilitating, if not actively aiding, the spread of Islam. In the German case there was even a deliberate policy at one time of encouraging Islam. In German East Africa the German authorities, installed there in AD 1891, deliberately established schools to educate the coastal Muslims, with a view to using them as junior civil servants to staff their administration. These clerks, many of whom were posted up-country, carried their Islam with them to areas it had not previously reached.

The British made no such deliberate attempt to involve Muslims in their administration although it is not apparent that they deliberately excluded them either. They simply relied on recruiting those who were best suited to their purpose, predominantly those trained in Christian mission schools. In contrast to the situation in northern Nigeria where, from the start, the British had positively cosseted Islam, their attitude in East Africa was generally to leave it to its own devices.

Education

In general, the education provided by the colonial administrations was a hindrance to Islam rather than a help. It was primarily secular but being often dispensed by Christian missionaries it was inseparable from some degree of proselytising. From the standpoint of present-day Islamic fundamentalists, colonial education is now perceived as having been a deliberate strategy aimed at destroying Islam.[22] A more realistic assessment is that the colonial authorities – at any rate the British and the Germans – simply introduced an education system designed to serve their own, largely secular needs, without any deliberate intention to influence Islam one way or the other. It was the Muslims' own, understandable, reluctance to receive such an education, and not their deliberate exclusion from it, that largely accounts for the disability they subsequently suffered, when independence found them disadvantaged against the better-educated Christians. But whatever may have been the underlying intention of the colonial educators, there is no doubt that secular anglophone education corroded the sacerdotal Arabic literacy of Islam by rendering it obsolete for everyday purposes.

The separation of government and religion

The threat to Islam was not merely that secular education led either to the emergence of a class of secularised Muslims or a Christian elite. A deeper factor was also at work. Religion and politics are inseparable in Islam; so, too, are religion and government. The sultan is both an administrator and the guardian of the moral integrity of the Islamic state. The *qāḍī*, the Muslim magistrate, presides over the administration of a religious law. But the colonial administrators, following a pattern that had become firmly established throughout the Western world at this time, at once separated religion and administration. Thus Muslims, Christians and pagans were governed indifferently according to a secular civil code. Islamic law was not usually abandoned entirely in those areas where Islam was entrenched since such Muslim communities were usually allowed some autonomy in the law of personal status and, in some circumstances, even in Islamic criminal law. But the *Sharī'a* ceased to be universal, as it had been under the writ of the old sultanates. Islam is a seamless cloak. Such rents in its fabric damaged it sorely. A consequence of this, which was widespread across East Africa, was that the custodianship of Islam passed more and more out of the hands of the traditional Muslim ruling hierarchy – the sultan, the *qaḍīs* and the *imāms* – and passed into those of the leaders of the *Ṣūfī ṭuruq*. These people were traditionally unburdened by administrative duties of state, their role being wholly devotional, mystical and thaumaturgic. It was to them that the East African Muslims now turned increasingly, for their education and for moral and, even on occasions, political support. To an extent, therefore, their influence tended to make it even more difficult for the Muslims to adjust to the increasingly secular environment that encroached upon them as a result of the colonial occupations.

Another consequence of the separation between religion and government was that, in some situations, it encouraged a return to ancient tribal divisions. The concept of the Islamic *umma*, the universal Islamic community, is one the power of which should not be underestimated. There is no doubt that the medieval sultanates did bind people of different ethnic and social origins together by a common religious and cultural bond – even if slavery did lie at the root of this process. When this was broken down by the colonial administrations, there was a tendency for tribalism to reassert itself. Consequently, Islam under the colonial regimes tended to lose the universalist characteristics conferred upon it by the *umma*. It became increasingly particularist, identified with specific tribes and areas. It was a long time before the new concepts introduced by the colonialists – first that of imperial commonwealth and subsequently that of independent nation-state – replaced the ancient one of the Islamic *umma*. Present-day Islamic radicals argued with much evidence to support them, that in the hearts of the Muslim masses, as opposed to their supine modernist rulers, they never have.

ISLAM IN THE NEW NATION-STATES OF EAST AFRICA (*C.* 1961 TO THE PRESENT DAY)

As in the case of West Africa, so also in that of East Africa, independence produced a proliferation of nation-states.

Kenya

Kenya, the first East African country to gain independence in 1961, was historically that part of the littoral and its hinterland dominated by the medieval trading town of Mombaṣa. It thus inherited a strong Swahili Islamic culture along the coast while its Northern Frontier Province encompassed nomadic Muslim Somalis. Some Muslims were also to be found inland, around Lake Victoria, brought there by the thirteenth/nineteenth-century ivory trade. Although the British allowed the Kenyan Muslims a measure of autonomy in their laws, Christian missionaries were also most active in Kenya, especially in the field of education. Despite some attempts at Islamic revivalism, the Kenyan Muslims entered independence at a disadvantage to the African, mission-educated Christians.

The Mau Mau rebellion of 1952–60 placed the Kenyan Muslims in a dilemma. They could hardly side with Mau Mau pagans any more than they could identify themselves with European colonialists. Most therefore simply stood aside. Under Kenyatta's rule as President the Muslims were left alone to regulate their own affairs; but after his death, secular and Christian opinion gained ground. The Law of Succession Bill, which Kenyatta had largely ignored, was reactivated and both tribal custom and Islamic law were made subservient to the secular code. The result has been an increasingly pronounced division between Kenyan Muslims and Christians, especially Christian secularists, and a rise in Islamic activism.

This situation has also drawn in certain Islamic superpowers, for example Saudi Arabia and Iran who compete for the allegiance of Kenya's Muslims through propaganda and fund Islamic activism there.

Estimates of the proportion of Kenyans who are Muslims vary from certain optimistic Islamic sources, which claim thirty per cent or more,[23] to more sober estimates that put the Muslims at not more than six per cent.[24] Such estimates are almost certainly too conservative. The probability is that Islam in Kenya is both expanding numerically and becoming more militant under the influence of the wider Islamic fundamentalist movement.

Zimbabwe

Prior to the colonial era, Zimbabwe comprised a medieval African kingdom with its capital at Great Zimbabwe. Both Muslims and Portuguese penetrated into this kingdom and left mixed-blood communities of Muslims and Christians behind them. These were, however, largely wiped out by the pagan Africans in the seventeenth and eighteenth centuries AD. Islam then almost died out. It has subsequently been represented by an African people, the Varemba, who display evidence of early contacts with Islam that have coloured their culture but who certainly cannot be regarded as fully Muslim. Some Yaos are also present in Zimbabwe. Their Islam is firmer than that of the Varemba. They are strict *Sunnīs* of the Mālikī rite.

There is also a community of Indo-Pakistani Muslims in Zimbabwe who are *Sunnīs* of the Hanafī rite. They have been responsible for the building of many mosques and for other welfare activities. Both the Indo-Pakistanis and the Yao Muslims are engaged in an attempt to win back the Varemba to full Islam. In this they enjoy the financial and propaganda assistance of the Saudi Arabians and the Libyans. The official figure for the Muslim presence in Zimbabwe is less than one per cent, though this figure begs the question as to whether the Varemba are to be regarded as Muslims or animists.

Uganda

Since Uganda has no coastline, it did not partake of the Swahili culture of the Middle Ages, instead owing its Islamic contacts to the establishment of trade links with the coast in the mid-nineteenth century AD. It thereupon became a cockpit for a struggle between Muslim traders, French Roman Catholics and British Protestants for the allegiance of the *kabakas*, the traditional rulers of the Bugandas. The Protestants, with their greater resources, won and the territory was subsequently largely converted to Christianity. As elsewhere, the Muslims have been disadvantaged by their reluctance to avail themselves of secular education, dispensed mainly by Christian missionaries. During the era of Idi Amin, ruler of Uganda from 1971 to 1979, the Muslims improved their position somewhat but suffered a setback in the aftermath.

There is a significant community of Indian Muslims in Uganda, who are Ismā'īlī followers of the Agha Khan. Despite the latter's substantial welfare programme for the benefit of the whole Muslim community, much tension exists between the African population – Muslim and non-Muslim alike – and these Indian Muslims. This tension, caused by the Indians' greater prosperity compared with Africans, came to a head during Idi Amin's regime.

Muslims as at 1984 made up 6.6 per cent of the total population. Muslim sources claim that Islam is expanding at the expense of indigenous animism. On the other hand, Islamic values and culture appear to be increasingly at risk from the new technological and secular environment that Ugandan modernists now seek to promote. Thus Islam wins on the animist side but loses in the contest with secular modernism.

Tanganyika

The territory known until 1964 as Tanganyika is geographically the littoral and hinterland dominated during the Arab–Persian, Portuguese and Ottoman periods by the offshore islands of Pemba and Zanzibar, and by Kilwa. Islam along the coast is therefore of ancient origin. It had led to the development of a strong Swahili Islamic culture there long before the colonial era, though the penetration of this culture inland occurred only after *c.* 1298/1880, when Arab traders along Lake Victoria spread Islam among the local Yaos.

As German East Africa, the territory was the location of the well-known 'Meccan Letter' incident. The German authorities of the day became aware, *c.* 1908, of a letter purporting to come from Mecca, that was circulating among the African population and causing considerable unrest. It contained inflammatory material of a messianic tenor and urged the Muslims to rise up against their infidel oppressors. The Germans took alarm and they adopted stern measures including execution of ringleaders to suppress the unrest this letter excited. In the end, it was traced back, not to Mecca but to a certain Muhammad b. Khalfan al-Barwani, known as 'Rumaliza'. This person was a Zanzibari ivory and slave trader whose profitable activities had been disturbed under German rule. He had forged the Meccan Letter – or had it forged – and circulated in the hope of arousing a mahdist *jihād* to drive the Germans out.

While Islam is now strictly observed among the Swahili speakers of the coast, inland it is less so, to the extent that Schildknecht has referred to the 'bantuization' of Islam, a phenomenon similar to the 'mixing' described in the West African case and universally characteristic of 'Islam-on-the-fringes'.[25] Pilgrimage to Mecca is often beyond the means of these inland Muslims. They turn instead for expression of their beliefs to the *Ṣūfī* orders, which have flourished in a modest fashion in this area.

There also grew up a substantial community of Asian – mainly Indian – Muslims in Tanganyika. As elsewhere in East Africa, their social and racial exclusiveness works to their disadvantage, while their conspicuous prosperity gives rise to fierce African resentment. This is unfortunately not mitigated by the major contribution to the economy that they make or by their generosity in mosque-building and other welfare projects.

As elsewhere in East Africa, the African Muslims of Tanganyika suffered, *vis-à-vis* the Christians and secularists, as a consequence of their unwillingness to embrace anglophone, secular education. To some extent their disadvantageous position has been ameliorated by the recent interest in Tanganyika (now Tanzania) of the Islamic superpowers. These now provide bursaries for the education of Muslims in overseas Islamic centres. They also circulate propaganda and news of events in the wider Islamic world, in an attempt to encourage the extension of Islam.

Present-day Tanzania, the successor state to Tanganyika, or more accurately the government of Julius Nyerere, has incurred odium in the Islamic world for its enforced union of Zanzibar and Tanganyika, to form Tanzania. This is regarded by most Muslims as having wilfully destroyed the ancient Islamic identity of Zanzibar. The proportion of Muslims in Tanzania in 1984 is given as 32.2 per cent.

Zanzibar

The early history of Zanzibar is obscure. There is some evidence that Muslims may have been present there as early as 500/1106–7 and that their presence continued into the seventh/thirteenth century.[26] But they may have been there under the patronage of local African rulers.

By the eighth/fourteenth century Zanzibar was clearly a Muslim settlement subject to the ruling Shīrāzī dynasty in Kilwa. By the following century it had become an independent Islamic sultanate. It was taken over by the 'Umānīs during the eleventh/seventeenth century, to become the capital of the 'Umānī empire and the main trading centre of the Indian Ocean.

After a colonial interlude in which it passed through German and British hands, it became, in 1963, an independent Islamic state under its own Muslim sultan. In 1964 the sultan was overthrown as a consequence of popular African distrust of the 'Umānī elite which he represented, and the 'People's Republic of Zanzibar' was set up. Shortly after, as a result of a violent campaign involving troops from Tanganyika led by the notorious John Okello, it was joined by an Act of Union with Tanganyika, to form the 'United Republic of Tanzania'.

Muslim opinion generally insists that this union was imposed on the Muslims of Zanzibar by Nyerere, a militant Christian, and his henchman, Okello, against the will of the Zanzibari people, and that it has been followed by a deliberate campaign to extinguish the Islamic character of Zanzibar under a secularist constitution. The Tanganyikans have their own, exculpatory version of their action.[27]

While it is true that tension has long existed between the African population of Zanzibar and their 'Umānī overlords, there is little doubt that the Tanganyikan take-over has been greatly resented in the Islamic world at large, as well as by most Zanzibari Muslims. Such actions on the part of the Tanganyikans as the establishment of a brewery there, seem particularly provocative.

To some extent the demands of the Zanzibari Muslims for the restoration of their autonomy have been conceded since the initial union took place. None the less, it is clear that, for better or for worse, the union of this former, almost exclusively Muslim island of Zanzibar with a mainland nation-state that has been traditionally pagan and Christian, and is now increasingly secularised, has gravely damaged the ancient Islamic culture of that island.

Mozambique

When the Portuguese were evicted from all their possessions north of Cape Delgado they maintained a footing in the territory of Mozambique and formally declared it part of Portuguese India in AD 1751. In the late nineteenth century AD Mozambique became part of Portuguese East Africa and then an overseas province of Portugal in 1951. By this time the Muslim population consisted of the coastal Muslims, firm in the Faith, substantial Muslim communities in the north of the hinterland and inland tribal elements more or less tinged with Islam but still largely animist.

An independence movement, the Frente de Libertação de Moçambique (FRELIMO) was formed in 1968, which engaged in armed resistance to the colonial power. Independence was gained in 1975. This resulted in a Marxist one-party state, which immediately provoked armed opposition. A civil war has been fought, on and off, since that time. The situation of the Muslims in these developments has been ambiguous. FRELIMO was dominated by an educated Marxist elite of Christian origin but hostile to all religion. Anti-Portuguese sentiment caused some Muslims to give cover to FRELIMO guerrillas but lack of representation in FRELIMO and the Muslims' hostility to the anti-religious policies of the Marxists, alienated Muslim opinion from them. As in other African civil wars where Marxism has been the revolutionary ideology, the Muslims have largely stood aside. They have suffered persecution none the less.

The true level of adherence to Islam in Mozambique is difficult to assess. It was a centre for considerable activity on the part of the Qādiriyya *ṭarīqa* during the late thirteenth–fourteenth/nineteenth century. At the present time the proportion of Muslims is generously estimated by some Muslim sources at fifty-five per cent;[28] other more sober sources estimate it at no more than thirteen per cent. Once again, the discrepancy probably turns on whether certain tribal groups that display traces of Islam but are clearly not fully converted, are to be classed as Muslims or as something else. Mozambique Muslims are said to look to the world-wide Islamic resurgence to reassert the power of Islam there. None the less, a generation of Marxism has set up powerful secularist strongholds that even Islamic fundamentalism may now find hard to breach.

Malawi

Present-day Malawi was historically part of the hinterland of Mozambique. It lay on the edge of Swahili Islam. Around 1256/1840, Muslim Swahilis, known locally as Jumbes, who were seeking ivory, set up a small Muslim enclave on the western shore of Lake Nyasa. They formed a commercial alliance with the local Yaos, who in consequence went over to Islam in substantial numbers. By *c.* 1287/1870, the Yao chief, Makanjila III, had adopted Islam. These Muslim Yaos proved to be the most tenacious opponents of the Christian missionaries who moved into the territory *c.* AD 1859, partly in an effort to suppress the slave trade, which went hand in hand with the ivory trade and upon which was based the prosperity of the Swahili Jumbes and their Yao allies. Fighting broke out between them and the forces of the African Lakes Company *c.* AD 1887. Although the Yaos were officially 'pacified' in the ensuing campaign – their economy and their social structure were destroyed, both of which were squarely based on the slave trade and the institution of slavery – they remained fiercely attached to Islam. This attachment caused them to resist strongly the Western-style education offered by the missionaries and the colonial authorities. Consequently, they became increasingly disadvantaged over against the non-Yao African Christians.

The most reliable estimate of the religious composition of the present Malawi population is: Protestant Christians fifty-five per cent, Roman Catholic Christians twenty per cent and Muslims twenty per cent.[29] However, this takes no account of an undoubtedly substantial number who claim nominal adherence to one or other of the two Abrahamic religions but in fact still remain faithful to the ancestral animism. In northern Malawi, Christianity now appears to dominate Islam. Nkhotakota is the main centre of Islam at the present time.

Congo

The present Congo was, until the end of the nineteenth century AD part of that vast African hinterland, the domain of African kingdoms untouched by Islam. The penetration of Islam there was part of the wider movement of Swahili-Arab Muslims into the interior, in search of ivory and slaves, that developed during that century. In consequence Swahili trading posts were set up, which attracted local Africans from the bush to settle. Once settled they adopted Islam not because of active proselytising on the part of the Swahilis, but by cultural contagion. These trading posts quickly assumed the character of Muslim settlements, though they seldom claimed the status of sultanates. Indeed, they often depended on the patronage of local African chiefs who shared their profits.

Prominent among these Swahili ivory traders and slavers was the notorious Aḥmad b. Muḥammad b. Juma b. al-Murjirbī, commonly known as Tippu Tip. He was originally a subject of the sultan of Zanzibar. In the course of an adventurous career, which included accompanying the British explorer Stanley into unknown territory, he set up what did amount to his own sultanate at Utetera, in the Upper Congo. For a time he enjoyed the patronage of the Belgians, who by now shared possession of the territory with the French. But this alliance with the infidel alienated other Swahili Muslim interests in the area. Fighting broke out and by 1313/1895, Tippu Tip's sultanate had dissolved into disorder. The heritage of Tippu Tip and the other Swahili-Arabs was clusters of faintly islamised Africans known as Wangwana, who peopled their settlements.

During the colonial era the Belgians, influenced by strong Catholic interests, were on the whole hostile to Islam. The Muslims were neglected, especially in the field of education. They did, however, come under the influence of *Ṣūfī shaykh*s who penetrated into the Congo during the 1930s.

The Muslims of the Congo have in recent times tended to keep their distance from the politics of that troubled state. They took no significant part in the independence struggle and were virtually ignored by Lumumba and other Congo leaders of Christian origin.

Around 1985, the Muslims amounted to a mere four per cent of the total Congo population.[30] Like other Muslim minority groups in the present East African nation-states, they are the object of external Islamic fundamentalist interest, that seeks a resurgence of Islam in black Africa.

One may sum up the situation concerning Islam in the east African nation-states as follows. Where these states have a coastline along the Indian Ocean, the anciently established Swahili–Islamic culture remains dominant along a narrow coastal strip, although inevitably, like Islam world-wide, it has to contend with the onslaught of the secular, technological culture of the day. In the interior, Islam is by and large the recent introduction of the nineteenth-century ivory and slave trade, and of Muslim communities of mainly Indian origin who migrated into these areas during the colonial period. Muslim minorities have to compete both with animists and with better-educated Christians and secularists. A characteristic of these inland areas is the partially islamised culture of animist groups that have failed to convert fully to Islam. Apart from anything else, these groups tend to distort statistics purporting to describe the religious composition of the East African nation-states.

All these East African nation-states have recently attracted the attention of Islamic superpowers: Saudi Arabia, Libya, Iran, et al., as well as international Islamic revivalist movements, all of whom hope to promote a revival of Islam in black Africa, but who frequently compete with each other to their common disadvantage. It would be imprudent to predict what the outcome of such revivalist initiatives may be, but they have certainly received a considerable boost as a result of the collapse of world-wide communism. This is seen by the Muslims as the demise of *kufr*, materialistic unbelief.

ISLAM IN SOUTH AFRICA (AD 1652 TO THE PRESENT DAY)

Cape Coloureds et al.

Islam in South Africa is a different phenomenon from Islam along the East African littoral, which may be regarded as giving way to the coastline of the Cape just south of Maputo (Lourenço Marques). There were no medieval settlements of Arabs or Persians along that coastline. Apart from certain faintly islamised animist groups that drifted in from Mozambique from the middle of the twelfth/eighteenth century, the Lemba and the Balemba, South African Islam is the direct consequence of the importation by the Dutch settlers of AD 1652, of Malays, Javanese and some Bengalis, from the Dutch East Indies. Many of these people had been converted to Islam by Arab traders as from the eighth/fourteenth century. They now brought their Islam with them and were settled by the Dutch in and around Cape Town, *c.* AD 1694. They are therefore frequently known as 'Cape Coloureds'.

Some 200 years later, another wave, this time of Indian labourers and shopkeepers, entered South Africa. Many were Muslims. Their settlement was more dispersed than that of the Cape Coloureds. They tend to be most numerous around Durban and East Natal.

The early Cape Coloureds were largely shut off from outside Islamic contacts. The building of the Suez Canal, finished in 1869 later gave them easier access to Mecca, for Pilgrimage which stimulated a programme of mosque-building and Islamic revivalism in and around Cape Town.

The Indian Muslim community has fared better because of its links with the Ismāʿīlī Muslims of East Africa, which brings them the patronage of the Agha Khan. As elsewhere in Africa, these Indian Muslims are highly exclusive. They do not normally mix with the

Cape Coloureds, nor do they mix with the faintly islamised Lemba and Balemba. South African Muslim intellectuals on both sides of the ethnic divide are, however, now endeavouring to overcome this and, in particular, are engaged in a campaign to draw the Lemba and Balemba more closely into full Islamic observance. Surprisingly, in view of their historically disadvantageous social and political status, the 'Malays' or Cape Coloureds have made a significant contribution to Afrikaans culture. Many of their words have found their way into the Afrikaans lexicon. They have also influenced South African food habits.

A new hermeneutics of the Koran

One of the most interesting aspects of Islam in South Africa is the manner in which African Muslim intellectuals there are endeavouring to reinterpret Islam in the light of the overarching apartheid issue. This tendency is strongly reminiscent of Christian 'Liberation Theology', and takes as its text the several verses of the Koran that refer to *al-mustaḍʿafūn*, 'the weak' or 'downtrodden' in its various grammatical forms (Koran 8:26; 4:98 and *passim*). It attempts to impose a new hermeneutics upon these verses in such a way as to refer them to the issue of apartheid, in a manner favourable to the South African blacks. This notion is pursued further when the Koranic Ibrāhīm (Abraham) is made symbolic of the abandonment of family and particular tribe for the sake of a wider, common identity within an Islam held to be at one with the anti-racist ideology.

The next stage of this hermeneutical declension turns on *Sūra* 28, *al-Qiṣaṣ*, 'The narrative' [of Moses and the Exodus], where Pharaoh of Koran 28:4 symbolises the perceived 'white racists' while 28:5–6 is taken to be divine assurance of victory for the African nationalists. Furthermore, what these Muslims regard as the 'liberation' of Meccan society from the postulated tyranny of the pre-Islamic Meccan establishment (in fact, its offence appears to have been its wish to continue in its ancestral cult and its determination to protect its markets) is radicalised to fit the South African context in a manner that flatters the mandatory progressivist and anti-racist requirement.

One may question whether such ancient, decontextualised scriptural references can be successfully adapted to fit modern socio-political contexts – and even whether the attempt to do so is morally honest. None the less, there is no denying the intellectual agility of this new hermeneutical gymnastic of the South African Muslims.[31]

NOTES

1. Oliver (ed.), vol. 3, p. 192, citing al-Mas'ūdī's *Murūj al-dhahab.*
2. Ibid., p. 192.
3. Brice, William C., ed. cit., Bibl., pp. 8Ce and 11Ce.
4. Oliver (ed.), vol. 3, p. 192.
5. Al-Idrīsī's map can be consulted in Brice, ed. cit., p. 1.
6. Ibid., p. 1.
7. Oliver (ed.), vol. 3, p. 190, f.n. 1.
8. Gibb, op. cit., Bibl., p. 112.
9. Oliver (ed.), vol. 3, p. 220, f.n. 1.
10. Chittick, ibid., pp. 201–4, gives a detailed account of the founding of the Shirāzī dynasty and of the local traditions associated with this.
11. Gibb, op. cit., p. 112.
12. Oliver (ed.), vol. 3, p. 205.
13. Gibb, p. 112. For 'Yufi' one should read 'Zambezi' in the light of present-day research.
14. Ibid., p. 379.
15. See Map 1 and J. E. G. Sutton's recent seminar paper cited in Bibl., and the bibliography he gives.
16. See f.n. 8 above.
17. Oliver (ed.), vol. 3, p. 231.
18. Gibb, p. 112.
19. Knappert, J., 'Islamic poetry of Africa', loc. cit., Bibl.
20. Gibb, p. 112.
21. Oliver (ed.), vol. 3, p. 231.
22. See e.g. Malik N'Daiye's essay 'Nationalism as an Instrument of Cultural Imperialism – A Case Study of French West Africa' in M. Ghayasuddin (ed.), Bibl., for an example of this Muslim argument.
23. See for instance Mzee Abdullah, 'Pope visits Africa to boost Roman Catholic minority' in Kalim Siddiqui (ed.), *Issues in the Islamic Movement 1985–1986 (1405–1406)*, Bibl., p. 43.
24. See Rabiatu Ammah, loc. cit., Bibl., p. 18. *The Cambridge Encyclopedia* (1990) s.v. Kenya gives Christianity 66 per cent and local beliefs 26 per cent, thus leaving the Muslims no more than 8 per cent.
25. In Kritzeck and Lewis (eds), p. 241.
26. See Knappert's 'A Short History of Zanzibar' in *Annales Aequatoria*, 13 (1992), p. 17.
27. What purports to be the general Muslim consensus is set out by Kettani, M. Ali, loc. cit., *Journal of the Institute of Muslim-Minority Affairs*, 4/1 and 2, pp. 104–19; see also Siddiqui (ed.), *Issues 1983–1984*, pp. 83–4, 160–3 and 198–9. The Tanzanian government's view is set out in Omari., loc. cit., Sicard (ed.), *BICMURA*, 2/2, 1984 (see Bibl. under Omari).
28. See for instance Iqbal Asaria's essay 'Back seat for Muslims in Mozambique' in Kalim Siddiqui (ed.), *Issues 1981–1982*, p. 299.
29. Crystal, David (ed.), *The Cambridge Encyclopedia*, 1990, s. v. Malawi. Rabiatu Ammah, loc. cit., citing figures relating to *c.* 1980, gives a smaller figure of 16.2 per cent for the Muslims.
30. Ammah, Rabiatu, loc. cit., p. 17.
31. I am indebted to C. du P. le Roux's informative article cited in Bibl., for the information on this issue given above, although the presentation and comments are my own.

7

African Islamic Literatures

The foregoing account has considered the political, social and theological expressions of Islam in Africa, but there is another aspect that has so far been touched on only briefly – the emergence of Islamic literatures in African languages. These literatures provide an accurate guide, if not always to the chronology of Islamic penetration, at least to the depth to which Islam has entered into the host societies.

CLASSICAL ARABIC LITERATURE OF AFRICAN ORIGIN

As Knappert points out in his study of the Islamic poetry of Africa,[1] there are two levels of Islamic literature in African Islam. First, there is the scholarly level of the learned African *'ulamā'* who write in classical Arabic. This literature is not essentially different from its counterpart anywhere in Islam. At first much of it was copied directly from existing sources, by way of extracts, summaries and the like. Later, the African *'ulamā'* began to compose original works in classical Arabic in which they attempted to interpret the *Sharī'a* in the light of African conditions; and to explain Islamic theology against the background of prevailing African animism. Typical of such endeavours are the works of the thirteenth/nineteenth-century Fulānī scholars of Hausaland studied in Chapter 4 above.[2] Local historical chronicling was another literary activity undertaken in classical Arabic that was widely practised in both West Africa and East Africa during the Middle Ages.[3]

VERNACULAR WRITTEN LITERATURES

Arising from this indigenous classical Arabic tradition there developed a vernacular tradition of African Islamic literature, composed in one or other of the major African languages – Swahili, Fulfulde, Hausa and so on. It is of two kinds: literature that was written down and literature that remained an oral tradition.

The main written vernacular literatures are those in Swahili, Fulfulde, Hausa, Harari – a language of the Ethiopian Muslims – and the Berber dialect Zenaga. In each of these cases the literatures required the development of forms of the Arabic script modified to a greater or lesser extent according to the phonetic requirements of the language. In the Hausa case, this modified script was known as *ajami*, from Arabic '' J M', 'foreign'. It came to be widely used by others as well as the Hausas to describe the use of the Arabic script to record languages other than Arabic. Various rough and ready diacritical marks were invented, in addition to those already existing in classical Arabic, to serve the phonetic needs of particular African tongues.

The dates at which these *ajami* scripts and the literatures they record first emerged are uncertain. Paper perishes rapidly in the African climate and in the conditions under which it was stored during the Middle Ages. Knappert traces the first extant written literature in Swahili back to *c.* 1062/1652.[4] Written Islamic literature in Zenaga, a language of the Saharan Berbers, can be traced back to *c.* 1112/1700, although it may be much older.[5] A written literature in Fulfulde is likely to have arisen somewhat later, in the twelfth/eighteenth century, perhaps under the influence of neighbouring Zenaga.[6] Hausa written literature is reputed to have emerged later still, during the thirteenth/nineteenth century, as part of the process of drawing the Hausa peasantry more closely into Islam, that gathered pace after the successful *jihād* in Hausaland during the early years of that century.[7] Harari written Islamic literature is limited to the town of Harar, in eastern Ethiopia, which is the main centre of Islam in that otherwise largely Christian area. Being a Semitic language, Harari is easily written in the Arabic script, and some existing manuscripts can be dated back to *c.* 1060/1650.[8]

Content and format of the vernacular written Islamic literatures

The major vernacular Islamic literatures – Swahili, Zenaga, Fulfulde and Hausa – share certain characteristics of content and format. They are mainly in verse, Fulfulde and Hausa entirely so. Their content is drawn in the first instance from the Koran and *tafsīr*, that is classical Arabic commentary upon that scripture. They consist typically of descriptions of divine punishment and reward (Hausa *wa'azi*, Swahili *waadhi*, both from Arabic *wa'ẓ*, 'warning', 'admonition'). Frequent in this category are poems about *dunyā* (Arabic 'world'), which are Islamic *memento mori*. They personify the world as a painted harlot, or a fractious mare that throws her rider. The poet dwells on the transitory nature of worldly pleasures and on the untrustworthiness of the world. Equally popular in all these vernacular written Islamic literatures is a category known in Hausa as *madahu* (Arabic *madh* or *madīh*, 'panegyric'). In Swahili it is usually described as *kasida* (Arabic *qaṣīda*, 'ode'). This comprises praise to the Prophet Muhammad that closely follows the imagery and content of such classical Arabic verse compositions as the *Burda*, the *'Ishrīniyya* and other classical Arabic panegyrics to the Prophet Muhammad described in the context of North African Sufism in Chapter 1 of this book (pp. 35–7). Such vernacular panegyric is closely associated with the spread of popular Sufism in African Islam, both west and east. Equally popular in both traditions are poems written to celebrate the Prophet's birthday (Arabic *mawlid*). Instructional poems, to teach the people the elements of Islamic theology, are also frequent as too are works on Islamic astrology.

But perhaps the most popular category of all, at any rate in Swahili and Hausa, are poems celebrating the Prophet's *isrā'*, his miraculous night journey from Mecca to Jerusalem upon the mythical riding beast al-Burāqa, described in Chapter 1 above, and his subsequent *mi'rāj*, 'ascension', through the seven heavens to the throne of Allah. Such poems abound in both Hausa and Swahili. They are often remarkably close to one another in sequence and imagery, which suggests that both arise from a common classical Arabic prototype. The following are some examples of the themes, or genres in several African languages that illustrate their common Islamic origins. First is an instructional poem in Islamic theology, composed *c.* 1211/1797 and translated from Zenaga:

> I have beseeched my God who is my Lord,
> Who reigns eternal, who lives without need,
> Omnipresent, He owns unmeasured space.
> Devoid of form He needs no attribute ...[9]

Here is another example of a theological poem, this time from Hausa, which dates from *c.* 1950:

> The Lord God is One, the Unique,
> Wherever you seek Him you will find Him.
> Say, He, Allah, is One,
> Allah is He on whom all depend,
> He begets not nor is He begotten,
> And there is none like Him[10]

Here is an example of *madīh*, panegyric to the Prophet, based on the classical Arabic *Burdah* mentioned in Chapter 1, but composed in Fulfulde:

> More shining than all the pearls or rubies is Muḥammad,
> More beauty than all the gold or silver has Muḥammad,
> More splendour than all the moonshine or sunlight has
>   Muḥammad,
> More sweetness than the purest honey has Muḥammad,
> More quenching for the thirst than water is Muḥammad.[11]

Here is another example of *madīh*, this time from Hausa:

> Heaven is loftly but you know it does not reach
> So high as to equal the glory of Muḥammad,
> The throne of heaven is beneath him in respect of glory
> ...

His light exceeds the light of the moon on the fourteenth day of
the month,
Because there is no light like the light of Muḥammad.[12]

The following is an example, from Hausa verse, of the *mi'rāj* story, described above, in which the Prophet ascends to heaven in the company of the Angel Jibrīl (Gabriel):

In the night, on a Monday Gabriel came to Aḥmad,
He said 'The King greets you, He is calling,
You are to mount al-Burāqa, O Prophet Muḥammad.
...
At the farthest lote tree Gabriel stopped,
And Muḥammad said, 'O Gabriel, do you leave me here alone?'
Gabriel said, 'O trustworthy one, Muḥammad,
Do not fear, you shall not fear today'.
...
Then he crossed screens and rivers of light,
And he came before the King who had created Muḥammad,
...
He went to heaven and returned to Mecca in one hour,
His wife Khadīja had not turned in her sleep before he alighted,
Aḥmad.[13]

The same *mi'rāj* story is equally popular in Swahili where, as Knappert points out, its final episode is often that of the Prophet's death.[14] This takes the form of a final ascent, again in the company of Gabriel, to Paradise, which rehearses the lifetime *mi'rāj*:

Thus spoke the angel to God's messenger,
'My brother, wise apostle of the Lord!
Please listen to these last words you will hear
from me while you are still alive on earth:
Come with me to my Paradise: it is home!
The birds are singing divine melodies,
The trees are all in bloom and full of flowers
of every colour that the rainbow shows
I have adorned the gardens and the paths.
The prophets of the past wait eagerly
to welcome you as soon as you arrive.[15]

Other favourite themes of Swahili and Zenaga written literature are the popular classical romances and folkloric cycles such as the romance of Banū Hilāl, the saga of Sayf b. Dhī Yazan and the Islamic version of the Alexander cycle, together with other folkloric themes mentioned in Chapter 2 above. These exist, too, in Hausa but here they appear to have been confined to the oral tradition in that language, perhaps because paper in the western Sudan was scarce and expensive and was therefore reserved for recording didactic religious material.

The strong similarity in content and format that exists across the written vernacular Islamic literatures of Africa testifies to the depth to which Islam has penetrated into the life-style of the people, who still cherish these literatures to the present day; and to the remarkable evenness with which Islamic mainstream culture has imposed itself upon what were originally diverse indigenous African societies ranging from cattle nomads to primitive agriculturalists and hunter-gatherers.

MANDE, SONGHAY AND SOMALI

These three languages never developed written vernacular Islamic literatures. Each language community had a strong tradition of local writing in classical Arabic, that is to say Mande, Songhay and Somali *ʿulamāʾ* have long composed their tracts and their chronicles in that language and have recorded them in the Arabic script. But they failed to adapt that script to producing such literature on any significant scale in their ancestral tongues. There may be many reasons for this – and different ones in each case. One may be the ancientness of Islamic contacts and the subsequent fading of popular Islam before its literary influence reached the point where a written vernacular literature was needed. This seems to apply in the Mande case. For in Mali, where this language was spoken, a small Muslim scholarly elite arose, that presided over a much larger community where Islam was faint and seriously diluted with surviving animism. There seems to have been insufficient middle ground to nurture a popular written Islamic literature. The popular literature remained entirely oral – the province of *griots*. It certainly exhibits Islamic influences, particularly echoes of the heroic Islamic folklore cycles. But these are little more than tinges and traces. They testify to the faint Islam of the Mande-speaking people. They cannot be regarded as demonstrating any solid grounding of Islam among them. A similar situation is to be observed among the Songhays, typically the practitioners of mixed Islam during the Middle Ages. Here again a learned elite centred around the university mosque of Timbuktu, dispensed a classical Islamic learning that seems to have established no more than a patchy hold over the commonalty.

Another factor in both these cases may have been the absence of a powerful reform movement. As was pointed out above (pp. 110–111), both the Fulanis and the Hausas experienced such a reform movement during the twelfth/eighteenth and thirteenth/nineteenth centuries. This drive towards Islamic reform or revivalism was a strong incentive to creating a didactic vernacular literature available to the common people, a thrust similar, perhaps, to that which set off the pamphleteering of the Christian Reformation in sixteenth-century Europe and the Methodist evangelical movement in England in the eighteenth century AD. Of course the common people of Africa were largely non-literate and most of them could not read the Arabic script even when it recorded their mother tongues. But they could understand it when it was read to them by those who could read that script. Had the message been read to them in classical Arabic, it would of course have been incomprehensible to them. There is, therefore, little doubt that a strong movement of Islamic reform or revivalism was a spur to the production of vernacular written literatures in Africa while its absence discouraged the emergence of such literature. Although the Mande and Songhay-speaking people did experience jihād in the nineteenth century AD, it went less deep than in the case of the Hausas and Fulari.

In the Somali case full Islam was the ancient possession of a small circle of *ʿulamāʾ* often trained in Mecca. Beyond their circle Islam was in many cases somewhat nominal, perhaps no more than the allegiance in name of the clan chief. Moreover, the Somalis were nomads. Despite its romantic nomadic associations diligently fostered by certain ruling Islamic lineages such as the Saudis, Islam tends to sink deeper roots among townsmen and villagers than it does among pastoralists.

One should also mention the Yorubas of West Africa, a people who have evolved a long tradition of African statehood of their own which is based on an indigenous African religion and owes nothing to Islam. They were, however, situated on the edge of the empire of Mali and some were influenced by the medieval Islamic influences flowing from that Islamic state. Later, in the fourteenth/nineteenth century, a Yoruba Islamic emirate emerged as a breakaway state from the old pagan Yoruba empire. The result has been that certain Yoruba *ʿulamāʾ* have been prolific composers in classical Arabic, yet in this case too no significant vernacular written Islamic literature developed. The Muslim Yorubas have evolved an oral tradition of Islamic origin and there are certain Islamic traces in Yoruba oral literature but these are faint and have in no way extinguished the pre-existing, non-Islamic culture of this literature.[16]

NOTES

1. 'The Islamic poetry of Africa', *Journal for Islamic Studies* No 10, 1990.
2. See Sulaiman Musa, 'The Main Objectives of the Literary Works of

Shaykh 'Uthman b. Fudi', CSIC Papers No 9, September, 1992, Centre for the Study of Islam and Christian–Muslim Relations, Selly Oak Colleges, Birmingham, who lists the Arabic works of this Muslim reformer.

3. For instance the tenth/sixteenth-century Timbuktu chronicler Aḥmad Baba (see Oliver (ed.) vol. 3, p. 92 and *passim*) and the Borno chronicler Ibn Fartuwa of the same century (ibid., p. 292). See also ibid., p. 417 for an account of Arabic scholarship in Timbuktu during the tenth/sixteenth century.
4. Loc. cit., p. 134.
5. Ibid., p. 105.
6. Ibid., p. 112.
7. See Hiskett, 1975 for a comprehensive study of the history of Hausa vernacular verse.
8. Knappert, loc. cit., pp. 109–10.
9. Ibid., p. 105.
10. Muhammad Sani Aliyu, 'Shortcomings in Hausa Society as Seen by Representative Hausa Islamic Poets from *ca*. 1950 to *ca*. 1982', MA dissertation, Bayero University, 1983, p. 6.
11. Knappert, loc. cit., p. 117.
12. Hiskett, 1975, p. 45.
13. Ibid., pp. 54–5.
14. 'The Mawlid', *Orientalia Lovanensia Periodica*, 19, 1988.
15. Knappert, *Handbook of Swahili literature*, New York, 1992, p. 92.
16. See Hiskett, 1984, pp. 112–15 for a more extensive study of Yoruba Islamic tradition.

8

Reflections and Uncertainties

To attempt to reach conclusions concerning Islam across Africa, from the Mediterranean to the Indian Ocean, is like peering into a kaleidoscope. No sooner does one pattern emerge than a thought, a forgotten factor or a sudden reservation intervenes and the whole pattern changes. The purpose of this chapter is therefore not to offer firm conclusions; there are none. It is simply to review certain outstanding aspects, and then to pose questions that the reader may attempt to answer for him or herself.

The triumph of the Christians?

The Muslims had a fixed and perhaps rather wooden view of the European colonialists as 'Christians'. Yet it is remarkable that, from Tangier to Maputo, these Christians, for all their fire-power and organisation, and the physical domination this brought them over the Muslims, did not succeed in shaking by one iota the Islamic faith of the millions of Muslims they governed. Indeed, whatever the Islamic fundamentalists may now aver to the contrary, it is questionable whether the British and the Germans, at any rate, ever wanted to. Be that as it may, there were no mass movements of Muslims over to Christianity. The Christian missionaries, for all their zeal, beat their heads against a brick wall as far as the Muslims were concerned. This is a most eloquent testimony to the strength of Islam, and to the hold it continues to exert over the Faithful even in the most adverse circumstances.

But it also raises another question. Were the Muslims right to regard their conquerors as 'Christians'? Or was this simply a medieval notion to which they clung too long? Would they have achieved a fuller understanding of their own plight if they had recognised at once that they were not, in fact, challenged by Christianity in the way that their forefathers had been challenged by Christian Crusaders, but by a new phenomenon: post-Christian secularism? If so, the fact that the Christian missionaries got nowhere is beside the point, for they, too, were fighting ancient, anachronistic battles. What does matter is to what extent the Muslims have succumbed, not to Christianity but to what the colonists really brought in their baggage trains: secular pluralism that confronted the transcendental unitarianism of Islam. That opens up a very different story.

Islamic theocracy at bay

When one surveys the course of Islam in Africa, one is impressed by the power of what Dr Hasan Askari has deftly termed 'the long-forgotten dimension of eschatology' – forgotten that is by the West but not by Islam.[1] For throughout Islamic Africa, from the North African *Ṣūfīs* and marabouts of the fifth/eleventh century, through Aḥmad Grañ in East Africa during the tenth/sixteenth century to the thirteenth/nineteenth-century *jihād* of the Fulani in Hausaland, and the *Mahdiyya* in the Nilotic Sudan, Muslims have appealed to transcendental, not man-made values in order to determine the nature of the political system under which men should live. They are, of course, not wholly unique in this. Menelik II's campaigns of the late nineteenth century AD in Ethiopia demonstrated an equal eschatological fury of a Christian kind. But Professor Askari is surely correct when he suggests that the eschatological dimension is, by and large, no longer a major political determinant in the secular West.

The current resurgence of Islamic theocracy, on the other hand, is simply a present-day appeal to the medieval values of eschatology. It clearly seemed to many observers *c.* 1960 that a number of new-fangled ideologies – nationalism, socialism, modernism – had finally triumphed over traditional Islam to the extent of reducing it from a total way of life to a mere cultural memory. Yet such a view has proved to be badly awry. In Algeria, Islamic theocracy has risen again, after a mere thirty years. All that now prevents it from asserting itself is the power of the gun; it is questionable how long that will be effective. Elsewhere in North Africa the reassertion of Islamic theocracy has been less emphatic. But there is no doubt that powerful forces are at work, in an attempt to restore it, that become progressively more threatening.

In Nigeria the thrust for a full Islamic theocracy has been such that the Federal government has been forced increasingly to break up the artificial entity known as Nigeria, into an increasing number of largely autonomous states, in an attempt to forestall this. One feels it is only the considerable strength of the Nigerian Christian minority, and the presence of the military constantly in the background, that blocks the Muslim theocratic drive. In Mali, Mauritania and elsewhere in the West African hinterland, powerful Toureg separatist forces struggle with the same end in view (see Map 6).

In East Africa the thrust towards Islamic theocracy is muted, owing to the fragmented nature of Islam in that area and the considerable Christian and pagan resistance to it. None the less, it gathers pace, fuelled by funds and propaganda from the world-wide Islamic *umma*.

But perhaps the most startling triumph of all for Islamic theocracy in tropical Africa is to be found in the Nilotic Sudan. All the early chatter about Sudanese nationalism, and the barely concealed aspirations in some quarters of the British Sudan Education Service that they could engineer a strain of Islam that leaned more towards *The New Statesman* than to the Koran, have become sand in the wind. After some thirty years of deplorably ineffective democratic government punctuated by military *coups*, the Sudanese, with General al-Bashir at their head, with the *Sharī'a* firmly restored as the law of the land and with al-Turabi's Sudan Charter as their banner, have rekindled the fires of the *Mahdiyya* without restraint and, it would appear, without hindrance. Meanwhile, John Garang forlornly seeks help from the OAU, from Ghana and from other Christian African states, that is not forthcoming. One may ask: how far will resurgent Islamic theocracy go in Africa? And are there any countervailing forces that may yet stand in its way?

Democracy in Africa: The Muslim rejection

Dr Kalim Siddiqui, Director of the Muslim Institute, London, is also a leading spokesman for the International Islamic Movement, an Islamic fundamentalist organisation which is influential in Africa and to which prominent African Muslims belong. In a series of fierce and lucid publications he distils the universalist attitudes and principles of fundamentalist Islam. He has described democracy, together with nationalism, socialism and capitalism as 'the greatest political *kufr* [unbelief] in the modern world'.[2] Elsewhere, he argues that it cannot be held 'that because there is *shūrā* [consultation] in Islam, modern democracy is "Islamic"'.[3] On the contrary, 'the political party framework as found in western democracies is divisive of the society and therefore does not suit the *Ummah*'.[4] In another place he concludes: 'It is quite clear that one *Ummah* must mean one Islamic movement, leading to one global Islamic State under one Imam/Khalifa',[5] and he speaks scathingly of those Islamic modernists who seek to establish 'a liberal and democratic nation-state with a few cosmetic "Islamic" features'.[6] He warns that they 'must realise that their [Western] education had equipped them to serve the political, social, economic, administrative and military systems that we must destroy'.[7]

Dr Siddiqui is of course not an African but he does represent a world-wide Islamic tendency. His are surely sentiments that would be endorsed by the winning Front Islamique de Salut in Algeria, by the Islamic Tendency movement in Tunisia, by the *'Yan Izala* in Nigeria, especially such leaders of Muslim thought as 'Umar Abdullahi and Ibraheem Sulaiman and by the powerful Muslim Brotherhood in

Egypt and the Sudan. For instance, Sulaiman has written that:

> the failure of democracy once again, in the Nigerian political drama reinforces the hard truth that the attempt by Nigeria to seek to establish herself on 'the debris of Western imperialism' as Professor Abdullahi Smith puts it, is an absolutely futile exercise[8]

and in reference to the events of the immediate post-civil war period in Nigeria that:

> It should have been clear to every conscious mind ... that all past efforts to solve Nigeria's problems without reference to the sacred Sharia, and to Islam have failed.[9]

He praises the efforts of the late Nigerian Head of State Murtala Mohammed (1975–6) who 'had started to give the Shari'ah its rightful place in Nigeria'.[10] Elsewhere he writes that 'Secularism supplants the Islamic laws with those of its own and defaces the sanctity of the Muslim Society'.[11] Such sentiments are certainly echoed by the banner-waving students who repeat Siddiqui's dictum that democracy is *kufr*, and by countless dissatisfied Muslim groups elsewhere in Africa whose aspirations have not achieved the same prominence as the more spectacularly evident tendencies.

It would be unwise to underestimate the appeal, let alone the compelling logic of these arguments. With monotonous regularity, democracy in Africa has belied its early hopes and has proved to be the overture to corruption, civil war and military dictatorship. Nigeria has suffered eight military *coups*, successful and unsuccessful, since independence. The egregious Shagari administration in that country, which fell unlamented in 1983 and was replaced by that of the ferocious General Buhari, himself to fall victim to a *coup* less than two years later, must lend force to the Muslim fundamentalists' arguments. So, too, does the ugly see-saw of suborned 'democracy' and military tyranny that has bedevilled the Nilotic Sudan. Zanzibari Muslims can hardly be expected to look favourably upon a democracy that has destroyed their ancient civilisation and delivered them over to brewers and American tourists. Whatever may seem to be the rights and wrongs of the case to non-Muslim observers, Saharan Touregs cannot be expected to settle down contentedly under a democratic system that subjects them to the government of those who were so recently their slaves. And so on. There is ample reason why African Muslims should embrace the fundamentalist doctrine that democracy is *kufr* and that *shūrā* offers no transpontine path to pluralist government by universal adult suffrage.

A curious aspect of the Muslim attitude to democracy is the frequency with which newly independent African nation-states with

Muslim majorities have none the less insisted on inserting the word into their state names. Thus the Anglo–Egyptian Sudan became the 'Democratic Republic of the Sudan'; Somaliland became the 'Somali Democratic Republic'; Algeria became the 'Democratic and Popular Republic of Algeria' and so on. To some extent this reflects the initial victory of the small and, as it has turned out, unrepresentative westernised elite whom Siddiqui has so roundly castigated. They have simply adopted the socialist stance that a one-party state in the alleged interest of 'the people' is *ipso facto* a democracy. To some extent, too, it also reflects the rather defiant position of some Muslims that their *shūrā* is just as good as the infidels' universal franchise. Both positions are now becoming increasingly untenable, as the fundamentalists persuasively reject the concept of democracy, lock, stock and barrel and insist that *shūrā* is a Koranic and transcendental concept that is in no way the bedfellow of secular democracy.

And the non-Muslim African enthusiasm for it

Yet the fact is that all over those parts of Africa where Islam is not the hegemonic culture, or where strong non-Muslim minorities are still able to challenge that hegemony, a tide is running in favour of this very democracy that Islamic Africa so angrily rejects as *kufr*. Of course, it is true that many eminent Muslim names appear on the roll of those prepared to swim with the democratic tide. But they are surely those whom the Sudanese *Ikhwān* and other Islamic radicals would regard as sinfully trifling with liberalism, as even al-Turabi once was. And *kufr* or not, the popular clamour for democracy grows in volume day by day.

In Nigeria, President Babangida, himself a Muslim but head of a pluralist military government that includes a strong Christian representation, is preparing a 'Political Transition Programme' of immense complexity intended to introduce yet a third attempt at a democratic multi-party system for the Federation. Among those that will compete this election when the time comes is the powerful Social Democratic Party, an African simulacrum of European parties of the same or similar names. Ghana is engaged in much the same exercise, which has thrown up a Democratic Alliance of Ghana (DAG), a London-based pressure group opposing Jerry Rawlings's programme of democratic reforms, which it believes to be inadequate. A Co-ordinating Committee of Democratic Forces also opposes Rawlings, the present Ghanaian Head of State, for similar reasons. In Chad the Mouvement pour la démocratie et le développement (MDD) challenges the rule of Idris Déby. Gambia has its People's Democratic Party (PDP) that will contest the forthcoming elections announced recently by President Jawara. A correspondent for *West Africa* magazine comments of Gambia, a typical Islamic area of the weak Malian tradition, that 'Democracy and multi-partyism are commodities that Gambians have taken for granted'.[12]

Togo has a plethora of political parties claiming a democratic identity – Union des Forces Démocratiques (UFD); Convention Démocratique des Peuples Africains (CDPA); Union Togalaise pour la Démocratique (UTD) and Parti Démocratique du Renouveau (PDR). Guinea Bissau has a Frente Democratica Social (FDS); a Partido da Unidade Social Democratico (PUSD) and a Movimento da Unidade Democratico (MUDE), all contesting its first presidential and legislative elections in 1992. The Congo has its Union des Forces Démocrationes (UFD) and a Rassemblement pour la Démocratie et le Développement (RDD). In Kenya the externally based United Movement for Democracy in Kenya, the internally based Forum for the Restoration of Democracy and the underground Union of Patriots for the Liberation of Kenya all regard the recent moves of President Daniel Arap Moi towards multi-party government as too limited and insincere.

While some of these groups no doubt represent tribal and factional interests whose commitment to democracy might be more honoured in the breach than in the observance, were they to gain power, there can be no doubting the drive among the African masses for popular democracy. It is significant that democracy is so often equated with development, for which these masses hunger. Professor Jibril Aminu, Nigerian Minister for Oil and President of OPEC in 1991, and who is himself a Muslim, though one who would hardly be approved of by Kalim Siddiqui, gave it as his opinion that

> democracy, and its presentday inseparable twin, market economy, are most likely to be the ruling order in most of these [African] countries by the end of the Decade, if not sooner.[13]

In a most informative article, 'Africa's Democratic Experiments', the magazine *West Africa* points out that the republics of the Sudan and of Somalia are alone in having, apparently, rejected the multi-party system and a democratic constitution. All the other forty-two independent tropical African states that it lists are engaged in measures ostensibly designed to implement such pluralist democratic systems, though *West Africa* is realistic enough to cast doubt on the sincerity of some of these attempts. Moreover, it does not mention the powerful Muslim minorities – or in some cases majorities – that fiercely oppose such initiatives. None the less, the article gives striking evidence of a great press of popular opinion that is dragging along even the most reluctant by their coat tails.[14]

Whether these bright new hopes have a better chance of success than earlier African endeavours at pluralist democracy is not within the competence of this book to predict. What is of its concern is: for how long in the face of such a mass movement, and with what expectation of success, can the radical Islamic position be maintained, that democracy is *kufr*? Before one answers too readily that the continental tide towards democracy is unstoppable, it is well to remember Algeria, the Republic of the Sudan, Somalia, the Toureg separatists in Mali and the banner-waving students in northern Nigeria. All of these demonstrate that the popular pull towards democracy may still face fierce Islamic resistance, the outcome of which is imponderable.

African unity and Islam

The issue of democracy had begun to exercise the minds and consciences of African Muslims even before the end of the colonial period. For instance, as was pointed out above, the Nigerian establishment, *Sunnī*, Mālikī, Qādirī and highly conservative but not yet fundamentalist in the current ferocity of that tendency, had settled for a form of Islamic 'constitutional monarchy' not dissimilar to that which obtains in Morocco. It was able, for the time being, to envisage a federation in which Christians also participated as equal partners – though there was always an underlying yearning that, in Allah's good time, Islam, with its evident transcendental superiority, would somehow or other extend its mantle over all.

But there was another straw in the wind of those days, barely perceived at that time, but which has become increasingly evident over the years. It now poses yet another challenge to Islamic theocracy: it is the idea of African unity. Around 1960 this was regarded by most traditional Muslims as something wholly temporal, if not downright irreligious, with which they wanted nothing to do. The idea of 'unity' with African polytheists and African Christians who, in the Muslims' view, ought by rights to have become Muslims generations ago, was unacceptable, to say the least. For them, union was envisaged in terms of ever-closer cultural and political links with the Arab Middle East, and with the non-Arab Islamic *umma* beyond.

For many colonial officials – the present writer was certainly no exception – the idea of African unity was regarded as the pipe-dream of African intellectuals who had drunk too deeply of the left-wing journals so generously available to them in British university common rooms. Among them, Kwame Nkrumah, the archetypal forward African intellectual, was the prime mover.

Yet the dream has survived, despite all the upheavals that have racked the African continent since it was first broached. In June 1991, at Abuja, soon to become the new Federal Capital of Nigeria, the twenty-seventh summit of the Organisation of African Unity (OAU) took place. It led to the adoption of a treaty establishing an African Economic Community by the year 2025. This development, in the words of one who reported it, is 'Africa's response to the challenge posed by the emerging world of trade blocs'.[15] But the report goes on to observe that:

> Within Africa itself, the Abuja Treaty poses a challenge to the concept of regionalism and gives a new lease of life to the existing sub-regional economic communities ... which hold a special place in the progressive establishment of the new Pan-African Community.[16]

Elsewhere, the report comments:

> Abuja reflects the essential elements of a democratic framework, and recognises the importance of popular democracy if development is to be sustained.[17]

In February 1992, President Ibrahim Babangida of Nigeria, himself a nominal Muslim,

> called upon fellow heads of state in Africa to ratify the treaty signed in Abuja last year calling for the setting up of the African Economic Community.[18]

In Ghana it is reported that:

> At least four groups have emerged, all claiming to be mobilising people towards the realisation of Nkrumah's ideas ...[19]

Foremost among these is that of African unity. The new government of Ethiopia, insofar as it has any real authority, now attempts to give renewed salience to the OAU, of which the late emperor Haile Selassie was the founder. A leading article in *West Africa* of 4–10 May 1992 remarks:

> It may be banal to repeat a much-preached but seldom practised truism, that for Africa it is only unity – the submerging of sovereignty through progressive integration – that can spearhead the fight against the perpetual dependence which seems to be part and parcel of the present international system.[20]

Whether such a united African community, which has surrendered its individual sovereignties to some centralist bureaucracy, is really much nearer to practical realisation than it was in Nkrumah's heyday, is a matter of opinion. It is also true that some Muslims are willing to participate in multi-party politics. Indeed, a person bearing an Islamic name was Chairman of OAU at the time of writing. But none of this alters the fact that if African unity, based upon democratic pluralism as its exponents insist it must be, were ever to become a reality, it would sound the death knell for the unitary, transcendental, theocratic *umma* for which radical Muslims so ardently yearn. The Muslim viewpoint is vigorously propagated by several powerful Islamic propaganda organisations financed largely with Saudi and Libyan oil money, that exist for the purpose of Islamic *daʿwa*, missionary activity, and whose message appears to be incompatible with the democratic pluralism that lies at the root of African unity. One of these is 'Islamic Call' (*al-daʿwa al-islāmiyya*) founded in Libya in 1972, which operates widely across West and East Africa and purports to offer essentially Islamic, not Western solutions to Africa's social and economic problems. Another is the 'Islam in Africa Organisation' founded as a result of the Islam in Africa Conference held in Abuja, Nigeria in November 1989. Its aims are set out in its Preamble, being

> determined to sustain the momentum of global Islamic resurgence and further encourage cooperation, understanding and the brotherhood of the Ummah; and desirous of forging a common front to unite the Ummah with a view to facing the common enemy – the imperialist and zionist forces of domination and secularization, illiteracy, poverty and degradation – and to rediscover and reinstate Africa's glorious Islamic past.

It is influential in Nigeria, Niger, Gambia, Mauritania, Senegal, Tunisia, Libya, Tanzania, Sudan and Tunisia. Also important in promoting the Islamic viewpoint is the international Organisation of Islamic Conference (OIC) described in Chapter 4 as at the centre of a constitutional crisis in Nigeria in 1986 although, as Hunwick points out, this organisation is somewhat ambivalent in its attitude towards co-operation with non-Islamic bodies.

What the outcome of such activities may be it would be rash to predict. Perhaps African Unity will get no further than the talking shop and will never become a real threat to Islamic aspirations. None the less, it does seem clear that a conflict of ideas of a very basic kind is currently taking place in Africa, between Islamic radicals on the one hand, and on the other, secular modernists, both Muslims and non-Muslims. It is not at present certain that any *modus vivendi* will emerge between them.[21]

Secular literacy: the fundamentalists' forlorn response?

Such literacy was referred to above as 'the poisoned chalice', a hemlock that destroys the divinely inscribed Arabic literacy that has so elegantly sustained Islam for 1,400 years. It has been discussed at length above, but one question may be examined again in the light of the fundamentalists' response. Was secular literacy – an ungodly and often unlovely manifestation against which the Muslims so understandably complain – really the rude imposition of malign imperialists intent on destroying Islam? If there had been no colonial occupations, would Muslims in Africa still be rubbing along contentedly, literate in classical Arabic, intact in Islam and untainted by the wider secularism that profane literacy brings? Or is it the case that secularism in the wider world, which owes nothing directly to colonialism, would inevitably have borne down upon Africa, with much the same consequences that the fundamentalists now so resentfully lay at the door of the departed 'colonial masters'? At any rate, a seminar organised by the London Muslim Institute in August 1983, entitled 'State and Politics in Islam', and which represents the views of the International Islamic Movement, recommends 'that Arabic be made the international Islamic language, and asks all Muslim people to learn it'.[22] This represents an attempt by this world-wide Islamic Movement to redress the loss of Arabic literacy which is complained of by so many Muslim radicals in particular instances. Examples from Africa are Malik N'Daiye who laments the demise of that literacy in French West Africa, and Ibraheem Sulaiman who deplores that: 'Arabic, which was the official language in both the Sokoto Caliphate and the Sultanate of Borno was abolished, and English imposed on Nigeria'.[23]

All of the Islamic propaganda (*da'wa*) organisations described above have as part of their aims the revival of Arabic literacy in Africa. One can receive these endeavours with scholarly empathy, while at the same time wondering whether such attempts to turn back the arrow of time as these organisations propose can any longer be successful in restoring the ancient verities of Islam to their former glory?

Roads to conversion

Conversion to Islam across the African continent has not been uniform. The purpose of this section is to reflect upon the various roads by which Africans have been brought into the Faith.

The first, most obvious road is that of military conquest. This achieved the early, massive conversions of Egypt, and the whole North African littoral, to Islam. One may suspect that these conquests were in some measure the plucking of fruits that were already ripe for picking. None the less, there can be no doubting the preponderant persuasion of the sword in setting up conditions that brought such conversion about.

Elsewhere, in tropical Africa, such once-and-for-all conquest has been rare. The Almoravid campaigns, once assumed to have been crucial in bringing Islam to the Niger Bend, are now widely believed to have been minor affairs that had limited consequences. It was not until the era of the great *jihāds* that the sword once again gained ascendency over other, more peaceful means of persuasion.

In West Africa, conversion has taken place overwhelmingly as a consequence of trade. Islamic bills of exchange, credit extended by Muslims to those who profess Islam in order to be worthy of such trust, and the compelling argument of a precise table of Islamic weights and measures were the means by which West Africans were brought to Islam in increasing numbers, over the generations.

In East Africa, trade, too, was the factor that first brought Muslims and non-Muslims together. But here a biological factor also intervened. It was one that was not entirely absent on the West African side but proved much more potent in the East African case. This was concubinage on a substantial scale between Muslim males and animist African women. The reason for the salience of this biological mode along the east African coast is surely that Arab and Persian Muslim merchants tended to settle permanently, or semi-permanently, on the littoral and the offshore islands. In West Africa, however, where incidently, the climate is much less pleasant than on the east coast, they came by trans-Saharan caravan from North Africa and Egypt. When their business was done, they went back the way they had come. On the east coast, in contrast, initial trade contacts led to long-term settlement and interbreeding, from which there emerged the characteristic Swahili culture described above.

Both these roads to conversion were slow, pervasive and generally benign. Apart from the initial enslavement of the pagan Zanj, conversion came by way of social contacts and cultural assimilation, not by the arbitrament of force. Such slow, organic, passive forces are surely unexceptional. They have a human dignity and a quiet inevitability that are lacking in the ugly social engineering with which the secular West so often tries to wreak its will. There is much evidence that they are still at work, slowly and often unseen, below the glitzy surface of multi-party democracy, African unity and all the other modern shibboleths that bewitch the imagination of contemporary Africa. They may in the end prove more powerful than these.

Jihād, which represents a return to the earlier, violent mode of conversion by conquest, is the road that characterised the tenth/sixteenth century in Ethiopia and the thirteenth/nineteenth century in West Africa and the Nilotic Sudan. Muslims habitually glamourise this method of conversion by presenting it as 'fighting in the way of Allah', and they seek to give an aura of reasonableness to it by pointing out that '*jihād* of the sword' is never resorted to before 'preaching *jihād*' has been tried and failed. Some will also insist that *jihād* of the sword is never resorted to until the Islamic community has first been the victim of attack by non-Muslims, but this is simply not borne out by the facts of history. The reality is that behind the whole notion of *jihād*, even 'preaching *jihād*', there lies an assumption of surpassing intellectual arrogance. It involves the demand that non-Muslims should accept what the Muslims undoubtedly sincerely believe to be true: that the Koran is the direct revealed Word of God. No allowance can be made for the fact that, for non-Muslims, whether African animists or any other category of non-believers, this is simply not self-evident, that it may indeed seem downright incredible. Neither doubt nor scepticism have any legitimate intellectual standing in Islam. The only alternative allowed to non-believers in the classical Islamic system is to accept the status of *dhimmi*, non-Muslim tributary subject of the Islamic state: or if they are pagans, to become enslaved.

The resort to *jihād* is also habitually defended by the allegation that the non-Islamic culture is tyrannous, while Islam equates to justice. Thus Shehu Usman Bugaje, in his 'Foreword' to Ibraheem Sulaiman's book, writes that:

> Islam has consistently and persistently stood on the side of the weak and the oppressed, checked the excesses of the corrupt and the strong and insisted on the establishment of justice, equity and fairness in human society.[24]

And, as is the way of the Muslims, he has a Koranic verse ready to hand to clinch his argument:

> And did not Allah check one set of people by means of another, the earth would indeed be full of mischief: but Allah is full of bounty to all the world (2:251).

Yet the difficulty again arises that such Islamic certainties exclude the right of the non-Muslim to disagree: to insist, for instance, that the Islamic *Sharīʿa* is in many important respects neither just nor fair, or to retort that for those whose recent forefathers were enslaved by the Muslims, such grandiloquent claims are sawdust in the mouth.

The reality of *jihād* of the sword is that, unlike the other roads to conversion discussed above, it involves the assertion by force that Islam is, to quote the Sudanese *Ikhwān*, 'a universal ethical imperative'. It brooks neither argument nor compromise. This of course, lies behind the Islamic conviction that democratic pluralism is *kufr*. Such pluralism necessarily involves choice, which may be contrary to the Divine imperative. This the Muslim cannot concede.

Jihād of the sword is still a reality that infuses the works of such present-day Islamic radicals as ʿUmar Abdullahi and Ibraheem Sulaiman. They glorify the Fulānī *jihād* and the *persona* of Shaykh ʿAbd Allāh b. Fūdī, who conducted it in the field. A similar reality informs the Sudan Charter, now being tragically acted out in the southern Sudan. It may reasonably be seen behind the fierce campaigns of Toureg separatists against the black Africans of Mali, Mauritania and Niger, although the latter have certainly not used their new democratic powers in a conciliatory manner.

There is little doubt that the frustrations that understandably now assail radical Muslims by way of the onslaught of profane literacy, popular democracy and the drive for African unity that fly in the face of the divinely ordained *Imām/Khalīfa* under whose sole rule man should live, leaves these Muslims feeling that they have no other recourse against the advancing forces of *kufr* than to resort to armed *jihād*. Kalim Siddiqui, that articulate spokesman for Islamic fundamentalism world-wide, who is listened to respectfully across Islamic Africa, expresses this feeling in the following passage:

> Just as the power and influence of *kufr* in the modern world is global, so are the bonds of faith and destiny of the Muslim *Ummah*. History has come full circle. The global power of *kufr* waits to be challenged and defeated by the global power of Islam. This is the unfinished business of history, so let us go ahead and finish it.[25]

In an African context Ibraheem Sulaiman expresses the same basic radical Islamic concept of two essentially conflicting and irreconcilable ideologies when he writes that 'There are two civilisations competing for supremacy in Nigeria today: Islam and European civilisation' and goes on to insist on the Muslim's 'eternal obligation' not merely to live as an individual Muslim but to strive to set up a state consistent with Islamic theocratic principles.[26]

There may be behind these brave words the ring of desperation – though they have clearly been heeded with gusto, if with varying degrees of success by the Algerians, the Muslim Sudanese, the Touregs and the Nigerian *'Yan Izala*, while others wait in the wings. One asks oneself whether, despite such rhetoric, the Muslims must, in the end, simply succumb to kufr because it is now, apparently, so overwhelmingly the force majeure? Is it then the case that Islam will gradually be reduced to a personal belief system, bereft of its social, political and legal institutions and subservient to the secular pluralist democracy which so many non-Muslim Africans insist is the way of the future? Or will the Muslim masses be finally aroused, as they were in Algeria and, like the northern Sudanese and the Saharan Touregs, turn again to the sword to finish the unfinished business of history, in the manner Allah intends? Or may there after all be a compromise that is as yet hardly in sight whereby Islamic theocracy in Africa learns to adjust itself to the exigencies of the modern world?

NOTES

1. Loc. cit., in Kerr, David and Hasan Askari (eds), Bibl.
2. *Issues … 1983–1984*, p. 13.
3. Ghayasuddin (ed.), Bibl., p. 14.
4. *Issues … 1983–1984*, p. 48.
5. Ghayasuddin, p. 4.
6. Ibid., p. 9.
7. Ibid., p. 9.
8. 'The Moment of Truth in Nigeria', *Impact International* 13–26 April 1984.
9. Ibid.
10. Ibid.
11. 'Islam and Secularism in Nigeria: An Encounter of Two Civilisations', *Impact International* 10–23 October 1986.
12. 10–16 February 1992, p. 69.
13. *West Africa*, 16–22 December 1991, p. 2,087.
14. 25–31 May 1992.
15. *West Africa*, 2–8 December 1991, p. 2,014.
16. Ibid., p. 2,014.
17. Ibid., p. 2,014.
18. *West Africa*, 10–16 February 1992, p. 249.
19. Ibid., 2–8 December 1991, p. 2,004.
20. *West Africa*, 4–10 May 1992, p. 745.
21. This issue of a possible *modus vivendi* between Muslims and non-Muslims on the one hand and Muslim fundamentalists and moderate Muslims on the other is discussed by P. J. Ryan, 'Islam and Politics in West Africa: Minority and Majority Models', *The Muslim World*, LXXVII, 1987; also in John Hunwick, 'An African Case Study of Political Islam: Nigeria', *Annals of the American Academy of Political and Social Science*, vol. 524, 1992 and in Julie Lawson, 'Nigerian historiography and the Sokoto jihads', MA dissertation, School of oriental and African Studies, London, 1989, as well as in P. Clarke, 'Islamic reform in contemporary Nigeria: methods and aims', *Third World Quarterly*, vol. 10, No. 2, 1988. The Islamic propaganda organisations described here in outline may be studied in greater detail in Hunwick's paper 'West Africa and the Wider World of Islam: Networks and Organizations', 05/10/93, published by Northwestern University.
22. *Issues … 1983–1984*, p. 50.
23. Loc. cit., *Impact International*, 10–23 October 1986.
24. Op. cit., vii.
25. *Issues … 1983–1984*, p. 23.
26. Loc. cit., *Impact International*, 10–23 October 1986.

Bibliographic Essay

The quantity of scholarly writing on Islam in Africa is huge. This Essay, and the accompanying Select Bibliography, do not set out to encompass the whole of it, merely to indicate a small number of key books that will enable the reader to expand upon the broad survey of Islam in Africa undertaken in this short work. Most of these books contain their own specialist bibliographies, with the help of which more detailed studies can be undertaken. There are in addition a large number of articles in learned journals that bear on aspects of Islam in Africa, especially in the modern era. A selection of what seem to me the more relevant of these to issues discussed in this book is also included in this Essay, though it represents only a tiny proportion of what is available. For more information on this availability the reader should consult the Abstracts in Sicard (ed.) *Bulletin on Islam and Christian–Muslim Relations in Africa* (henceforth *BICMURA*), which provide up-to-date running lists.

For North Africa an appropriate starting point is the series of scholarly chapters in Holt, et al. (eds), 2A, by Tourneau, Mantran, Raymond and Nouschi. These give considerably greater detail, especially on dynastic history, than has been possible in this book. Volume 2B of Holt, et al. (eds) contains a comprehensive bibliography on 'North Africa' (pp. 895–7). Among the works listed there, Dupont and Coppolani, *Les confréries religieuses musulmanes*, is an old but reliable account of the *Ṣūfī ṭuruq*. A more recent work is Drague, *Esquisse d'histoire religieuse de Maroc*. For the era of the Amīr ʿAbd al-Qādir, Emerit's *L'Algérie à l'époque d'Abd-el-Kader* is valuable. On the question of North African nationalism Hahn, *North Africa: Nationalism to Nationhood* is provocative, though its conclusions do not necessarily match those proposed in this study. The general evaluation of Sufism in North Africa, Spain and elsewhere, is comprehensively dealt with in Arberry's chapter 'Mysticism', Holt, et al. (eds), *The Cambridge History of Islam*, 2B.

Learned articles on Islam in North Africa are legion. Fierro's interesting study, 'The Polemic about *karāmāt al-awliyā'* and the Development of Sufism in al-Andalus (fourth/tenth–fifth/eleventh centuries)'; may usefully be studied in conjunction with my own discussion of Sufism in Chapter 1 of this book. Peter von Sivers 'The realm of justice: Apocalyptic revolts in Algeria (1849–1879)' is a fine scholarly study of Algerian revolts against the French occupation seen from the religious viewpoint and in considerably greater detail than could be undertaken in the present broad study. On modern Algeria H. Roberts, 'Radical Islamism and the dilemma of Algeria nationalism' traces the rise of Islamic radicalism against the background of nationalism and is recommended, as is also L. Hanisch, 'The denunciation of mysticism as a bulwark against reason: a contribution to the expansion of Algerian reformism 1925–1939' and M. Shirazi, 'Regulating the family in Algeria' which considers the reform of family law and its relation to the *Sharīʿa*.

On Morocco students are recommended to read J. Benomar, 'The Monarchy, the Islamic Movement and religious discourse in Morocco' which examines the relation of Islamic radicalism to the monarchy and its policies, and A. Tazi, 'Morocco's commitment to Islam, long-standing feature of Moroccan diplomacy' which assesses the role of Islam in Moroccan foreign relations.

For Tunisia, G. Last, 'Gedanken Über Liebe, Ehe und Geburtenregelung in Tunisien' considers the destructive effects of modernism on human and social relations. M. Shirazi, 'Political thaw in Tunisia' examines the rise of the Islamic Tendency in Tunisia and M. Boulby, 'The Islamic challenge: Tunisia since independence' is comprehensive and useful. J. Degos, 'Les marabouts Africains à Bordeaux' gives an interesting account of marabouts working among Muslim immigrants in France.

For Egypt the student should certainly begin with Bernard Lewis's 'Egypt and Syria' in Holt, et al. (eds), 1A. Lane-Poole's *History of Egypt in the Middle Ages'* is a reliable standard work. For Egypt in the context of the Ottoman empire Wittek's *The Rise of the Ottoman Empire* is recommended. Vatikiotis's *The Modern History of Egypt* is essential for the modern period. Among a vast number of learned articles on Egyptian Islam the student will find the following particularly useful: S. E. Ibrahim, 'Egypt's Islamic activism in the 1980s', M. Forstner, 'Die Muslimbrüder I' and K. A. Magd, 'The enduring legacy of the Ikhwan'. The latter gives an unusual assessment of what the author considers the constructive contribution of the *Ikhwān*. Mir Zuhair Husain, 'Hassan Al-Banna (1906–1949). Founder of the Ikhwan al-Muslimin' may also be consulted for a view of the founder of the Muslim Brotherhood in Egypt.

For the Nilotic Sudan, Holt's 'The Nilotic Sudan' in Holt, et al. (eds), 2A and Hrbeck's 'Egypt, Nubia and the Eastern Deserts' in Oliver (ed.), vol. 3, are both excellent starting points. A more detailed study is Holt, *A Modern History of the Sudan*, which is highly recommended. The recent history of the Sudan has attracted an immense contribution of learned articles. The student may usefully consult the Abstracts in various issues of *BICMURA* for running lists of these. Of particular interest to readers of this book may be W. J. House, 'The Status of Women in the Sudan' and H. Makki, 'Sudan's road to Islamic State' which traces the rise of the Islamic National Front and its relations with the *Ikhwān*. S. Begum, 'The Process of Islamisation in Sudan' is a useful critical study of the introduction of the *Sharī'a* by Numeiri.

West Africa has a substantial bibliography on Islam. I suggest students consult my *The Development of Islam in West Africa* and, for the period of the Fulani *jihād*, my *The Sword of Truth*. Other essential basic works are Levtzion, 'The Western Maghrib and Sudan' in Oliver (ed.), vol. 3 and Humphrey Fisher, 'The Western and Central Sudan' in Holt, et al. (eds), 2A. See also my 'The Nineteenth-century Jihads in West Africa' in Flint (ed.), vol. 5. To list articles relating to Islam in all the nation states of West Africa is beyond the scope of this Essay. Several have already been cited in the Notes to Chapter 4. In addition I recommend A. R. Doi, 'Political role of Islam in West Africa with special reference to Uthmān dān Fodio' and L. Kaba, 'The pen, the sword and the crown: Islam and revolution in Songhay reconsidered, 1464–1493'. S. Ottenberg, 'Two new religions, one analytic frame' is an interesting study of the interaction of Islam and Christianity in Sierra Leone, as is also Ibrahim Cole's 'Muslim-Christian Relations in Sierra Leone'. A. Dery, 'The Advent of Islam in Ghana' is a useful study of modern Islam in that country and its representative organisations, while *West Africa* No. 3,480 of 30 April 1984 contains a short but useful comment on an attempt to achieve Muslim unity in Ghana. M. Shirazi, 'Same old story as Senegal turns down Muslim party' is a brief but informative comment on the attempt to exclude Islamic parties from the political process in Senegal, while *West Africa* No. 3,411 of 20 December 1982 records President Diouf's attempts to win support from the *Ṣūfī ṭuruq*.

Ethiopia and the Horn are best studied in Tamrat, 'Ethiopia, the Red Sea and the Horn' in Oliver (ed.), vol. 3. Sanceau's *Portugal in Quest of Prester John* tells the fascinating story of this curious medieval preoccupation, which could only be touched on in the present work. Tamrat's *Church and State in Ethiopia 1270–1527* is a valuable account of Ethiopian history from the Christian standpoint, while Trimingham's *Islam in Ethiopia* tells it from the Islamic side. Early Somali history is treated largely under Ethiopian history. H. S. Lewis's 'The Origins of the Galla and Somali' is a useful study, as is also I. M. Lewis, *The Modern History of Somaliland*. A. S. Bemath's useful article 'Sayyid Muhammad 'Abd Allah Hassan and the Somali Rebellion of 1899–1920' seeks to link this rebellion to the situation in Somalia in modern times. Y. M. Aberra, 'Muslim institutions in Ethiopia: the Asmara Awqaf' considers the economic situation of Muslims in Eritrea while E. D. Hecht, 'Harar and Lemu: a comparison of two East African Muslim societies' compares and contrasts two Ethiopian Muslim groups.

For the study of Islam in East Africa the student may begin with Chittick's comprehensive 'The East Coast, Madagascar and the Indian Ocean' in Oliver (ed.), vol. 3. The development of Swahili Islam, especially from the literary viewpoint, is best studied in Knappert's scholarly contributions and more especially his *Four Centuries of Swahili Verse*. James De Vere Allen, *Swahili Origins*, is a recent, most controversial account of this subject. So too is Nurse and Spear, *The Swahili: Reconstructing the History and Language of an African Society*, which argues that the origins of Swahili culture are more ancient than the arrival of the Arabs on the East coast. For the Portuguese period Newitt's *Portuguese Settlement on the Zambesi* is a recent, informative study. Articles on Islam in East African nation-states abound. Among the most useful are D. S. Bone, 'Islam in Malawi', a comprehensive study of Islam in that country. The journal *Arabia* No. 22 of June 1983 contains a brief report on the activities of the Islamic council of Mozambique which throws light on the present state of Islam in that country. Islam in Kenya is considered by H. Bogner, 'Begegnungen mit Muslims in Mombasa' while Y. A. Eraj, 'The Qur'an School and the Basic Development of Children of Muslim Minorities I–IV' considers the education and other aspects of the lives of Kenyan Muslim children. M. Samiullah, 'Muslims in Kenya: Problems and Possible Solutions' is also a useful study. T. A. Gadir, 'Little unity in Uganda's big diversity' considers the place of Islam in the multi-religious society of Uganda while S. I. Kiggunda and I. K. K. Lukwago consider 'The Status of the Muslim Community in Uganda' with special reference to the era of Idi Amin. Tanzania has attracted a great deal of learned comment as a result of its experiment in *ujaama*. S. D. Govig, 'Religion and the Search for Socialism in Tanzania' is informative, while H. M. Batibo's 'The Important Contribution of Arabic to the development of Kiswahili' emphasises the role of Arabic literacy in the development of the Swahili language. S. A. Fundi, 'Islam and Muslims in Tanzania' considers the educational situation of Tanzanian Muslims. Ephraim Mandivenga, 'Islam in Tanzania: A General Survey', published in 1990, is a most recent assessment.

While the general bibliography on South Africa is immense and much of it contains incidental information on Islam there, Islam as a central issue is less well served. Probably the most convenient account with which to begin is Blij's chapter in Kritzeck and Lewis (eds). The subject may then be pursued through the bibliography given in his footnotes. Articles on Islam in South Africa are more numerous. Among the most interesting are F. Esack, 'Three Islamic strands in the South African struggle for justice' and A. Gamiet, 'Afrikaans: The Muslim medium' which considers the development of Arabic literacy in the Cape and its influence on Afrikaans; also S. E. Dangor, 'The Beginning of Islam in the Cape' which is a useful historical study. C. du P. le Roux's important article has already been cited in the Notes to Chapter 6. Students may also find G. Lubbe, 'Islam in South Africa: Enemy or Ally' of interest for its examination of Muslim–Christian relations in South Africa.

The Islamic literatures of Africa may best be studied in the several specialist works and articles by Knappert listed in the Bibliography and, for the Hausa side, in my *History of Hausa Islamic Verse*. Also useful in establishing the patterns of Arabic literature which the African Muslims followed are René Basset, *La Bordah du Cheikh El-Bouṣiri* and H. A. R. Gibb, *Arabic Literature*. H. T. Norris's *Shinqītī Folk Literature and Song* and his *Saharan Myth and Saga* are both seminal studies of Berber literature. C. H. Robinson's *Specimens of Hausa Literature* is an early but still useful study of this subject.

Among more general works covering Islam in Africa as a whole is, first and foremost, Kritzeck and Lewis (eds). This work comprises a series of essays by experts covering all the main geographical areas of Africa, together with certain wider issues such as 'Nationalism and Modernism', 'The Legal Tradition' and so on. Martin's *Muslim Brotherhoods in Nineteenth-century Africa* is a most useful study of the history and role of the *Ṣūfī ṭuruq* in Africa. Students would also do well to consult A. Arteche 'Islam y opciones fundamentales de las comunidades Christianas en el Africa negra'. Those who may not be able to read this in the original will find an excellent English review article by Redmond Fitzmaurice in *BICMURA* 2/2, 1984. Students may also usefully consult O. H. Kasule, 'Islamic Dawa in Africa: methods and strategy' for an informative account of how the present Islamic revivalist movement is conducted.

The rise of the Salafist tendency, the Muslim Brotherhood and Islamic fundamentalism are all covered in scholarly fashion in Choueiri's *Islamic Fundamentalism*. This book has, of course, wider horizons than just Africa. The three articles by M. Forstner, K. A. Magd and Mir Zuhair Husain, listed under Egypt, are also relevant to the study of the Muslim Brotherhood generally. K. D. Willis, 'Fundamentalist Islam' is also useful and so too is J. L. Esposito, 'Islamic resurgence'.

Brice (ed.) has been cited more than once in the foregoing pages. His learned compilation gives a striking visual impression of how Islam has spread across Africa, century by century. It is also most useful in tracing the expansion of trade over the centuries, and for its representation of the world maps of al-Idrīsī and al-Sharfī.

The admirable series edited by Sicard, *BICMURA*, contains frequent valuable articles on aspects of Islam in Africa with a particular slant towards Christian–Muslim relations, and students will do well to keep abreast of these publications. They should also familiarise themselves with both Ghayasuddin (ed.) 1986 and the several volumes of *Issues in the Islamic Movement*, edited by Siddiqui. These are a series published on an annual basis which set out the Islamic fundamentalist viewpoint on a large number of world events involving Islam, many of them concerning Africa. While the interpretations and conclusions expressed in these volumes are frankly those of Islamic fundamentalists – therein lies the value of the series to the student – the books also contain a wealth of factual information that is often difficult to track down in other sources.

I have included several references to the magazine *West Africa* in Chapter 8 above, and in this Bibliographic Essay. This publication is most useful for bringing oneself up to date with West African politics and current affairs, and indeed those of Africa generally. It seems to me, however, to be written very much from the viewpoint of southern, Christian and secular West Africans. It is therefore less informative than it might be, and sometimes quite astray when dealing with issue that have to do with Islam.

Apart from the specific acknowledgements made here and elsewhere in this book, I am indebted to all the authors listed in this Essay for my own understanding of Islam in Africa.

Select Bibliography

BOOKS AND THESES

Abdullah, Mzee, 'Pope visits Africa to boost Roman Catholic Minority' in Kalim Siddiqui and Ghayasuddin (eds), *Issues in the Islamic Movement 1985–86*, London, 1987.

Abdullahi, Shehu 'Umar, *On the Search for a Viable Political Culture: Reflections on the Political Thought of Shaikh Abdullahi Dan Fodio*, Kaduna, 1984.

Affendi, Abdelwahab El-, *Turabi's Revolution: Islam and Power in the Sudan*, London, 1991.

Aliyu, Muhammad Sani, 'Shortcomings in Hausa Society as Seen by Representative Hausa Islamic Poets from *c.* 1950 to *c.* 1982', MA Dissertation, Bayero University, 1983.

Allen, James de Vere, *Swahili Origins*, London and Nairobi, 1993.

Arberry, A. J, 'Mysticism' in Holt, et al. (eds), *The Cambridge History of Islam*, 2B.

Asaria, Iqbal, 'Back Seat for Muslims in Mozambique' in Kalim Siddiqui (ed.), *Issues in the Islamic Movement 1981–1982 (1401–1402)*, London, 1983.

Basset, René, *La Bordah du Cheikh Bouṣiri*, Paris, 1849.

Blij, Harm J. de, 'South Africa' in Kriteck and Lewis (eds), *Islam in Africa*.

Braybooke, Lord (ed.), *The Concise Pepys*, Ware, 1988.

Brice, William C. (ed.), *An Historical Atlas of Islam*, Leiden, 1981.

Chittick, Neville H., 'The East Coast, Madagascar and the Indian Ocean' in Oliver (ed.), *The Cambridge History of Africa*, vol. 3.

Choueiri, Youssef M., *Islamic Fundamentalism*, London, 1990.

Crowder, Michael (ed.), *West African Resistance*, London, 1971.

Crystal, David (ed.), *The Cambridge Encyclopedia*, Cambridge, 1990.

Cuoq, Joseph M., *Recueil des sources arabes concernant l'Afrique occidentale du VIIIe siècle*, Paris, 1975.

Drague, G., *Esquisse d'histoire religieuse de Maroc*, Paris, 1951.

Dupont, O. and X. Coppolani, *Les confréries religieuses musulmanes*, Algiers, 1897.

Emerit, M., *L'Algérie à l'époque d'Abd-el-Kader*, Paris, 1951.

Fisher, H. J., 'The Western and Central Sudan' in Holt et al. (eds), *The Cambridge History of Islam*, 2A.

——, 'The Eastern Maghrib and the Central Sudan' in Oliver (ed.), *The Cambridge History of Africa*, vol. 3.

Flint, John E. (ed.), *The Cambridge History of Africa*, vol. 5, Cambridge, 1976.

Ghayasuddin, M. (ed.), *The Impact of Nationalism on the Muslim World*, London, 1986.

Gibb, H. A. R., *Ibn Battuta: Travels in Asia and Africa 1325–1354*, London, 1929–63.

——, *Arabic Literature*, London, 1962.

Hahn, L., *North Africa: Nationalism to Nationhood*, Washington, D.C., 1960.
Hiskett, M., *The Sword of Truth: The Life and Times of the Shehu Usuman Dan Fodio*, New York, 1973.
——, *A History of Hausa Islamic Verse*, London, 1975.
——, 'The Nineteenth-century Jihads in West Africa' in Flint (ed.), *The Cambridge History of Africa*, vol. 5, 1976.
——, *The Development of Islam in West Africa*, London and New York, 1984.
Holt, P. M., *A Modern History of the Sudan*, London, 1961.
Holt, P. M., 'The Nilotic Sudan', in Holt, et al. (eds), *The Cambridge History of Islam*.
Holt, P. M., Anne K. S. Lambton and Bernard Lewis (eds), *The Cambridge History of Islam*, 1A, 1B, 2A, 2B, Cambridge, 1970.
Hrbeck, Ivan, 'Egypt, Nubia and the Eastern Desert' in Oliver (ed.), *The Cambridge History of Africa*, vol. 3.
Kanya-Forstner, A. S., 'Mali-Tukolor', in Crowder (ed.), *West African Resistance*.
Knappert, J., *Traditional Swahili Poetry: an Investigation into the Concepts of East African Islam*, Leiden, 1967.
——, *Myths and Legends of the Swahili*, London, 1970.
——, *Four Centuries of Swahili Verse*, London, 1979.
——, *Islamic Legends*, Leiden, 1985.
——, *Handbook of Swahili Literature*, New York, 1992.
Kritzeck, James and William H. Lewis (eds), *Islam in Africa*, New York, 1969.
Lane-Poole, S., *History of Egypt in the Middle Ages*, second edition, London, 1914.
Lawson, Julie, 'Nigerian Historiography and the Sokoto jihads', MA Dissertation, School of Oriental and African Studies, London, 1989.
Levtzion, Nehemia, 'The Western Maghrib and the Sudan', in Oliver (ed.), *The Cambridge History of Africa*, vol. 3.
Lewis, Bernard, 'Egypt and Syria' in Holt, et al. (eds), *The Cambridge History of Islam*, 1A.
Lewis, I. M., *The Modern History of Somaliland*, London, 1965.
Lubeck, P. M., 'Islamic Protest under Semi-industrial Capitalism: Yan Tatsine Explained' in Peel and Stewart (eds), *Popular Islam South of the Sahara*.
Mantran, R., 'North Africa in the Sixteenth and Seventeenth Centuries' in Holt, et al. (eds), *The Cambridge History of Islam*, 2A.
Martin, B. G., *Muslim Brotherhoods in Nineteenth-century Africa*, Cambridge, 1976.
N'Daiye, Malik, 'Nationalism as an Instrument of Cultural Imperialism – A Case Study of French West Africa' in Ghayasuddin (ed.), *The Impact of Nationalism on the Muslim world*.
Newitt, M. D., *Portuguese Settlement on the Zambesi*, London, 1973.
Norris, H. T., *Shinqiti Folk Literature and Song*, Oxford, 1968.
——, *Saharan Myth and Saga*, Oxford, 1972.
Nouschi, André, 'North Africa in the Period of Colonization', in Holt, et al. (eds), *The Cambridge History Of Islam*, 2A.
Nurse, Derek and Thomas Spear, *The Swahili: Reconstructing the History and Language of an African Society 800–1500*, Philadelphia, 1985.

Oliver, Roland (ed.), *The Cambridge History of Africa*, vol. 3, Cambridge, 1977.
Peel, J. D. Y. and C. C. Stewart, *Popular Islam South of the Sahara*, Manchester, 1985.
Raymond, André, 'North Africa in the Pre-colonial period' in Holt, et al. (eds), *The Cambridge History of Islam* 2A.
Robinson, C. H., *Hausaland or Fifteen Hundred Miles through the Central Sudan*, London, 1896.
——, *Specimens of Hausa Literature*, Cambridge, 1896.
Sanceau, E., *Portugal in Quest of Prester John*, London, 1943.
Siddiqui, Kalim (ed.), *Issues in the Islamic Movement 1981–1982 (1401–1402)*, London, 1983.
——, *Issues in the Islamic Movement 1983–1984 (1403–1404)*, London, 1985.
——, *Issues in the Islamic Movement 1984–1985 (1404–1405)*, London, 1986.
——, and M. Ghayasuddin (eds), *Issues in the Islamic Movement 1985–1986 (1405–1406)*, London, 1987.
Sulaiman, Ibraheem, *A Revolution in History*, London and New York, 1986.
Tamrat, Taddesse, *Church and State in Ethiopia, 1270–1527*, Oxford, 1972.
——, 'Ethiopia, The Red Sea and the Horn' in Oliver (ed.), *The Cambridge History of Africa*, vol. 3.
Tourneau, Roger le, 'North Africa to the Sixteenth Century' in Holt, et al. (eds), *The Cambridge History of Islam*, 2A.
Trimingham, J. S., *Islam in Ethiopia*, London, 1952.
——, 'The Expansion of Islam' in Kritzeck and Lewis (eds), *Islam in Africa*.
Vatikiotis, P. J., *The Modern History of Egypt*, London, 1969.
Wittek, P., *The Rise of the Ottoman Empire*, London, 1938.

ARTICLES AND SEMINAR PAPERS

Abdin, A. Z., al-, 'The Sudan Charter – National Unity and Diversity' in Sicard (ed.), *BICMURA*, 6/1, 1988.
Aberra, Y. M., 'Muslim institutions in Ethiopia: the Asmara Awqaf', *Journal Institute of Muslim Minority Affairs*, 5/1, 1984.
Ammah, Rabiatu, 'New Light on Muslim Statistics for Africa' in Sicard (ed.), *BICMURA*, 2/1, 1984.
Anon, 'Islamic Council of Mozambique', *Arabia*, no. 22, 1983.
Arteche, A., 'Islam y opciones fundamentales de las comunidades Christianas en el Africa negra', *Misiones Extranjeras*, no. 78–9, 1983.
Askari, Hasan, 'Religion and Development: Search for Conceptual Clarity and New Methodology – The Case of Islam' in Kerr, David and Hasan Askari (eds), *Newsletter*, Centre for the Study of Islam and Christian-Muslim Relations, Selly Oak Colleges, Birmingham, no. 13, May 1985.
Batibo, H. M., 'The Important Contribution of Arabic to the Development of Kiswahili', *Islam Today*, vol. 2, 1984.
Begum, S., 'The Process of Islamisation in Sudan', *The Straight Path*, 4,112, 1984.
Bemath, A. S., 'Sayyid Muhammad ʿAbd Allah Hassan and the Somali Revolution 1899–1920', *Al-Ilm*, vol. 4, 1984.
Benomar, J., 'The Monarchy, the Islamic Movement and religious discourse in Morocco', *Third World Quarterly*, 10/2, 1988.
Bogner, H., 'Begegnungen mit Muslims in Mombasa', *Orientdienst-Information*, no. 79, 1983.

Bone, D. S., 'Islam in Malawi', *Journal of Religion in Africa*, 13/2, 1982.
Boulby, M., 'The Islamic challenge: Tunisia since independence', *Third World Quarterly*, 10/2, 1988.
Christelow, Allen, 'Religious Protest and Dissent in Northern Nigeria from Mahdism to Quranic Integralism', *Journal of the Institute of Muslim Minority Affairs*, 6/2, 1985.
Clarke, P., 'Islamic reform in contemporary Nigeria: methods and aims', *Third World Quarterly*, 10/2, 1988.
Cole, Ibrahim, 'Muslim-Christian Relations in Sierra Leone', *BICMURA* 1/4, 1983.
Dangor, S. E., 'The Beginnings of Islam in the Cape', *Al-Ilm*, vol. 4, 1984.
Degas, J., 'Les marabouts africains à Bordeaux', *Hommes et migrations*, no. 1,051, 1983.
Derry, A., 'The Advent of Islam in Ghana', *Al-Islam*, 7/4, 1983.
Doi, A. R., 'Political role of Islam in West Africa with special reference to Uthmān dān Fodio', *Al-Ilm*, vol. 41, 1984.
Effat, Rajia, 'The Problems of Women in Egypt', Fifth International Conference on the Unity of the Sciences, Washington, D.C., 1986.
Eraj, Y. A., 'The Qur'an School and the Basic Development of Children of Muslim Minorities', I–IV, *The Muslim World*, 21/27–30, 1984.
Esack, F., 'Three Islamic strands in the South African struggle for justice', *Third World Quarterly*, 10/2, 1988.
Esposito, J. L., 'Islamic resurgence', *Pro Mundi Vita Bulletin*, no. 109, 1987.
Fierro, Mirabel, 'The Polemic about *karāmāt al-awliyā'* and the Development of Sufism in al-Andalus (fourth/tenth century–fifth/eleventh century)', *Bulletin of the School of Oriental and African Studies*, LV/2, 1992.
Fisher, H. J., 'Conversion Reconsidered: Some Historical Aspects of Religious Conversion in Black Africa', *Africa*, XL, 111/1 1973.
Fitzmaurice, Redmond, 'Islam and Christianity in Africa', *BICMURA*, 2/2, 1984.
Forstner, M., 'Die Muslimbrüder', *CIBEDO-Texte*, no. 32, 1983.
Fundi, S. A., 'Islam and Muslims in Tanzania', *Yaqeen International*, 31/17, 1983.
Gadir, T. A., 'Little Unity in Uganda's big Diversity', *Arabia*, no. 22, 1983.
Gamiet, A., 'Afrikaans: The Muslim medium', *Arabia*, no. 23, 1983.
Govig, S. D., 'Religion and the Search for Socialism in Tanzania', *Journal of African Studies*, 14/3, 1988.
Hanisch, L., 'The denunciation of mysticism as a bulwark against reason: a contribution to the expansion of Algerian reformism 1925–1939', *Maghreb Review*, 11/5 and 6, 1986.
Hecht, E. D., 'Harar and Lemu: a comparison of two East African Muslim societies', *Trans-African Journal of History*, vol. 16, 1987.
Hiskett, M., 'The Maitatsine Riots in Kano, 1980: An Assessment', *Journal of Religion in Africa*, 17/3, 1987.
House, J., 'The Status of Women in the Sudan', *The Journal of Modern African Studies*, 26/2, 1988.
Hunwick, J., 'An African Case Study of Political Islam: Nigeria', *The Annals of the American Academy of Political and Social Science*, vol. 524, November, 1992.
——, 'West Africa and the Wider World of Islam: Networks and Organizations', paper published on 10 May 1993 by Northwestern University.

Husain, Mir Zuhair, 'Hassan Al-Banna (1906–1949). Founder of the Ikhwan al-Muslimin', *Islam and the Modern Age*, 17/4. 1986.
Ibrahim, S. E., 'Egypt's Islamic activism in the 1980s', *Third World Quarterly*, 10/2. 1988.
Kaba, L., 'The pen, the sword and the crown: Islam and revolution in Songhay reconsidered 1464–1493', *Journal of African History*, 125/3, 1984.
Kasule, O. H., 'Islamic Dawa in Africa: methods and strategy', *The Universal Message*, 5/10–12, 1984.
Kepel, Gilles, 'The Teaching of Sheikh Faisal' in J. S. Nielsen (ed.), *Research Papers*, no. 29, March, 1986.
Kerr, David and Hassan Askari (eds), *Newsletter*, Centre for the Study of Islam and Christian–Muslim Relations, Selly Oak Colleges, Birmingham (occasional publication).
Kiggunda, S. I. and I. K. K. Lukwago, 'The status of the Muslim community in Uganda', *Journal Institute of Muslim Minority Affairs*, 4/1 and 2, 1982.
Knappert, J., 'The Mawlid', *Orientalia Lovanensia Periodica*, 19, 1988.
——, 'The Islamic Poetry of Africa', *Journal for Islamic Studies*, no. 10, 1990.
——, 'A Short History of Zanzibar', *Annales Aequatoria*, 13, 1992.
Lange, Dierk, 'Progrès de l'Islam et changement politique au Kane Kānem du XIe au XIIIe siècle: un essai d'interprétation', *Journal of African History*, XIX, 4, 1978.
Last, G., 'Gedanken Über Liebe, Ehe und Geburtenregelung in Tunisien', *Al-Islam*, no. 6, 1982.
Lewis, H. S., 'The Origins of the Galla and Somali', *Journal of African History*, VII, 1966.
Lubbe, G., 'Islam in South Africa: Enemy or Ally', *BICMURA*, 3/1, 1985.
Magd, K. A., 'The enduring legacy of the Ikhwan', *Arabia*, No. 32, 1984.
Makki, H., 'Sudan's road to Islamic State', *Impact-International*, 14–27, October, 1988.
Mandivenga, Ephraim, 'Islam in Tanzania: A General Survey', *Journal Institute of Muslim Minority Affairs*, 11/2, 1990.
Musa, Sulaiman, 'The Main Objectives of the Literary Works of Shaykh 'Uthman b. Fudi', GSIG Papers No. 9, September, 1992, Centre for the Study of Islam and Christian–Muslim Relations, Selly Oak Colleges, Birmingham.
Nielsen, J.S., (ed.), *Research Papers*, Centre for the Study of Islam and Christian–Muslim Relations, Selly Oak Colleges, Birmingham (occasional publications).
——, *News of Muslims in Europe*, a periodic news sheet published by Centre for the Study of Islam and Christian–Muslim Relations.
——, 'Muslims in Europe: An Overview' in Nielsen (ed.), *Research Papers*, no. 12, 1981.
Omari, C. K., 'Christian-Muslim Relations in Tanzania – The Socio-Political Dimensions' in Sicard (ed.), *BICMURA*, 2/2, 1984.
Onaiyenkane, John, 'The Shari'a in Nigeria: A Christian view' in Sicard (ed.), *BICMURA*, 6/1. 1988.
Ottenberg, S., 'Two new religions, one analytic frame', *Cahiers d'études Africaines*, 24/4, 1984.
Roberts, H., 'Radical Islamism and the dilemma of Algerian nationalism', *Third World Quarterly*, 10/2, 1988.

Roux, C. du P. le, 'Hermeneutics – Islam and the South African Context', *Journal for Islamic Studies*, no. 10, 1990.
Ryan, P. J., 'Islam and Politics in West Africa: Minority and Majority Models', *The Muslim World*, LXXVII, 1987.
Samiullah, M., 'Muslims in Kenya: Problems and Possible Solutions', *Al-Islam*, 7/2, 1983.
Shirazi, M., 'Same old story as Senegal turns down Muslim Party', *Arabia*, no. 22, 1983.
——, 'Political thaw in Tunisia', *Arabia*, no. 37, 1984.
——, 'Regulating the family in Algeria', *Arabia*, no. 37, 1984.
Sicard, Sigvard von (ed.), *Bulletin on Islam and Christian–Muslim Relations in Africa* (*BICMURA*), Selly Oak Colleges, Birmingham.
—— (ed.), 'The Violent Politics of Religion and the Survival of Nigeria', a seminar paper published in *BICMURA*, 6/1, 1988.
Sivers, Peter von, 'The realm of justice: Apocalyptic revolts in Algeria (1849–1879)', *Humaniora Islamica I*, 1973.
Sulaiman, Ibraheem, 'The Moment of Truth in Nigeria', *Impact International*, 13–26 April 1984.
—— 'Islam and Secularism in Nigeria: An encounter of two civilisations', *Impact International*, 10–23, October, 1986.
Sutton, J. E., 'Lords of the International Gold Trade in the 1320s and 1330s: al-Hasan b. Sulaiman of Kilwa and Mansa Musa of Mali', African History Seminar, 6 May, 1992, School of Oriental and African Studies, London.
Tazi, A., 'Morocco's commitment to Islam, long-standing feature of Moroccan diplomacy', *Islam Today*, vol. 2, 1984.
Whiteman, Kaye (ed.), *West Africa Magazine*, London, weekly publication.
Willis, K. D., 'Fundamentalist Islam', *The Christian Science Monitor*, 76/170, 1984.

Index

9445